W9-AER-687

MEDIA, CONSCIOUSNESS, AND CULTURE

COMMUNICATION AND HUMAN VALUES

MEDIA, CONSCIOUSNESS, AND CULTURE

Explorations of Walter Ong's Thought

**edited by Bruce E. Gronbeck
Thomas J. Farrell
Paul A. Soukup**

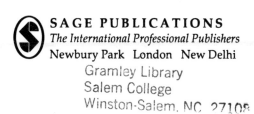

SAGE PUBLICATIONS
The International Professional Publishers
Newbury Park   London   New Delhi

For information address:

SAGE Publications, Inc.
2455 Teller Road
Newbury Park, California 91320

SAGE Publications Ltd.
6 Bonhill Street
London EC2A 4PU
United Kingdom

SAGE Publications India Pvt. Ltd.
M-32 Market
Greater Kailash I
New Delhi 110 048 India

Printed in the United States of America

Library of Congress Cataloging-in-Publication Data

Media, consciousness, and culture : Explorations of Walter Ong's thought
    / edited by Bruce E. Gronbeck, Thomas J. Farrell, Paul A. Soukup.
        p.   cm. —(Communication and human values)
    Includes bibliographical references and index.
    ISBN 0-8039-4025-4
    1. Ong, Walter J.   2. Communication.   3. Rhetoric.   4. Mass media.
    5. Consciousness.   I. Gronbeck, Bruce E.   II.   Farrell, Thomas J.
    III.   Soukup, Paul A.   IV.   Series: Communication and human values
    (Newbury Park, Calif.)
P92.5.O54M42   1991
302.2—dc20   90-27759
                                                                                                CIP

FIRST PRINTING, 1991

Sage Production Editor: Judith L. Hunter

Contents

Part III: Media Studies

Part IV: Studies of Consciousness

Foreword

During its modern history communication research has swung back and forth between two different models for understanding its subject: In one rendition communications is seen as a mode of information, in another as a mode of production. While the first model is deep in the sinews of American history, its modern inspiration was directly technological: the development of electrical machines beginning with the telegraph and climaxing in servo-mechanisms for firing guns, opening doors, and, via computer control, regulating all sorts of processes. The inspiration for the second model was industrial and architectural: the 19th-century factory with its organization of workers and managers and the struggle (sometimes coercive, sometimes ideological) between them—a site and struggle Marxism worked into a master narrative.

The mode of information and the mode of production have enchanted, indeed bewitched, several generations of scholars. While they now constitute orthodox models and while much has been learned from them, they have the combined disadvantage of bleaching out the extraordinary phenomenological diversity of communication—the actual found diversity of language, meaning, signification, technology, identity, and social relations—into the whitened bones of senders, messages, receivers, and feedback loops. Despite surface differences, both models—the mode of information and the mode of production—focus on a control mechanism view of communications, and the binary oppositions at their core—transmitter and receptor in one, bourgeoisie and proletariat in another—are mere inversions of one another. Both see communications as emancipatory if and when the social process is cured of certain imperfections: purged in one case of a corrupting imperfection of language and the irrational, cured in the other case of a corrupting imperfection of ownership and control. To put it positively, communication could be liberated—restored to its true vocation—if only a language of pure rational cognition or a mode of pure communal ownership could be discovered. Neither of the liberations anticipated in theory and desired in fact has arrived and, as a result, we have cooked up compensatory alternatives in which communication is conceived as a means to therapeutically cure our anxieties or solipsistically pursue our pleasures.

The long attempt to unhook from these orthodox views has assumed the generic name of cultural studies but this intellectual mansion itself has many rooms. British cultural studies—though national identity is somewhat deceiving here—has done one turn or another on poststructural Marxism in order to dislodge the binarism of base and superstructure, bourgeoisie and proletariat, code and message. A second version of cultural studies, and one ultimately more congenial to North America, can be traced to at least one source: the gathering at the University of Toronto, as the 1940s turned into the 1950s, of a then obscure assemblage of scholars.

Harold Innis, Marshall McLuhan, Northrop Frye, and Eric Havelock were a loose and disjointed group and hardly aimed at what they wrought: the creation of a distinctive North American version of communication theory. Nor were they without precedent, for it is hardly possible to understand the outcome of their encounters without taking into account the earlier work of Patrick Geddes, Lewis Mumford, John Dewey, Robert Park, and others in the Chicago School of Sociology, along with the omnipresent shadow of Kenneth Burke.

Nonetheless, the work of the Toronto group proved decisive because it shifted the axis of study away from the mode of information and the mode of production. "Shifted away" is too strong; rather, they created another track of intellectual life where technologies of communication could be studied historically and rhetorically, not merely as expressions or addenda to the mode of production or information but also as forms of cultural creation, transmission, and preservation—modes of cultural production, which are also and more than modes of information.

Since that founding moment when cultural studies was given a decisive North American articulation—centered in technology, organized around the simultaneous and interpenetrating vectors of identity, social relations, and forms of productive life—important voices have been added from a variety of places: Jack Goody, J. David Bolter, Elizabeth Eisenstein, and Anthony Giddens to mention but a few. And now that the underlaborer, ground-clearing operation of post-structuralism has done its work, the relevance of the untranslatable French—Baudrillard, Derrida, and Foucault—to this undertaking has become clear.

Each of these writers works or worked within a distinctive national formation, within the boundaries of specific intellectual traditions and in light of specifically individual concerns. Jack Goody, for example, can only be understood against the backdrop of a British anthropological tradition, a reaction to Claude Lévi-Strauss and structuralism, and a personal project: By inserting the intervening mechanism of literacy between the oppositions of primitive and modern, myth and science, the concrete and the abstract, he attempts to restore the Primitive in all Reason and Reason within all Primitives.

Despite the idiosyncrasies of the voices involved, a collection of loosely articulated books and projects is adding up to a distinctive line of inquiry, often behind the backs of the writers involved. And, to finally get to the point of all this, no one has better defined that project, shaped its boundaries, given it coherence, mapped its problems, or humanely articulated its intent than Walter J. Ong, SJ. A colleague of McLuhan, and blessed with an estimable Jesuit education that forswears premature publication, Walter Ong is the intellectual equivalent of a long-distance runner with peripheral vision. While many contemporary writers on meaning, signification, and media have trained heavy guns on the relationship of the spoken and written word, Walter Ong early on absorbed from McLuhan and others the lesson that electronic communication was transforming the relations between talk and text, and thus our understanding of the entire embracing arc from the oral to the chirographic-typographic to the televisual. While he has, like many others, speculated on the long waves of causality stretching from cave paintings to comic books, Walter Ong, unlike many others, has also produced detailed, narrow-focused studies on Ramism and education, African drums and other so-called primitive modes of communication, psychoanalysis, and individual writers such as Jonathan Swift and Gerard Manley Hopkins. Within the extended length and width of his scholarship, Walter Ong has never lost his own distinctive voice and concerns: the analysis of the steady, progressive interiorization of consciousness, the problematic status of religious symbols and the sacred in a secularizing world of nonsacred media, the deeply agonistic, oppositional yet often ritualized conflicts that are the everyday stuff of social life.

In a distinguished, diverse, yet doggedly extensive and coherent set of books and articles, he has enriched our understanding of the history, trans-formation, continuities, and discontinuities of the variable practices of com-munication. His emphasis on the technology of communication has never been a form of simple technological determinism. Rather, he has recognized that technology, through the constitution of social practice, both imagines and sediments forms of human consciousness and social relations.

The essays that follow celebrate Walter Ong's singular achievement, but they do more than that. They also extend and critique his work—sometimes rather piously, sometimes less reverently—and, so much the better, enhance and deepen the valuable intellectual tradition Walter Ong, with some distinguished predecessors and contemporaries, did so much to create.

James W. Carey

Preface

The communications revolution of the twentieth century has involved more than an electrifying of interhuman contact. In part as cause, in part as effect, in part as associated events, it has been accompanied by wide-ranging changes in all the psychological and social aspects of life. Not only do we think of ourselves and others differently now, but we also look upon societies and transsocial relationships in wholly new ways, thanks to the communications revolution; it has occurred amid technological, psychological, social, and ultimately conceptual transformations, forcing us to see ourselves, others, and the universe in radically altered ways. Poised at the threshold of a new millennium, we mythify a brave new world wherein television extends our vision and computers rewire our central nervous systems; both inspire moral preachments and paeans to their operations and applications.

The communications revolution and, more precisely, the various revolutions in communication over the centuries, have provided focus for the work of Walter J. Ong, SJ (1912-). In his attempts to define various communication media precisely in terms of their groundings in consciousness and their uses in society, he has woven together the three concepts that are comprised in the primary title of this book. Others have pursued relationships between mind and messages psycholinguistically; sought to specify the ties between messages and their contexts sociolinguistically; and worked out ways of relating mind to contexts, self to society. Few, however, can compare with Ong and his ability to simultaneously look inward and outward when theorizing communication and critically examining communicative artifacts.

Ong's has been an extraordinary career in humane studies. His work has combined virtues found in his mentors: His grounding in original texts and social practices has been as secure as that of his Harvard doctoral adviser, Perry Miller, and yet his speculative elan and daring rival that of his Saint Louis University M.A. adviser, Marshall McLuhan. His spirit is controlled yet free; his intellectual style is that of the critic—tied to text-events and yet unfettered in its search for the vantage points from which to see and understand those practices in fresh ways.

Nowhere are these habits better illustrated than in his most successful book, *Orality and Literacy* (1982b). Ong's orality-literacy theorems in that work were constructed out of both concrete events and new theorizations. While others (and Ong himself in earlier works) had pioneered studies of the shifts in consciousness and culture that accompanied the movement from a dominating orality to a dominating literacy in the Western world, *Orality and Literacy* is the book that captured the imagination of the widest readership. As of this writing, it has already been published in eight languages, and a string of other authors has followed in Ong's footsteps over the past few years.

John Miles Foley (1985) has annotated more than 1,800 books and articles treating the oral tradition; additionally, he edited a *festschrift* in honor of Milman Parry (Foley, 1987a) and, as editor of *Oral Tradition*, coordinated the publication in that journal of a *festschrift* in honor of Ong (Foley, 1987b). Together with his work honoring Albert B. Lord (Foley, 1981), he has worked hard to focus scholarly attention on three of the most productive students of orality and to assemble materials all can use in pursuing the orality-literacy theorems. He also has authored a monograph on the history and methodology of oral composition theory (Foley, 1988) and edited a collection with contributions by Ong and Lord (Foley, 1986).

The list of others working in this area during the 1980s and 1990s is prodigious. Jeff Opland (1983) studied aspects of Xhosa oral praise poetry in contemporary South Africa, while Kevin B. Maxwell (1983) examined the current impact of literacy on the oral culture of the Bemba in Zambia. Sylvia Scribner and Michael Cole (1981) studied the syllabic writing system of the Vai in Liberia. Bruno Gentili (1988) called attention to the dimension of performance in oral poetry in ancient Greece from Homer to the fifth century BCE, and Ward Parks (1990) followed up Ong's treatment of male contesting in oral cultures with a detailed analysis of the Homeric and Old English traditions and a discussion of the Sanskrit epic, Mahabharata. Paul Zumthor (1990) analyzed aspects of oral poetry from antiquity to the present. Warwick Wadlington (1987) followed Ong's leads in discussing Faulknerian tragedy, and Sandra M. Gilbert and Susan Gubar (1987) employed his thought to articulate a feminist approach to literary criticism.

In theological and religious studies, Northrop Frye (1982) worked from Ongian notions about cultural history in examining the history of the interpretation of the Bible. Werner H. Kelber (1983) investigated the implications of orality and textuality for understanding the oral and written Gospels. Pheme Perkins (1980) examined the crisis of Gnosticism in the early church in terms of orality and literacy. Frans Jozef van Beeck (1979) explored orality as such in Christology, and he later used Ong's work to account for certain tendencies in theological writing in recent centuries (van Beeck, 1989). While Jesse M. Gellrich (1985) surveyed the idea of the book in the Middle Ages, Brian Stock (1983) studied several major theological controversies during the eleventh and twelfth centuries in terms of contrasts between orality and literacy, with special reference to textually defined discourse communities. David Toolan (1987, pp. 87-147) used Ong's work to discuss particular aspects of Hinduism, Judaism, and Christianity.

Among students of rhetoric, of course, Ong's work is broadly cited and extended. Richard Leo Enos (1988) examined the literate quality of Cicero's legal rhetoric, and John D. Schaeffer (1990) used leads in Ong to situate Vico's treatment of rhetoric. Patricia Bizzell and Bruce Herzberg (1990) use Ong's work extensively in discussing rhetoric and education in the Renaissance, although they fail to mention that Ong and Charles J. Ermatinger have published an English translation of Milton's *Logic* (1982), which was composed and published originally in Latin. The essays Enos (1990) gathered in another Sage anthology examine oral and written communication from antiquity to the present, while works edited by David R. Olson, Nancy Torrance, and Angela Hildyard (1985) investigate the nature and consequences of learning to read and write—a subject Myron C. Tuman (1987) also has explored in depth. A controversial application of the orality-literacy hypothesis developed by Havelock (1978, 1982) and Ong has been proposed by Thomas J. Farrell (1983) in an article about IQ, orality, and literacy; an issue of *Pre/Text* was devoted to discussing the controversy (Swearingen, 1986, pp. 117-208). Other journals also have devoted issues to examining orality-literacy theory: *New Literary History* (Cohen, 1984-85, pp. 1-206), *Cultural Anthropology* (Biesele & Tyler, 1986, pp. 131-256), *Visible Language* (Olson & deKerckove, 1986, pp. 248-361), *Interchange* (Olson, 1987, pp. 1-173), and *Semeia* (Silberman, 1987, pp. 1-145).

More generally, Jack Goody (1986) formulated a comprehensive view of the impact of writing on the organization of society; it synthesized and extended his previous groundbreaking studies, now available in collected form (Goody, 1987). Neil Postman (1985) presented an analysis of the negative consequences of television on public discussion, working from Ong's studies of orality and literacy; Joshua Meyrowitz (1985) used Ong's discussions of the relationships between media and both consciousness and culture to ground his study of the impact of electronic media on social behavior. Henry Sussman (1989) and Stephen Tyler (1987) integrated Ong's work in their forays into deconstruction; Michael Heim (1987) and Philip Leith (1990) used Ong in their attempts to better understand word processing and artificial intelligence, respectively. Robert K. Logan (1986) as well as Ivan Illich and Barry Sanders (1988) have provided nontechnical, historical surveys of issues associated with the orality-literacy hypotheses developed by Havelock and Ong. Overall, as Leith has written, "Ong's text has been used in many areas: philosophy, literature, linguistics, in the history of memory systems and the history of medicine, in anthropology, sociology, psychology, theology, education, and intellectual and culture studies generally" (1990, pp. 74-75)—not to mention, of course, Leith's own field of computer science.

Who is this scholar with such a broad following? He is a descendant of an early American settler, Francis Ong, who arrived at the Massachusetts Bay Colony in 1631 in the company of Roger Williams; Ong certainly came upon his interest in Ramism honestly, given such roots. But not all New Englanders remain there. Walter's grandfather, Richard Marshall Ong, was born in Madisonville, Ohio, and after the Civil War (in which he had one brother in the Union Army and another fighting for the Confederacy), moved to New Orleans, where he married Mary Virginia Jackson, a native of New Orleans whose family roots were in Tennessee. One of their children, Walter Jackson Ong, moved to Kansas City, where he married a third-generation Missourian of German Catholic descent, Blanche Eugenia Mense. Their children, Walter Jackson Ong and Richard Mense Ong, were brought up Catholics. Walter Sr., raised an Episcopalian by his mother (his father was Methodist), frequently attended Catholic services with his wife and children and was received into the Catholic Church before his death.

With this Catholic family background, Walter Jr., from fourth grade on to his doctoral studies at Harvard, was under the tutelage of Catholic educators. The Kansas City, Missouri, area was his home, where he attended Rockhurst High School and Rockhurst College. After graduation in 1933, he worked in the printing business, entered the Society of Jesus in 1935 at the Missouri Province novitiate, St. Stanislaus Seminary, and then continued his higher education: a licentiate in philosophy (1940), an M.A. in English (1941), and a licentiate in theology (1948), all from Saint Louis University, and, after teaching and research assignments (two Guggenheim Fellowships), his Ph.D. in English from Harvard in 1954.

That fall, he settled in to teaching English (later called Onglish by his students) at Saint Louis University, even today his primary home. He was named Professor of English in 1959, and Professor of Humanities in Psychiatry in 1970, from which he codirected a joint program for M.D.s in psychiatry and Ph.D. candidates in English. He was named University Professor of Humanities in 1981. In these posts he continued an active career on fellowships, lectureships, and visiting professorships, all the while publishing nearly 400 articles, monographs, chapters, and books. He was made a Chevalier dans l'Ordre des Palmes Académiques by the government of France and is a Fellow of the American Academy of Arts and Sciences. (For more background, see Lumpp, 1987a.)

This anthology, however, does more than lionize a powerful, even dominant, American critic and intellectual. Rather, this work takes as givens the importance of Ong's conceptualizations and the richness of the research program he and others have maintained in support of those views. In problematizing media, consciousness, and culture in particular ways and in attacking the resultant problems in a unique fashion, Ong has provided footings for other theorists, historians, and critics. The essays that follow add to, quarrel with, explain, and even shamelessly use Ong's thoughts as intellectual struts at key points in their arguments. In those varied relationships with him, the authors offer the most sincere form of scholarly encomium: They make Ong foundational to their own projects, in the process advancing contemporary rhetorical, literary, and communication studies along productive paths.

In respect to the thrusts of both Ong's writings and those of our authors, this book is organized into four parts. Part I stands as orientation. The essays conceptualize him in two ways, one around the themes of media, consciousness, and culture, and the other around specific ideas and concepts developed by Ong across time. The problematics that unify this book are set out first. Part II illustrates the breadth of Ong's understanding of rhetorical studies, with essays working on typical issues in the history and contemporary study of rhetorical processes. In Part III are found studies working from the most famous aspects of Onglish, his conceptualization of media and mediational processes; these essays, again, run the gamut from historical to contemporary theoretical study, befitting Ong's own approaches to mediation. Part IV takes us into the topic so often omitted in contemporary rhetorical and communication studies, consciousness; four essays come with reforming force, demanding that current scholarship deal more forthrightly with the problematic of consciousness in psychoanalytical, epistemological, and sociological ways.

The four-part organization provides a kind of map for studying various communities of thought. The careful reader will find the roads running between these communities. David Payne's rhetorical understanding of character from Part IV could serve as a moral grounding to the questions of voice discussed in Part II, just as Annabelle Sreberny-Mohammadi's analysis of Iranian subcultures could be informed by Payne's work. Ruth El Saffar's and Thomas Farrell's explorations of consciousness in Part IV expand issues raised in Noël Valis's discussion of joyousness in Part II and in Silverstone's venture into television and the unconscious in Part III. And, of course, both Anthony Palmeri, in Part II, and Philip Leith, in Part III, treat Ong's revolutionary analysis of Peter Ramus, while David Heckel's work on the trans- formative power of print in sixteenth-century scientific writing parallels Leith's effort to capture the transformative power of computeriza- tion in twentieth-century science. These cross-divisional associations are to be expected in a work that revolves around the gridlocked ideas of com- munication, consciousness, and culture.

This anthology, then, stands as a syllabus for a course in contemporary theories of discursiveness—the variety of communicative modes throughout the history of Western thought, and the relationships between those modes and the psychoculture of life. As an anthology, it can touch down but here and there in its scanning of history and its articulation of metacritical and theoretical ideas. Only in following a path from the references in the bibliography and out into the library will readers have a complete course of study. That is all one can expect from a good book: guidance into dialogues on matters of import. We hope we have provided the bases for such talk.

Regarding actual citations from Ong's writings, the works mentioned by the essayists span a period of 40 years. His earlier works follow the then-common practice of using gendered language. His later works use inclusive language, as in his classes he urges all to do, explicitly lecturing on this matter. With this explanation of the state of affairs, the editors have let all quotations from his works stand as in the original published texts.

The project has been helped along by many who deserve acknowledge-ment here. We must begin with Robert A. White, of Gregorian University in Rome, and David Eley, of the Jesuit Communication Project in Toronto, for initiating the effort and helping in the search for authors and editors. Review-ing tasks fell not only to the editors but also to Thomas D. Bacig, James H. Fetzer, William A. Gibson, Eleanor M. Hoffman, Yolande J. Jenny, Virginia T. Katz, and Kenneth C. Risdon of the University of Minnesota-Duluth; Richard Leo Enos of Carnegie-Mellon University; William J. Kennedy, Cornell University; David R. Payne, University of South Florida; Donald G. Marshall, University of Illinois-Chicago; members of the Project on Rhetoric of Inquiry at the University of Iowa; an audience at a Speech Communication Association panel, where papers by Anthony Palmeri, David Payne, and Bruce Gronbeck were presented and queried; and Walter J. Ong of Saint Louis University, who provided everything from correction of Latin to full commentary on various papers.

Much technical assistance was provided the editors. For assistance in locating references, thanks go to Martha L. Eberhart at the University of Minnesota-Duluth and Cynthia Bradley at Santa Clara University; also at UM-D were William A. Gibson, Malcolm Kendall, Nancy J. Korby, Kenneth C. Risdon, and Barbara K. Williams, who offered technical help in the translating of word processing programs and the electronic transmission of material. Sue Brockopp, Kathleen H. Fitzgerald, Nancy J. Korby, and Barbara K. Williams at UM-D did word processing, as did Melanie Hesseltine at the University of Iowa. Ms. Hesseltine also maintained the networking files between the University of Iowa and the many authors who joined, stayed with, or left the project. Rita Elliott and Sandy Chiaramonte provided the office support at Santa Clara. In the spring of 1987, the Centre for the Study of Communication and Culture in London provided Bruce Gronbeck an Ong library and ideal working conditions for doing his essay; special thanks must go to Robert A. White, then the Centre's Research Director, and Maria Way, the secretary who kept the operation on an even keel. The University of Iowa Center for Advanced Studies also provided a working home for Bruce Gronbeck, giving him the solitude needed to write incidental materials. Institutional support for travel, electronic and express mail, phone, copying, and the like was graciously provided by the University of Iowa, University of Minnesota-Duluth, and Santa Clara University. Finally, both Sage-UK and Sage-USA deserve commendation. Sage-UK originally reviewed and endorsed the project; and then Sage-USA, especially editor Ann West, got the project off the ground. Special thanks, too, go to Marie Louise Pencheon as our main contact point with Sage Publications, Inc.

Other publishing companies were generous in granting permission for authors to use copyrighted materials from their books. Cornell University Press granted permission to use material from three of Ong's books: *Fighting for Life* (1981a), *Interfaces of the Word* (1977a), and *Rhetoric, Romance, and Technology* (1971). Ellis Horwood Ltd. graciously granted permission to reprint an edited version of Chapter 4 of Philip Leith's *Formalism in AI and Computer Science* (1990). Harvard University Press granted us permission to reproduce materials from Ong's *Ramus, Method, and the Decay of Dialogue* (1958a). Methuen and Company granted us permission to use material from Ong's *Orality and Literacy: The Technologizing of the Word* (1982b).

An anthology—especially one working so hard for an integrated yet complex account of communication practices and their relationships to mind and society—demands hard work from many. The senior editor graciously acknowledges the untotaled hours Thomas Farrell spent in electronic communication with authors, in bibliographical detail, and in editing; Paul

Soukup spent nearly as much time preparing for the electronic presentation of the manuscript to Sage, constructing an index and the permissions list, and editing selected essays. This book is a reflection of their selfless devotion to the man and the ideas that inspired it.

B.E.G.

PART I

Introductory Studies: Ong on Consciousness, Communication, and Culture

Introduction

BRUCE E. GRONBECK

Arguably, three problems are central to twentieth-century humane inquiry in general, rhetorical and communication studies in particular. First, following developments in British empiricism and German rationalism, eighteenth- and nineteenth-century epistemologists and rhetoricians concerned themselves with mind and the message-mind relationship. And, following Freud and Mead in the twentieth century, Western theorists of rhetoric and communication had to treat notions of consciousness and self in addition to questions of mind, finally throwing off mechanistic faculty psychology within the lifetimes of people still living.

Second, for centuries, rhetoric and public discourse about politics and society were matters of oral performance—face-to-face exchanges by power elites. By the nineteenth century, written discourse was given attention, and, with the coming of the twentieth-century electronic revolution, multiple media of communication had to be theorized in any complete treatment of discursive social practices.

And third, implicit in communication theory after Aristotle's *Rhetoric* was a concern for audiences and their social moorings. Rhetorical effectiveness was understood from the first to be related to people's values and idealizations. However, with the coming of the idea of "culture" (vis-à-vis "society") came a broadening of thought on audience; German theories of sociality, and British, American, and French work on the study of anthropology complicated our understanding of culture and forced a reconceptualization of rhetoric and public discourse. And thus it was that the twentieth century produced epistemological, communicative, and sociocultural revolutions at least as jarring as those of fifth- and sixth-century BCE Greece and of eighteenth-century England.

These are not the only problematics raised in twentieth-century human sciences, though they permeate social thought and certainly dominate theories of rhetoric and communication. These problematics can be stated more formally: (a) How is mind to be defined, and how does that definition inform basic understandings of self, spirituality, individuality, and the collectivity? (b) If distinctions among orality, literacy, and visuality are more than mere differences of channel, but in fact constitute independent modes of individual and collective experience, then what personal and social changes accompany large-scale shifts from one mode of communication to another? (c) If culture is thought of not simply as communal structure (politics) or as interpersonal relationships (sociality), but rather as common webs of understanding and behaviors acted out with others, then what is the relationship between the individual (self) and the collectivity (society)? And in what ways do social groups manage the forces of continuity and change in their lives?

Such questions face students of humane studies in this century. Walter Ong is an especially acute student of such matters. While not everyone agrees with his answers to these queries, few will dispute the proposition that his thinking has been penetrating and influential enough to demand being taken into account. That taking-into-account is our focus.

Questions about consciousness, communication, and culture are addressed in most of his works, and his answers are provocative enough to frame the extensions, amendments, and redirections of thought that are comprised in this book. In Part I, the essay by Bruce Gronbeck defines more fully Ong's views on consciousness, communication, and culture; he argues that Ong reframes and revitalizes rhetorical and communication theory around these three problematics. Among contemporary American students of communication and culture, Ong is depicted as the strongest student of consciousness, giving him a unique place in the pantheon of American culturalists.

While Gronbeck examines Ong's thought through three foci, Thomas Farrell offers a broader survey, isolating a more diverse set of ideas in his chronological survey of Ong's writings; he allows us, too, to see the unfolding yet the constant enfolding of earlier writings into later reconceptualizations of them. Especially interesting are Farrell's thoughts on Ong's so-called middle period, the least studied portion of his career; the trilogy of works that dominate the period reveals the flowering of Ong's thinking about media, mind, and society that in turn leads to the triumphant books of the third period: *Fighting for Life* (1981a), *Orality and Literacy* (1982b), and *Hopkins, the Self, and God* (1986a).

Part I thus stands both as an orientation to the seminal intellectual issues guiding this project and also as critical introductions to the scholar who helped frame them.

1

The Rhetorical Studies Tradition and Walter J. Ong: Oral-Literacy Theories of Mediation, Culture, and Consciousness

BRUCE E. GRONBECK

Old and New Rhetorics

Most will agree that classical rhetorical conceptions of communication processes governed the practices of public discourse and at least most approaches to interpersonal and artistic transactions among the educated for more than two millennia of Western civilization. The Greek and Roman views on rhetoric spread through the rest of Europe and controlled not only the *artes oratoriae* (arts of oratory in forensic, legislative, and ceremonial settings), but also the *artes praedicandi* (art of preaching), the *artes notariae et dictaminis* (formal and informal arts of letter-writing), and the *ars poetica* (art of poetic discourse). The classical rhetorical model of communication and composition was taught and naturalized across all formal modes of interpersonal learning.

Rhetoric perennially wrestles with conceptualizations of *mediation* (means of communicating between people), *culture* (social organization and tenets, its degree and kind of hold over individuals), and *consciousness* (the self or individuated mind and its orientations to exterior life). Such questions not only can structure any attempt to discuss classical, Renaissance, modern, or contemporary rhetorical theory, but will also organize the thrusts of this book.

The Old Rhetoric

As far as mediation is concerned, classical rhetoric's model of communication was unidirectional, univocal, and unilateral. It assumed that the one was addressing the many, that only the one would speak so as to achieve a

5

sense of conviction or proof (*pistis*) in others, and that the will to power lay in the hands of the rhetor. Classical rhetoric was a model of domination of the many by the one, and all of its machinery was built with domination in mind. While Aristotle certainly was sensitive to style and the niceties of language in Book III, and the varieties of emotional states of human beings in Book II, the muscle of his *Rhetoric* was in Book I and late Book II, in the proofs that would compel assent through the genera, general, and special *topoi* or lines of argument that could be forged in enthymemes, rhetorical proof forms. Rhetorics focusing on proofs generally are concerned with force or power. Even the non-enthymematic proofs—maxims, examples—were discussed in terms of their probative force. The art of public speaking was the art of public performance and leadership designed for great lawyers, politicians, and ceremonial spokespersons for society.

As for culture, with citizenship in Athens and Rome came a series of rights and responsibilities; citizens' behavior in part was governed by membership in the city-state, in Roman *communitas*. More important than the sociopolitical expectations that characterized these collectivities, however, were beliefs—the generally received opinions called by Plato *doxa*, by Cicero *mores*—that presumably were held in common by citizens. Collective commitments to such values created a pool of conventional wisdom orators could call upon when urging courses of action; the enthymeme could be the great engine of proof only in cultures where likemindedness, a collective *ethos* or character, could be assumed. Culture thus was a matter of common spirit or worldview, a homogenizing element that suppressed individuality in favor of collectivizing values and commitments. Commonplaces could be tools of persuasion only in societies comparatively coherent in thought, word, and deed.

Regarding consciousness, the third primal element, as one might expect from such understandings of mediation and culture, we find but minimal thought. Aristotle's understanding of *animal rationalis* yielded a compartmentalized mind that had, as far as one can tell from reading him, but a shadowy sense of self-consciousness. In the *Rhetoric*, proofs were of three kinds—*logoi, pathoi,* and *ethoi*—leading to a theory of mind susceptible to what we term logical, emotional or pathetic, and ethical or characterological proofs. More important, one sees in Aristotle little sensitivity to rationality as highly differentiated across individuals. All persons, because of natural capacities, presumably are susceptible to logical proofs; all persons, because of their common experiences, likely respond to particular situations with specific emotions; and all persons, because of their communal identifications, presumably value similar aspects of character. Consciousness in Aristotle seems a collective commodity, and the classical system of rhetorical argumentation was built around the generalizability of consciousness. Plato, Aristotle, Cicero, and Quintilian wrote in the plural. "We" and "they," not "you" and "I," were comprised in the audiences of ancient Greece and Rome and of the neoclassical rhetoricians of later epochs as well.

Precisely when this grand rhetorical construction of collective life broke down, precisely when the classical rhetorical model of education and public influence lost its power, is a matter of definition and dispute among contemporary scholars. Some, such as Marshall McLuhan (1962), see oral culture crumbling under the weight of the printing press, which brought new sensibilities, segmented rather than communal bases of knowledge, privatized power, and individuation of people. Walter Ong opts for roughly the same period, though he builds his argument around the visualist thesis, in which the arts of discourse are depicted as becoming "monologue arts" wherein "Speech is no longer a medium in which the human mind and sensibility lives" and wherein communication is governed "by silent written and printed documents more than by the spoken word" (1958a, pp. 287, 291). Logic and communication are not simply printed and linearized, but seen. And, as we shall see in more detail, Ong parlayed this argument from *Ramus, Method, and the Decay of Dialogue* (1958a) into a complete theory of cultural transformation.

Other scholars see changes of philosophy as more important to the diminution of rhetorical communication, culture, and consciousness. Both W. Samuel Howell (1971) and George Kennedy (1980), for example, see the rise of science and the new associationist philosophies and psychologies as destructive of classical rhetoric's edifice. Later writing by Ong (1986a) features the role of modernist thought, with its stress upon individuation, in vitiating rhetorical arts. To still others, for example Georges Gusdorf (1965), subjectivist philosophies of the twentieth century, those that concern themselves with knowing and feeling as they are shared between individuals, redefine "interpersonal" communication, and, by extension, root out the vestiges of power-based rhetoricized talk.

New Rhetorics

While the points and sources of reorientation are thus various, all agree that we have witnessed the emergence, at least in this century, of an array of new positions from which to theorize communication, culture, and consciousness. I. A. Richards (1936), with his concerns for meaning and language in the 1920s and 1930s, spawned the so-called New Rhetorics, rhetorical theories focused less on power and public persuasion than on meaning acquisition or rehearsal and the tactics of social cooperation and identification (Berger & Luckmann, 1966; Burke, 1950). In the New Rhetorics, meanings are reconstituted rather than created, and influence is more a matter of sharing than overpowering.

A focus upon the what-and-how of meaning by rhetorical and communication theorists, it must be noted, finished off the attempts of eighteenth- and nineteenth-century scholars to refurbish Aristotelian understandings of communication processes. True, Aristotle's definition of rhetoric—the faculty of discovering in any given case the available means of persuasion (*Rhetoric* 1355b)—became the grounding for the twentieth-century revival of rhetorical criticism among students of public speaking. But strong interests in meaning and interpretive processes made a complete neoclassical revival difficult to sustain even in speech studies after the early 1960s. Various approaches to rhetorical criticism were proffered, disintegrating the Aristotelian critical paradigm in most programs in rhetoric and communication. Like their brethren in "theory," rhetorical critics were wedded to multiple perspectives on communication processes.

In all of the conceptual turmoil, of one thing we can be certain: In the last quarter of the twentieth century, finally, Western rhetorical and communication theory has been released from the grips of the classical and neoclassical consensus, and has been segmented, multiplied, and revitalized. Pluralism characterizes the philosophical bases of communication studies, and perspectivism, the critical analyses of communication processes and artifacts. "Isms" and "ologies" are spread across the surface of communication studies, engraving their textures and enriching their coloration. "The rhetoric of fiction," "the rhetoric of motives," rhetoric viewed as "the study of misunderstanding and its remedies," "the rhetoric of goodbye," "the rhetoric of the used car lot," "beyond words," "the empathic communicator," "bridges, not walls," "the ethnography of speaking," "I-Thou," "the games people play," "oh, what a blow that phantom gave me!," "understanding media," "TV, the most popular art," "reading television,"—the cant and catchphrases of contemporary communication studies jar the ear and mind. Relativism seems just around the corner, confusion threatens to reign, and academician after alarmist commodifies this-or-that new theory of human discoursing in yet another book heralding the death of Old Rhetoric or the birth of the New Communication/Information Order. Those concepts central to the understanding of collective life—the problematics surrounding mediation, consciousness, and culture—are defined and redefined by nearly everyone in the human sciences. It is no wonder that universities cannot decide whether rhetoric and communication are social sciences, humane studies, skills, or "other" when it comes time to map the life of the mind.

Rather than despair, however, we ought to recognize that there is both loss and gain when a paradigm of long standing and widespread domination weakens and dies or evolves. The losses include those of orientation, durability, and educability; points of consensus, after all, can be inculcated, counted on, and used to organize at least pockets of life. The gains, though, for the contemporary mind conditioned to destabilization, complexity, and rampant perspectivism, probably are far greater than the losses. The refashioning of the old paradigm brings with it excitement, inventiveness, exploration, disputation, and even democratization if no one has a corner on truth and ideational power, which usually is the case in times of unfettered inquiry.

Exemplary of these virtues are the works of and reactions to Walter Jackson Ong, SJ. Ong is known to some as the greatest pupil of young McLuhan, to others as a creative scholar of the European Renaissance, to *litterateurs* as a Modern Language Association president and buoyant literary critic within a broadly psychocultural school, to the Catholic community as friend of Teilhard and a principal apologist for American Catholicism, and to most of the academy as the author of *Orality and Literacy* (1982b), his best-selling scholarly work, now in eight languages. Even more broadly, within the cross-disciplinary collegium of scholars interested in rhetorical and communication matters, Ong is a leading figure in American cultural studies. Distinctively American with its unusual grounding in classics, religious hermeneutics, the philosophy of sociology, and anthropology, this school of communication studies stands counterpoised to its Continental and British sisters. It has affinities with French semiotics and structuralism, and the breadth of its generalizations gives it the feeling of writings from the Frankfurt school, yet cultural studies in America is its own creature.

Cultural studies' American house comprises many rooms. Dwelling there are anthropologists in the tradition of Boas, social theorists riding in the wake of the American pragmatists, the pop culture critics who made Bowling Green State University famous in the 1960s, the psychopolitical students of Harold Lasswell, and the language-and-society scholars who battled the New Critics for supremacy in literature departments. A special room is reserved for the likes of Walter Ong. He presses to understanding relationships between modes or channels of communication and both culture and consciousness, and thence along with others to articulate the so-called orality and literacy theorems. He is central to a select group of interpreter-critics that seeks to reconceptualize social formations, the mechanisms that permit those formations to work, and ties between individual and collective consciousness.

The point is this: As was true for the old rhetoric, mediation or communication, culture, and consciousness are concepts around which many of the puzzles central to twentieth-century thought revolve, and Ong has articulated theories of communication, culture, and consciousness thrilling in their creativity, forceful in their documentation, and sweeping in their scope. Like McLuhan before him, he can be considered a probe; but more than that, the solidity of his scholarship and the precision of his mind give his ideas a heft that McLuhan's never acquired. And Ong has been a reinterpreter of the classical, medieval, Renaissance, and modern ages as much as he has been an oracle of the electronic age. His work on communication, culture, and consciousness is such that it can sustain diverse scholarly projects. This anthology will illustrate some of those types of pursuits. In this essay, I seek to find some of the grounding ideas that make reading and talking with Ong such a rich experience.

Ong's Revaluation of Rhetoric and Communication

Because of their concern with the human center of the cosmos in one way or another, the humanities seem particularly qualified to help man resituate himself in the universe by relating his interior and exterior points of reference. (Ong, 1967a, p. 140)

No doubt Ong's academic mission is a humane one. Even in his church-centered works there is a drive to integrate mind and body with the soul and to deal with the individual situated in social organizations and cultures. His graduate training was literary, as he worked with McLuhan among others while on an M.A. program in English at Saint Louis University, and especially with Perry Miller and Myron P. Gilmore while on his Ph.D. program at Harvard (Ong, 1958a; 1981b). Yet his broadly defined course of literary studies was much more flexible than, say, the then-fashionable New Criticism that is so often a target in Ong's writings. In a sense Ong followed McLuhan's jump from literary scholarship to cultural studies (Gronbeck, 1981). But Ong's approach to literary and then cultural studies followed that of Perry Miller, whose *The New England Mind* (two volumes, 1939 and 1953) was not only Ong's entry to Ramism but also a source of his habits-of-analysis as well. In Ong, as in Miller, there is always a movement from a text to the outside world of the culture and to the inside world of the mind. To say, then, that Ong's background and interests are literary is both to identify his humane outlook and yet not to narrow it whatsoever. He is, preeminently, a grand theorizer. He is fitting into the cosmos, as the epigraph that opens this section suggests, not only humankind's communication habits but also its entire existence. Ong's journey as a scholar of Peter Ramus, which culminated in his first rhetorical book, *Ramus, Method, and the Decay of Dialogue* (1958a), to that of the intellectual-social commentator so clearly visible in one of his last three books, *Fighting for Life: Contest, Sexuality, and Consciousness* (1981a), is not really the long trip it might appear to be. Ong's themes, at least many of them, remain constant. He often writes in a loop, circling out into some seemingly new territory only to come back to what are perennial questions about mediation, culture, and consciousness. Ong has been bestirred by these matters all of his intellectual life. The words *orality, literacy,* and/or *literature, consciousness,* and *culture* appear in primary and secondary titles of his works with purposive regularity. They represent themes that go back at least to Ong's M.A. education at Saint Louis University. Note the way he describes McLuhan's teaching before World War II:

> McLuhan sensed and conveyed the excitement in the air. In literature grown out of one's own immediate lifeworld, contrasts between consciousness and the unconscious can be studied more confidently and in greater detail than in literatures more remote in time and culture. Reciprocally, the strategies and finesse developed in dealing with contemporary texts called for greater critical sophistication in dealing with earlier literature. The movement first to the remote and then from the remote to one's in-close lifeworld marked other disciplines, too. At this same time, and in a somewhat parallel fashion, the sophistication once reserved for the study of high culture was being brought to bear on popular culture, and the techniques used by anthropologists in addressing so-called primitive peoples were being used to study the societies that the anthropologists had grown up in. . . . Because of their subject matter, McLuhan's courses in "Rhetoric and Interpretation" could be expected to convey a sense of the moral and social urgency of literature as well as a sense of the interaction of past and present. His courses in English Renaissance literature did the same thing. (1981b, pp. 131-132)

Laid into this paragraph are the intellectual and, indirectly at least, the moral concerns that have created Ong's lifelong agenda. Those agenda seem to be centered on the following articulations of rhetoric's perennial questions:

1. What are the distinguishing features of *media of communication*, broadly understood? The "broadly understood" must be added when reading Ong, because he finds "media" a troublesome term:

> Unreflective reliance on models has generated the term "media" to designate new technological ways of managing the word, such as writing, print, and the electronic devices. The term is useful and I use it regularly here. But it can be misleading, encouraging us to think of writing, print, and electronic devices simply as ways of "moving information" over some sort of space intermediate between one person and another. In fact, each of the so-called "media" does far more than this: it makes possible thought processes inconceivable before. (1977a, p. 46; 1981a, p. 198, and 1982b, pp. 176-177)

The notion of "medium/media" is central to Ong's theories of rhetoric and communication because mediation is the primary negotiative concept essential to a contemporary theory of human individuality and collective existence. Given this century's interest in describing meaning-making processes, we must be able to explain how it is that human communication works.

2. What are the *psychodynamics* of selfhood? If British and European cultural studies turn outward to matters of social structure and political-economic power when contemplating communication processes (Fiske, 1987; Habermas, 1979), Americans often turn inward to trace the consequences of mediation processes for the individual self. As Ong says, he is interested in the "subtler effects of print on consciousness, rather than readily observable social effects" (1982b, p. 118). Over the past quarter-century, Ong almost always has ended his books and major monographs with a section on selfhood. So the last chapter of *Fighting for Life* is titled "Contest and Interiorization"; the last section of *Orality and Literacy,* "The Inward Turn: Consciousness and the Text"; and the last two pieces of contemplation in *Hopkins, the Self, and God,* "The Self-Confronting Self and God" and "Hopkins's Own Inscape." Discussions of psychodynamics appear regularly in Ong's writings because he knows the self, the "I" as he likes to talk about it, is a *dynamis*, is being driven by its own consciousness, the mediations available to it, and the cultural mores and social beings with which it is surrounded.

3. What is the relationship between *culture* and one's lifeworld? As has been suggested, a problem dominating twentieth-century thought in general is the relationship between self and society, consciousness and culture. Ong notes the "ontogenetic or individual growth of consciousness is meshed with phylogenetic growth" (1977a, p. 43), but *how*? This often is put as the problem of language, which many scholars want to define simultaneously as personalist and collectivist, as individual and shared (e.g., Havelock, 1986, p. 54). The sticking point for Ong is that he is dissatisfied with the linguistic bias of contemporary thought (e.g., 1982b, chap. 1; "The Vernacular Matrix of the New Criticism," 1962a, pp. 177-205). The negotiative process whereby the "I" makes sense of its own consciousness and cultural life is problematic, therefore, because we need prelinguistic notions, antecedent to and separable from the

idea of language, to describe the negotiations. Our ideas of written language limit us when it comes time to discuss orality as it existed before literacy. So how can we recover a sense of what Ong calls "primary orality," collectivities operating interactively without written media?

4. Finally, what are some of the *implications* of the interactions of mediation, consciousness, and culture for varied facets of human existence? While Ong is interested in mediation, consciousness, and culture per se, as primary problems facing any contemporary scholar in the liberal arts tradition, his inquiries never stop at the point of theoretical formulation. His training went beyond the philosophy and theology of the Jesuits, beyond the literary theories of McLuhan's Cambridge education. His is the soul of the critic, the interpreter of concrete human events and agents. Ong is driven to explore the implications of his theorizing in: the Church's life in this world (1957, 1959); the construction of narratives ("The Writer's Audience is Always a Fiction," 1977a, pp. 53-81); the study of new and old media of communication ("African Talking Drums and Oral Noetics," 1977a, pp. 92-120; the section on "Post-Typography: Electronics," 1982b, pp. 135-138); the evolution of cultural institutions forced by changes in mediation (studies of sports, politics, and business in 1981a, pp. 149-183); relationships between evolution theory and communication theory (1960a; Part II of 1967a); such effects of print as the birth of modern science (1982b, p. 127). The concept of noetics—of the sum total of mental activity influenced by ontogeny, phylogeny, cultural conditioning, and mediation processes—is so central to Ong because through its manifestations in any time and place he can trace out the personal and social implications of mediation.

Numerous other questions crisscross the books and essays of Walter Ong—studies of particular pieces of literature, St. Ignatius Loyola, Ramism, Romanticism, beatniks, the Boy Scouts. As a scholar who explores contemporary culture on many occasions, Walter Ong can be found chasing after the implications of everything from religious movements to the design of downtown St. Louis, Missouri, his home. Rhetoric's perennial questions endure, however, because they must be sought out and addressed not only by Ong but also by every generation witnessing rapid change and disorientation, fragmentation, and alienation. In a postmodernist or electronic age, Ong knows we face the forces of explosion and surface living. We must probe the ontological status of mediation when we face communication breakdowns and new forms of interaction; we must inquire into the nature of culture when we are presented with an array of social models; and we must probe our very self-conceptions when the "I" of existence is challenged, as in a time that has proclaimed the death of both God and ideology. Ong addresses such questions because if people do not, humanity individually and collectively will lose all bearings ("American Culture and Morality," 1967a, pp. 164-188).

Let us now more specifically examine Ong's thinking about mediation, consciousness, and culture to set up an evaluation of his contributions to culturally sensitive rhetorical and communication theory.

Mediation: The Orality-Literacy Theorems

Within a 12-month period in 1962 and 1963, Havelock notes (1986, pp. 24ff.), five important works were published: Lévi-Strauss's *The Savage Mind* (*La Pensée Sauvage*), Goody and Watt's "The Consequences of Literacy," McLuhan's *The Gutenberg Galaxy*, Mayr's *Animal Species and Evolution*, and Havelock's own *Preface to Plato*. These produced what Havelock talked about as "the oral-literate equation" (1986, passim), what Ong more generally discusses as "orality-literacy theorems" (1982b, chap. 7). The mathematical metaphors used here undoubtedly are appropriate, for both men advance some basic axioms as givens from which they deduce explanations for various characteristics of oral, written, electric, and other sorts of discourse (e.g., talking drums). Lévi-Strauss's *The Savage Mind* traversed the relationships between tribal myth and contemporary language, especially acts of naming; Mayr found language the great link between biology and society; Goody and Watt attended to the particular features of orality; McLuhan dealt with the sociopolitical and, to a lesser extent psychological, effects of the literacy revolution following the printing press; and in the Greek move to writing, Havelock discovered a key to fifth-century BCE Greece's cultural revolution.

In the terms "orality" and "literacy," as noted, we have more than mere media, more than "a pipeline transfer of units of material called 'information' from one place to another" (Ong, 1982b, p. 176). These terms, rather, comprehend the psychodynamics and sociodynamics that attend featured modes of intrapersonal and interpersonal mediation. So to Ong, in "primary oral culture"—culture that has known no literate modes of communication—thought and expression have a series of identifiable features. They are: (a) additive rather than subordinative, with details or items piled one upon the other; (b) aggregative rather than analytic, with ideas clustered on clichés and maxims that aid memory; (c) redundant or "copious," with much repetition of the "just said" to keep hearers and speakers on the same track; (d) conservative or traditionalist, with the culture's primary commitments frozen in narratives and aphorisms that can be memorized and repeated easily to the next generation, since there is no other way of keeping cultural history; (e) concrete in its processing of the lifeworld because the only way to test knowledge claims in nonabstract ways is referentially; (f) agonistically toned, with the testing process executed combatively; (g) empathetic and participatory rather than objectively distanced, with involving, personalized formulaic expressions rather than the objectification of the world that can accompany writing and printing; (h) homeostatic, with cultures living in a kind of permanent present, sloughing off the old that does not serve the here-and-now but retaining what is useful; and (i) situational rather than abstract, for oral language users cannot keep in mind abstractions that can be recorded on paper because memory is largely concrete (1982b, pp. 36-57). (John D. Schaeffer, 1990, nicely relates these features of oral discourse to a doctrine of common sense, *sensus communis*, as the foundation of community.)

Writing/print brings with it much more than mere ways of recording oral speech, although that, too, happens, leaving us with such discourses as orations and many strictly literary works that contain oral residues (e.g., "Oral Residue in Tudor Prose Style," 1971, pp. 23-47). Writing restructures consciousness, in the title of Chapter 4 of *Orality and Literacy*. Writing is a technology, an artificiality that exteriorizes thought; alienates the self from nature and even (by allowing for individuation) from other selves; allows for the development of lists, facts, science, and other marks of the exteriorization of knowledge; distances people by interposing texts between them, texts that, as Plato noted, cannot respond when interrogated; permitted the development of a nonrhetorical feminine style in discourse; and even produced totally reorganized societies (1982b, chap. 4; 1986b and "Transformations of the Word and Alienation," 1977a, pp. 17-49, on alienation and individuation; the essays and book on evolution already cited; "Latin and the Social Fabric," 1962a, pp. 206-219, and 1981a, pp. 129-148 on the feminine, which becomes associated with the rise of the vernacular; and "Transformations of the Word," 1967b, pp. 17-110, on social organization).

Electronic media—and Ong includes the telegraph, telephone, radio, sound motion pictures (because electronic sound is added to electrically projected vision), television, and computers—compose a further stage in humanity's evolution. Ong realizes that we are too much a part of the electronic revolution as yet to fully comprehend its psychodynamics and its social impacts. In the 1960s, he tends to discuss it along McLuhanesque lines (1967b, pp. 87-92); that leads him to think of electronic media in evolutionary terms, in terms of both the Freudian psychosexual developmental model

(1967b, pp. 92-110) and a sociobiological evolutionary model (1967b, pp. 103-104; "Evolution and Cyclicism in Our Time," 1967a, pp. 61-82; and 1981a, esp. pp. 9-12). "Transformations of the Word," first developed as the Terry Lectures for Yale in 1964, is perhaps Ong's most historicist conceptualization of the West's three-stage, linear evolution. In this period, he is busy breaking the back of cyclicist thinking and reconciling Darwinist evolutionary thought with Christianity.

Ong struggles to free himself from mere linearity, however, because he is convinced that change always brings with it residues from older cultural dispensations. Thus, the idea of phylogeny, of cultural developments in which stores of experience and knowledge are accumulated and passed on genetically from one generation to another, becomes appealing to him in the 1970s (1971, p. 10; and "Transformations of the Word and Alienation," 1977a, pp. 17-49). The key phrase moving out of the 1970s and into the 1980s, however, is "secondary orality." Ong believes that "The basic orality of language is permanent" (1982b, p. 7), by which he means that the great majority of the world's languages are not written, that traces of orality are present in all languages, and that reading normally consists in transmuting the inscribed word into sound, either interiorly in the imagination or exteriorly aloud (Gee & Ong, 1983). As early as "The Literate Orality of Popular Culture," Ong writes:

> Secondary orality is founded on—though it departs from—the individualized introversion of the age of writing, print, and rationalism which intervened between it and primary orality and which remains as part of us. History is deposited permanently, but not unalterably, as personality structure. (1971, p. 285)

Here is a hermeneutic understanding of mediation, one wherein the past is re-presented albeit in determinatively altered forms in current practice. So for example, "Secondary orality has generated a strong group sense, for listening to spoken words forms hearers into a group, a true audience . . . But secondary orality generates a sense for groups immeasurably larger than those of primary oral culture—McLuhan's 'global village' " (1982b, p. 136). And secondary orality has traces of the spontaneity that characterized primary orality, though, because we have absorbed the analyticity of print, "We plan our happenings carefully to be sure that they are thoroughly spontaneous" (1982b, p. 137). The agonistic practices of orality seemingly have returned in the form of televised political debates, but there are important differences:

On television contending presidential candidates do not stomp about a platform flailing their arms or even stand out in the open, like earlier orators metonymically claiming possession of a field, but install themselves behind protective lecterns for genteel exchanges of words projecting images of their self-contained selves instead of pacing up and down a rostrum flailing verbally at one another. They have texts in front of them—a state of affairs unknown to orators from antiquity through the Renaissance and beyond.

Writing governs our oral delivery as never before, and since, as has been seen, writing is interiorizing and nonforensic, the agonistic edge of oratory is dulled. (1981a, p. 142).

Ong thus, at times struggling for the right image or allusion, complicates his early linear model of mediational evolution, producing a kind of hermeneutic figure. In both *Fighting for Life* and *Hopkins, the Self, and God*, Ong completes his portrait of the present age by showing how the past is tied to the present in agonistic yet complementary tensions. While humankind undoubtedly has always valued historicity, following the spread of writing, it, in fact, could invent history proper, recorded chronicles and their interpretation (1977a, pp. 74-77; 1982b, pp. 96-101). Hence both histories and historicity, that is, both our view of sequences of past events as well as our inward sense of cyclical events, produce a noetic state in which technologically sophisticated media take on the status of secondary orality, and our cultures exist as the global villages McLuhan depicted (1968).

Ong's orality and literacy theorems, therefore, in good structuralist practice are founded on a duality. The two terms "orality" and "literacy" can be combined in different ways to produce a sophisticated analysis. They can be opposed, used with one modifying the other ("literate orality" and "oral literature"), employed adjectivally ("literate popular culture" and "oral noetics"), and even examined derivatively (with both orality and literacy seen as "transformations of the word"). Out of differentiation is born analyticity, and out of analyticity is born discriminative and hence critical scholarship— Ong's forte. While usually circumspect in its presence (e.g., 1982b, pp. 160-171), he flirts with postmodernist thought at the end of *Hopkins, the Self, and God*, because it allows him access to the "I" in ways more modernist and structuralist thought does not. Yet those flirtations are rare; he prefers to return time and again to his more totalizing orality and literacy theorems because they widen his vision and enlarge his insights so he can subsume under them both the self and society.

Consciousness: The Processes of Psychodynamics

As has been noted, Ong, as well as many other American students of culture, turns inward to the study of self, of the "I," of consciousness. Communication to Ong is to be studied in part to help us better deal with consciousness:

> Communication strikes deep into the consciousness. It is inadequate to think of communication, as we sometimes do, in terms of "contact." "Contact" suggests relationship in terms of surface. Communication is not the surface of life, but one aspect of life's substance. It is not expendable decoration, something added ad libitum to existence. Rather, when existence itself reaches a certain pitch with the advent of man, it entails communication. Man is a communicating animal. (1967a, p. 1)

Variously termed as "reflective self-possession expressed in the saying of 'I'" (1981a, p. 199), "the sensorium" (1967b, pp. 1ff.), "ego dominance" (1971, p. 15), "a base of response to existence" (1977a, p. 43), "Self in self, steepéd, and páshed" (Hopkins, quoted in 1986a, p. 3), consciousness is a pivotal notion to Ong. His principal study of consciousness is his 1986 *Hopkins, the Self, and God.*

The problem of the "I" to Ong is common to psychogenetics, phylogenetics, and cultural evolution. As for the first, he says, "Psychogenetically, in each individual the basic sense of self, of 'I' as a positive experience bordered by the opposed 'not-I,' comes into being with the early, but gradual, separation of the mother from the child, who has to learn that he or she has boundaries, exists amongst others" (1986a, p. 4). Second, phylogenetically, Ong sees patterns of self-consciousness, among other aspects of existence, carried down through generations ("Rhetoric and the Origin of Consciousness," 1971, pp. 1-22). And third, consciousness varies with cultural experience. Gerard Manley Hopkins, nineteenth-century Jesuit poet, could not have had his sense of selfhood without the advent of modern thought. Says Ong:

> This inward turning of consciousness . . . develops in counterbalance with the extreme outward turning implemented by the distancing or "objectivizing" technologies of writing, print, and computers, so that it is clear that self-consciousness is not the only feature marking the modern sensibility. . . . It has as concomitant and related phenomena the subjectivity or solipsism with which modern art and literature are often charged, the modern sense of alienation (the self feels itself in the extreme isolation of the nameless, pronominal "I") . . . a certain rejection of history (the "I," as earlier noted, is historically free-floating, though it can and eventually does bring vast reaches of history into itself), the

rejection of organized society (which relates named people in nameable structures) in favor of community (which relates people personally, on an I-you basis). (1986a, p. 130; cf. "Transformations of the Word and Alienation," 1977a, pp. 17-49)

All of this means that consciousness must work through relationships between "the two worlds, interior and exterior," which through time it has "become more and more capable of dealing with in verbalized detail" (1986b, p. 155). That working-through, to Ong, is ultimately the process of self-definition. Names are rhetorical, given to us by others; the "I" is self-understood:

The "I" identifies itself by its self-awareness and by this alone. The "I" has no name. Others know me as Walter, but of myself and to myself I am no more Walter than I am Tom or Dick or Harry, however much I may have accustomed myself to referring to myself or being referred to as Walter. To myself, I am simply "I." This "I" I alone can find. . . . All others besides myself, even father and mother, can contact this "I" only indirectly. . . . The "I" exists in a state of terrifying isolation. No matter how close another is to me, he or she can never break through into this center of my being, into what really matters. (1981a, pp. 194, 195, 196)

Yet, paradoxically, only such "I's" can open themselves and unite through love to one another to form true communities: "A human being is open to closure" (1981a, p. 198). The concept of psychodynamics, therefore, is extremely important to Ong. The processes of self-definition are manifold because, as noted, they work within psychogenetic, phylogenetic, cultural, and even one's own experiential realms as he illustrates in *Hopkins, the Self, and God,* where the poet's background as scientist is seen in his poetry. "When in the series of anthropoids and prehominids," believes Ong, "some beings appeared who were capable of the reflective self-possession expressed in the saying of 'I,' at whatever point they did so, the leap into human existence had clearly taken place" (1981a, p. 199).

Symbolization, therefore, is a key to the psychodynamics of self-defini-tion. And, of course, if symbolization is important, so are communicative modes—orality, literacy, electronics. Each of these variously distances in-dividuated selves from one another and their environment, and hence allows for stronger or weaker senses of selfhood. Psychodynamic mechanisms are crucially dependent upon the communicative modes of operations because each form of intrapersonal and interpersonal mediation seems adapted for particular levels of "innering" and "outering." Self-reflection, for example, requires an ability to distance oneself from one's "I"; that could occur only in the later stages of modernism, the later period of print domination, when self-consciousness could be distanced enough from mere existence (i.e., outered) so that it could look back at its privatized psyche contemplatively (i.e., innered). The poetry of Hopkins holds such fascination for Ong because in it can be observed these psychodynamics at work—an outered "I" looking back into the psyche and expressing the resulting vision, the sense of self-consciousness, in language. Later essays will treat consciousness more extensively. It is a key problematic for Ong because consciousness is finally our way into the cosmos. One of the many reasons Ong admires Pierre Teilhard de Chardin is because his *The Phenomenon of Man* is "synthesizing our awareness of the person with our knowledge of the evolutionary universe" (1967a, p. 144).

Culture: Foreground or Background?

As suggested, the problem of culture for Ong is a relational one. That is, he seldom discusses the idea of culture per se; he has little interest in institutions as cultural edifices and equal disinterest in boundaried definitions of peoples. It might be easy to assert that in his foregrounding of mediation and psychodynamics Ong backgrounds culture, making it but the field for the other forces of cultural evolution. That would be easy to say but not quite accurate. He really cannot offer the generalizations (theorems) he does about mediation and consciousness without holding some sort of theory of culture, however shadowy its definition. So what is that theory?

First, it is a broad vision, devoted to examining the most expansive contours of society in general. Ong seems interested in the patterns of *Geistesgeschichte* broadly conceived, not simply as "history of ideas" but more literally as the history of spirit. Ong uses the word *ethos* in its most generic sense, in reference to the fundamental character of a people ("Personalism and the Wilderness," 1962a, pp. 233-241). So the title essay of *The Barbarian Within* works a grand equation: insider:outsider as Greek:barbarian as scholastic:humanist as American:beatnik (1962a, pp. 260-285). Insiders and outsiders have contrasting spirits, counterpoised *ethoi*. Ong goes so far in "The Barbarian Within" to posit that culture is a kind of collective consciousness that characterizes a people at a particular time (see esp. pp. 284-285).

Second, as just suggested, Ong's theory of culture is really more time-bound than space-bound. Ong is maddeningly variable in his spatial definition of cultures. So in "The Barbarian Within," Greeks (Athenians), scholastics (European medieval scholars), Russians (citizens of the USSR), Americans (a geographically bounded peoples), American blacks (a racial group within the United States), and beatniks (a soft-edged group with only the loosest association with each other in the 1950s) are all talked about as "cultures"—and all in a single essay. Spatial associations seem to matter little, nor is consistency in physically defining analytical units important to Ong. The groups he identifies in "The Barbarian Within" are really defined temporally; these existed together in time and were bound together by common spirit or *ethos*, not other proximal relationships. Even temporal units are highly variable. The scholastics are defined as a group across centuries, while beatniks come and go culturally within a decade.

Third, Ong's segmentations are erratic because cultural change is his point of interest, and varied psychocultural changes can be studied across large expanses of time. Culture does not change in the twinkling of an eye, but, rather, revolutions occur in increments—almost literally one mind at a time—through long periods. Thus, the beatniks discussed in "The Barbarian Within" are simply symptomatic of outsiderness in the United States; other outsiders—Russians (pp. 276-277), Latin Americans (pp. 279-280), and American blacks (p. 282)—are discussed in one work. What really is being analyzed in the essay is the effect of insiderness/outsiderness on the American collective psyche, a struggle that has roots in the very colonization of the country. Ong thus has little interest in this or that segment of a specific society. Rather, he studies what Havelock terms "cross-cultural collisions" (1986, chap. 4), where "cross-cultural" is understood primarily as what an anthropologist would term intracultural phenomena, where such collisions can occur over multiple generations and where they can work themselves out in different ways for different corners of a population.

To Ong, then, a culture at base is defined noetically. The one and the many, self and society, "I" and "thou" merge in noetic activity, which is simultaneously individualized and collectivized. The word "psychoculture" encapsulates Ong's conception of "culture." The self and its society are assuredly separated, for of course the "I" of consciousness is isolated, even anonymous (1986a, p. 131). Yet, individuated consciousness and collective spirit are made from the same noetic material, for psychogenetics to Ong are always complemented and massaged by phylogenetics and cultural *ethoi*. The implicit (phylogenetic) and explicit (cultural) structures and notions of the past blend imperceptibly with the implicit (psychogenetic) and explicit (experiential) structure and notions of the presently existent "I." And thus, "the past is formative of the present" (1967a, p. 12). Ong ultimately values anthropology so highly and even sees himself as a kind of linguistic anthropologist, therefore, because American monists investigate cultures from both the inside and the outside:

Anthropology roots man in external environment, in time and space, descriptively and scientifically. Yet in doing so it in turn invites the relating of this external environment to man—which is to say, to an interiority, for it is in his possession of an inviolable interior, a personal conscious center, that man differs from other phenomena in the universe. *When anthropological studies become involved with man's interior (as they are more and more), they develop their present keen interest in communication* [italics added], which relates them not only to linguistic and literary studies, to psychology, sociology and philosophy, but also to something more directly religious—love itself. . . . I do not mean to suggest that anthropology has fully succeeded in linking man's interior with the external world, but only that it gives promise of some more unitary vision. (1967a, pp. 143-144)

Anthropology, to Ong, thus not only analyzes environment and society in time and space but, with hard work, also blends together the study of culture, consciousness, and communication—the three conceptual centers of humane studies. The italicized statement is Ong's hope for the triangulation of these three centers.

In the final analysis, culture is not simply field or backdrop to Ong, no matter how seldom he does explicit cultural analysis. He practices, in a cataloging of intellectual interests, cultural studies because a theory of culture allows him to bring together objective and subjective experience and to situate the individual within the world and then the cosmos—always his goal (1967a, p. 145).

Situating the Situator

Walter J. Ong is fond of classification. It is fitting, then, that we place him in and among the array of twentieth-century rhetorics and communication theories, in particular defining his contributions to cultural studies in America.

This century has had interpersonal communication processes theorized from a great number of perspectives: linguistic (Chomsky, 1965; Richards, 1936), social (Burke, 1950; Duncan, 1968; St. Clair & Giles, 1980), ethical (Ehninger & Hauser, 1984; Hoover, 1982), psychological (Berne, 1964; St. Clair & Giles, 1980), political (Bitzer, 1981; Edelman, 1964; Ellul, 1964), philosophical (Gusdorf, 1965; Habermas, 1979; Husserl, 1965; Perelman & Olbrechts-Tyteca, 1969; Toulmin, 1958), and cultural (Carey, 1989; Hall,1959). The examination of people, places, objects, processes, and concepts from varied perspectives, from axiomatic systems that guide the way we look at the world, I take to be a near-defining characteristic of contemporary

Western thought. Even such empirical philosophies as positivism are perspectival in that they are founded on articles of perceptual faith (the principle of verifiability) and on conceptual hierarchies (facticity and sense valued above metaphysics and non-sense). (See Ayer, 1946.) Once questions of symbolization and meaningfulness become central to inquiry, as they are for most scholars in the liberal arts traditions, perspectivism is almost inevitable. We have called Ong an American student of culture, thus identifying him with a humanistic perspective on communication and the human sciences. This school or viewpoint has been but vaguely demarcated in the literature and in this essay. James Carey (1989) has started and we have continued the project so as to more clearly specify Ong's primary contributions to intellectual life in the late twentieth century.

Where, then, does Ong fit among scholars interested in cultural understandings of rhetoric and communication? First, one ought to expect any member of this school to be concerned about the matters of communication, culture, and consciousness as we have defined them. And I think that is largely true. Among communication scholars in this tradition, Carey has written a grounding essay defining a cultural approach to communication studies that triangulates the three terms (1989, chap. 1). McLuhan's great aphorism, "The medium is the message," would have made no sense whatsoever without his understanding of synesthesia and other mental processes (Gronbeck, 1981). Harold Adams Innis's understanding of time- and space-bound cultures was rooted in not only studies of mediation but also a theory of knowledge and perception (Innis, 1972). Kenneth Burke, while more interested in communicative forms than mediation per se, nonetheless proposes a dramatistic theory of symbolic action that explains the ways in which meanings are enacted by social agents and shared through constituting documents (Burke, 1950).

While others could be mentioned, the purpose here is not to construct a formal school, but, again, to isolate Ong's contribution. It comes down, I think, to this: *Among American communication scholars, Ong is the strongest student of consciousness*, a student of culture one ought to examine along with the likes of David Riesman, Christopher Lasch, and Garry Wills. We normally, of course, associate Ong's work with mediation—with the visualist thesis of his work on the European Renaissance and with the orality-literacy theorems. No doubt that is proper. Yet not only have many others been working on the orality-literacy theorems, but it is often those others who have done the important textual analyses, the field work, that Walter Ong then summarizes and extends, as in *Orality and Literacy* and even in *Fighting for Life*. He certainly has done his version of field work (critical analysis) in such books as *Ramus, Method, and the Decay of Dialogue* and *Hopkins, the Self, and God*, but his boldest conceptualizing and theorizing occurs in works where he is not concentrating upon critical analysis of particular documents. It seems to occur when he takes yet one more run at understanding human consciousness in relationship both to individual situations and to collective activities, as in his trilogy of collected essays, *The Presence of the Word* (1967b), *Rhetoric, Romance, and Technology* (1971), and *Interfaces of the Word* (1977a).

Ong's attention to culture and consciousness, his conceptualization of psychoculture, is nuanced, not the kind of doctrinaire Freudian notions that fill, say, *The Journal of Psychohistory*. As noted, Ong is ever the eclectic, the intellectual scavenger who haunts multiple literatures in search of alternative understandings of consciousness-in-culture. His reconciliation of literary with psychocultural analysis is his hallmark, not only placing him within an American tradition of cultural studies, but making him perhaps the premier literary figure within it. The "transformations of the word" he so often discusses are attempts to rechart or refigure the idea of psychoculture as the bed for human textual (communicative) activity. His search for the ideal articulation of such transformations is endless in part because consciousness and culture are evolving, in part because they have been imported into numerous contemporary scholarly literatures and hence are regularly new-modeled, and in part because Ong's own spirit restlessly seeks to sketch the ultimate picture of *animal symbolicum*, a concept all great students of communication since Ernst Cassirer have sought to perfect.

Walter J. Ong, SJ, has been a prolific writer and a scholar whose influence has been felt across the full range of the human arts and sciences. Among the many twentieth-century statements on the human condition and its grounding in notions of communication, culture, and consciousness, Ong's is both backward-looking and forward-looking: a statement from a scholar with classical grounding and yet contemporary vision. He bridges both traditional rhetorical studies and contemporary communication studies in his effort to rethink mediation, mind, and social matrices. He straddles the social and literary traditions in typically American ways. He can be conservatively analytical, radically theoretical, and always, always, liberally humane.

2

An Overview of Walter J. Ong's Work

THOMAS J. FARRELL

As humankind moves toward the cosmopolis envisioned by Robert M. Doran (1990, pp. 355-386), world-cultural consciousness needs to emerge in more people, as Doran notes (pp. 527-558). World-cultural consciousness certainly emerged in Walter J. Ong, SJ. Ong has lectured widely about communication and related subjects across the United States and Canada as well as in Europe, the Middle East, Central and West Africa, North Africa, East Asia, and Latin America. Various books of his have been or are being translated into French, Italian, German, Spanish, Swedish, Romanian, Japanese, and Korean. Ong is surely a citizen in the emerging cosmopolis.

In the 1980s Ong published three important books. While *Fighting for Life* (1981a) and *Hopkins, the Self, and God* (1986a) grow out of concerns found in Ong's earlier works, *Orality and Literacy* (1982b) sums up central concerns of Ong's investigations in many of those earlier works. As the following survey of the early, middle, and late periods of his scholarly career shows, the study of orality and literacy has been a central concern of his work, although not his only one by any means. The late work often makes more explicit what was less explicit in earlier work. For example, Ong's discussion of the basic orality of language in *Orality and Literacy* (1982b, pp. 5-15) is more explicit about the oral base of language than is his treatment of language in his much earlier Master's study of Hopkins's sprung rhythm (1949). However, the point about the oral base of language is in effect implicit in that early study.

AUTHOR'S NOTE: In various parts of this essay, I have freely incorporated material from my own reviews in the following journals: *Philosophy and Rhetoric, College Composition and Communication, Cross Currents,* and *Review for Religious.*

In a similar vein, many of the themes developed in Ong's later work are part of *Ramus, Method, and the Decay of Dialogue: From the Art of Discourse to the Art of Reason* (1958a), which in this respect is his most seminal work. The polemic/irenic contrast developed in *The Presence of the Word* (1967b) is part of what Ong was pointing to in the subtitle about the contrast between the art of discourse and the art of reason, although the explicit terms *polemic* and *irenic* are not in the earlier work. By the same token, Ong's attention to agonistic structures in *Fighting for Life* (1981a) traces back to part of what he was pointing to in the subtitle of his book on Ramism, even though the term *agonistic* is not found in that early work.

However, if Ong's early works about Hopkins and Ramism are seedbeds for themes grown to full blossom in his later works, then the studies by Albert B. Lord (1960) and Eric A. Havelock (1963) are the soil and water that nourished the growth of the seeds of these themes in Ong's mind. But the themes were already there and ready to grow in Ong's mind. As a matter of fact, given what Ong had done in his works on Hopkins and Ramism, the studies by Lord and Havelock were a godsend. They enabled Ong to develop more explicitly his insights about orality and literacy.

The Early Period

Ong's sensitivity to the oral-aural dimension of communication is doubtlessly the most distinctive feature of his approach to the study of communication. His concern for the oral-aural dimension enables him to call attention to orality and voice, and it enables him to discuss orality-literacy interactions and contrasts as very few scholars can. How did Ong, a classics major at Rockhurst College in Kansas City (class of 1933), come to be so attuned to the oral-aural dimension of communication?

Ong's study of the "sprung rhythm" in the poetry of the Victorian Jesuit Gerard Manley Hopkins (1949) was originally written as his Master's thesis at Saint Louis University, under the direction of Marshall McLuhan, who taught the New Criticism at Saint Louis University from 1937 to 1944 but had not yet begun his work on the media (Ong, 1981b, p. 129). In that study Ong stresses that "Hopkins knew sprung rhythm because he heard it in English" (1949, p. 104). "Hopkins' entire discussion of his rhythm," says Ong, "evinces that he found something, his ears were opened, and once they were, he began to hear about him more and more evidence of the same thing" (p. 105). The rest of his long essay is devoted to explaining what Hopkins had come upon. Ong's attention to the oral-aural dimension of communication in this early study is significant because it marks a basic orientation for his scholarly work. It is also significant for another reason: In his study of Ramism with its visually arrayed dichotomies, Ong called attention to the visualization of the word; so Ong moved his attention from oral-aural phenomena in his Master's thesis to visual phenomena in his doctoral dissertation.

While Ong was studying at Saint Louis University from 1938 to 1941, McLuhan introduced him to the work of Peter Ramus, the Renaissance French philosopher and educational reformer. McLuhan had studied some of Ramus's works in graduate studies at Cambridge University, and he had come to know more about Ramism from Perry Miller's *The New England Mind: The Seventeenth Century* (Ong, 1981b, p. 134). Ong went on to do his doctoral dissertation at Harvard on Ramism under Miller. In 1958 Harvard University Press published Ong's two volumes on Ramism: *Ramus, Method, and the Decay of Dialogue* and *Ramus and Talon Inventory.* (Ong turned 46 on November 30 that year.) The latter volume carries the dedication, "For Herbert Marshall McLuhan, who started all this," to acknowledge that McLuhan had introduced Ong to the work of Ramus (Ong, 1981b, p. 134). But Ong developed his own insights concerning Ramism and print, as McLuhan noted in *The Gutenberg Galaxy* (1962).

To understand Ramism from Ong's standpoint, one needs to consider carefully the full title of his major work: *Ramus, Method, and the Decay of Dialogue: From the Art of Discourse to the Art of Reason* (1958a). In this highly original work, backed by the further massive documentation in its companion volume, *Ramus and Talon Inventory* (1958b), he aligns the art of discourse with oral-aural communication and the art of reason with print. As the subtitle indicates, Ramist method was pivotal in the larger movement from conceptualizing thought in terms of one person crying out to or addressing another person in discourse or dialogue, to conceptualizing thought as the activity of one person working inside himself or herself, with no dialogue, not even interior dialogue. The art of discourse to Ong was oriented toward public argumentation and thus was polemical, while the art of reason was oriented toward exposition and thus tended to be more private, irenic, and quiescent. The refutation of the actual or hypothetical adversarial position was a prescribed part of the art of oral discourse, as Aristotle noted in his *Rhetoric* (1402a-1403b, 1414b, 1418b-1419a). Consequently, in *Fighting for Life* (1981a, pp. 24-26, 121-134, 139-144), Ong aptly characterizes classical rhetoric as agonistic—contest-oriented, oriented toward adversativeness, built around a sense of being "up against it." But Ramism eliminated from the exposition of any "art" the standard refutation of possible adversarial positions in favor of oppositionless, quasi-monologic exposition, in which the method of following dichotomies to invent arguments supplanted arguing with actual or hypothetical adversarial positions. Adversaries were fended off or demolished by Ramus in separate published lectures apart from the "art" itself.

Ramus's reliance on method, a somewhat simplified logic as well as a means of invention, accentuated the concern for certitude by purporting to offer beforehand the proper form for the development of all thought, rather than allow the form to develop with the content of the thought. In actual practice deliberative rhetoric in the classical tradition involved reasoning from probable premises to probable conclusions. Ramus (1515-1572) followed the lead of Peter of Spain (c.1210-1277) and Rudolph Agricola (1444-1485), transforming the actual practice of rhetoric and logic, according to Ong. While Peter of Spain had developed an antecedent of modern symbolic logic out of probabilistic rhetoric, Ramus extended Peter of Spain's initiative in such a way in his *Dialectic* as to imply that good thinking proceeds from self-evident truths to a concern for certitude, instead of a concern for probability.

The genesis of Ong's thought in the early period of his scholarly life can be summed up by noting that it proceeds from a twofold development: acute attention to oral-aural and visual phenomena. While well-informed and confident in his claims, Ong maintains a sober and even staid tone in his publications and seemingly writes for a specialized scholarly audience. His subsequent efforts of the middle and late periods are characterized by a more lyrical tone.

The four collections of Ong's early period are not focused on orality-literacy contrasts, but explore contemporary culture. *Frontiers in American Catholicism* (1957) and *American Catholic Crossroads* (1959) treat issues in American Catholic culture and intellectual life, and religious-secular encounters in the modern world. *The Barbarian Within* (1962a) treats literary criticism and theory, teaching and communication, and personalism, existentialism, and outsiders. *In the Human Grain* (1967a) treats communications, evolution and cyclicism, and issues affecting Christian faith today. While Ong is clearly addressing a wider audience in these various essays than in his early studies of Hopkins and Ramism, he does not sound the lyrical tone found in *Knowledge and the Future of Man* (1968) and other works of the middle period.

In the Hopkins thesis, Ong engaged in the kind of close textual study characteristic of the New Criticism, only with reference to prosody rather than thematic matters. In the studies of Ramism, Ong emulated Perry Miller's broad approach to the study of cultural phenomena, but with special new foci of his own developed from massive reading in Ramus's and others' works in Latin before and after Ramus. When Ong was doing research on Ramism in various European libraries as a Guggenheim Fellow in the early 1950s, he stayed in the Jesuit house in Paris in which Pierre Teilhard de Chardin lived, where he read Teilhard's works for the first time (Lumpp, 1987a, p. 16). Ong was evidently encouraged by the convergence of Teilhard's thought with his own. In *Frontiers in American Catholicism* and *American Catholic Cross-roads,* Ong called attention to Teilhard's work. Had Ong not been encouraged by Teilhard's insights about the open-ended evolution of interiority in the cosmos, he may not have been as bold and daring as he was in his treatment of Ramism. Ramism's tendency to conceptualize thought as the activity of one person working inside himself or herself, with no dialogue, not even interior dialogue, served as the foil for Ong to develop his own insights about dialogue and interiority, not only in *Ramus, Method, and the Decay of Dialogue* but also in *The Barbarian Within.* The presence and growth of human interiority is arguably the most distinctive theme in all of Ong's work.

In addition to his two-volume study of Ramism, Ong also wrote about Ramism in connection with Hobbes and Talon's rhetoric in English (1951), the naming of Methodism (1953), the pre-Newtonian mind (1954a), Fouquelin's French rhetoric (1954b), Johannes Piscator (1954c), the transit to the modern mind (1955a), Cossart and du Monstier (1955b), Renaissance classroom procedure (1960b), the commercial mind (1961), a translation of Euripides (1964), Christianus Urstitius (1974b), and John Milton's textbook on logic (1982a). Moreover, he reviewed critical editions of two of Ramus's works (1965, 1966), wrote articles about Ramus for two encyclopedias (1967c, 1967d), and edited and wrote prefaces for reprints of two works by Ramus (1969, 1970). Ong's extensive treatment of Ramism is a singular achievement, the attainment of which enabled Ong to discover and formulate subsequent insights about the interaction of communication and culture and about male agonism.

The Middle Period

In 1960 *The Singer of Tales* by Albert B. Lord was published, and in 1963 *Preface to Plato* by Eric A. Havelock. These two books catalyzed Ong's thinking and in great part led to the development of his trilogy about psychocultural evolution and communication: *The Presence of the Word* (1967b), *Rhetoric, Romance, and Technology* (1971), and *Interfaces of the*

Word (1977a). In this trilogy Ong comes to identify four stages of psychocultural evolution based on shifts in communication: (a) primary oral culture, (b) manuscript or chirographic culture, (c) print or typographic culture, and (d) secondary oral culture, which is essentially literate but yet involves a new sensory mix because of electronic media that accentuate sound. Further, the computer, Ong points out, enables electronics also to extend almost beyond belief the visually based analytic processes encouraged by writing and print. He sees each of these four stages of culture as characterized by a different sensory mix.

To explain how the shift in the sensory mix occurs, Ong refers to the interiorization of literacy. That which is interiorized by the senses affects what is in the mind. Ong writes of the interiorization of literacy and literate modes of thought as proceeding by degrees, and he associates this gradual interiorization with the process of the individuation of consciousness. Ong also refers to residual orality and residual forms of primary oral thought and expression to account for the persistence of certain characteristics of primary orality even after the invention or introduction of vowelized literacy. The waning of primary orality proceeds by degrees. However, in order to be able to write about residual forms of primary orality in his trilogy, Ong would need to know the features of primary orality to a certain extent, and in order to write about the interiorization of vowelized literacy, he would need to distinguish features of literate thought. Lord and Havelock gave him the data he needed to discern the basic features of primary orality and vowelized literacy as he came to articulate these features in his trilogy.

In *The Singer of Tales,* Lord extends the analysis of recordings of Yugoslav poets begun by his teacher Milman Parry. Parry and Lord discuss what they call formulaic elements and formulas used by oral poets to compose "lines," as we would call them, as they perform. Lord also discusses themes or more or less predictable sequences of action used by oral poets to compose episodes in their narrative poems. Lord's study enabled Ong to see that primary oral thought and expression are formulary.

In other words, as Ong explains in *Interfaces of the Word,* if thought and expression were not formulary, primary oral people would not remember the thought expressed. Now, from his study of the history of rhetoric, Ong was familiar with the use of commonplace material in the rhetorical and literary tradition of the West. In *The Presence of the Word* (1967b, pp. 80-81), Ong discusses two kinds of commonplaces used in rhetoric: (a) cumulative commonplaces (e.g., sayings, proverbs, purple passages, set phrases, epithets, adages, maxims, apothegms, epigrams, *sententiae, exempla,* emblems, kennings, and standard parallelisms and oppositions), and (b) analytic commonplaces or *topoi* (i.e., common "logical" or analytic ways of approaching, inventing, and ordering material for presentation). The analytic commonplaces include definition, genus, species, wholes, parts, adjacents, relatives, comparisons, opposites, and witnesses, and "for a person, one might, by a kind of analytic process, consider his family, descent, sex, age, education, and the like" (Ong, 1977a, p. 149). Ong characterizes these as "concrete conceptualizations" (1958a, p. 104). What Parry and Lord call formulas and formulaic elements in oral narratives are similar to what Ong calls cumulative commonplaces, and what Lord calls themes in oral narratives are similar to what Ong calls analytic commonplaces. Thus Lord's work enabled Ong to align well-known features of the rhetorical tradition with features of the primary oral culture.

In *Interfaces of the Word* Ong focuses on one type of cumulative commonplace, epithets, to call attention to a difference between Spenser and Milton (1977a, pp. 189-212). Milton rarely uses epithets in the sense of standard, expected qualifiers, while Spenser frequently uses epithets, which correspond to formulaic elements in the Parry-Lord account of oral composing practices. However, on the level of larger formulary expressions (the equivalent of formulas in the Parry-Lord account), Ong finds that Milton relies on formulary expressions, whereas Hopkins, by contrast, employs more particular details (1986a, pp. 46-53). In other words, various types of cumulative commonplaces continued to be used long after the invention of writing, and later, of print.

In *Rhetoric, Romance, and Technology* Ong contends that formulary expressions dominated composing practices until the rise of Romanticism in the latter part of the eighteenth century (1971, pp. 255-283). Ong refers to these vestiges of primary oral composing practices as oral residue, and he attributes the eventual demise of formulary expressions to the gradual interiorization of literacy and literate modes of thought and the individuation of consciousness. Because formulary expressions capture the typical, not the particular or original, Ong connects the Romantic valorization of originality with the deeper interiorization of literacy. Later, in *Hopkins, the Self, and God* (1986a), he connects the Victorian accentuation of particularity with the yet deeper interiorization of literacy, noting that in Hopkins's case the emphasis on particularity had been prepared for and reinforced by the Catholic ascetical tradition, and particularly the Jesuit form of this tradition as centered in *The Spiritual Exercises* of St. Ignatius of Loyola.

Ong's appropriation of Havelock's work enabled him to establish other coordinates for the orality-literacy model. Havelock identifies concreteness with primary orality, and more abstract thinking with literacy. Havelock maintains that the primary oral cast of mind constituted the chief obstacle to the abstract classification of experience, the arrangement of cause and effect, the use of analysis, and scientific rationalism. The primary oral person was involved and committed to a given position on matters, whereas the fully literate person could be detached and look at matters from different points of view. Highly literate persons can examine experience and rearrange it, separate themselves from their experiences instead of just empathetically identifying with them, and stand apart from the object, reconsider it, analyze it, and evaluate it.

Oral discourse was attentive to the sensory (the concrete) and was more disposed to describing actions than to creating abstractions because people hearing what was said or sung could feel and follow concrete actions. Primary oral people, Havelock points out, could not see, hear, or taste categories, classes, relationships, principles, or axioms. The oral tradition according to Havelock did not analyze history in terms of cause and effect, factors and forces, objectives and influences, and the like because these analytical processes were not amenable to the psychodynamics of the remembering processes upon which oral composing is based.

In *The Presence of the Word* Ong describes the phenomena of the human word and sound. The word is sound, an event in time and space. It has long been axiomatic that sight is the most knowing sense, for it gives the most knowledge of actuality. Ong accepts this, but notes, "Sound is more real or existential than other sense objects, despite the fact that it is more evanescent" (1967b, p. 111). Thus the data from hearing have a feeling of liveliness not sensed from the data from sight. Data from all our senses feed into the sensory mix. The two most prominent types of sense data are sound and sight. Sight data situates the person in front of things, while sound situates the person in the middle of actuality and simultaneity.

Either sound or sight can dominate the synthesis of all data in the sensory mix. Domination by auditory vis-à-vis visual syntheses fosters different personality structures and different characteristic anxieties in persons, Ong claims. To support his claim about personality structures, Ong discusses religious, educational, commercial, and other practices associated historically with these two types of sensory syntheses as manifested in primary oral and literate cultures, respectively. Sound synthesis is associated with the tendency to believe and be instructed by established or received authority; visualist synthesis is associated with the tendency to question received knowledge and the drive to discover new knowledge. Visualism is associated with strong tendencies toward individualism, and audism, with a strong sense of social or corporate bonding. Sound unites groups of living beings as nothing else can, says Ong.

The essays in *Rhetoric, Romance, and Technology* develop ideas introduced in *Ramus, Method, and the Decay of Dialogue* and *The Presence of the Word*. Themes from the first book are reiterated but expanded in studies about Ramist classroom procedure, the commercial mind, Swift, the associationist philosophers, and John Stuart Mill. The studies of rhetoric and human consciousness, oral residue in Tudor prose style, Tudor writings on rhetoric, Latin language study as a puberty rite, and the art of memory echo motifs in *The Presence of the Word*. The essays on Romanticism and technology and on secondary orality elaborate ideas beyond his previous books.

Ong begins his treatment of Romanticism and technology by noting that knowledge storage and retrieval devices are of paramount importance in any culture. Primary oral culture relies on the living human memory to store knowledge in formulary expressions. Literate culture, by contrast, relies on writing, and later, printed books. When more knowledge was stored in books than ever before, the human mind was freed for other tasks. Both Romanticism and the technology of the Industrial Revolution, Ong suggests, resulted from humanity's accrued noetic control over nature. When vast supplies of knowledge had been stored in readily retrievable form in print culture, as they were in eighteenth-century encyclopedias, then this macro-development in the culture freed human energies for other pursuits. People were free to develop new technologies without fear of forgetting the old ones, just as they were also thereby free to celebrate what is romantically mysterious, different, original, strange, ineffable, inaccessible, and unknown because what was commonly known was safely stored in books. Persons in a primary oral culture could not take such risks for fear of losing what was known. They needed to devote their energies to remembering what was known, as stored in formulary expressions or commonplaces. The residually oral manuscript culture of the West also employed formulary expressions, at times with learned content. Print culture encouraged the collection of formulary expressions, as in Erasmus's *Adages*. Later in print culture Romanticism scorned formulary expressions. In the subsequent highly literate culture, commonplaces were eschewed as clichés. In our contemporary secondary oral culture, clichés are popularly used, but at the same time, undercut and mocked because of our relentless literacy.

In *Interfaces of the Word* Ong for the first time regularly differentiates manuscript or chirographic culture from print or typographic culture. In addition, he moves from using the terms *primarily oral* and *secondarily oral* to using the terms *primary orality* and *secondary orality.* In this collection of essays, Ong studies the evolution of the word in relation to a wide range of subjects: African drum talk; mother tongues and learned languages; Renaissance collections of commonplaces; epithets in Spenser and Milton; sense analogues for intellection; death (retrospectivity and closure) and written composition, with special attention to the futurity of the Bible; orality's accent on mimesis and literacy's sharpened focus on irony; Hemingway's tough talk as a way to fictionalize an audience; the New Critics' conception of the poem as a closed field; the "talked book" coming out of today's secondary orality; and closure and openness, with special reference to contemporary secondary oral culture. Ong's essay titled "The Writer's Audience Is Always a Fiction" was reprinted in *Interfaces of the Word* (1977a, pp. 53-81) from the January 1975 *PMLA;* it is probably the most frequently cited work by Ong.

While the essays in that collection expand themes found in the essays collected in *The Barbarian Within* and *In the Human Grain,* Ong clearly had discovered his thesis by the time he wrote those later essays. The thesis had been implicit in his various explorations up until then—the thesis that most major developments in culture and consciousness are related to the evolution of the word from primary orality through chirography and typography to the electronic transformations of the word today.

As the term *interfaces* suggests, Ong employs concepts of systems analysis to describe and explain the evolution of the word. In a nutshell, he associates primary orality with open-systems thinking because it projects openness and is open existentially. He associates vowelized literacy with closed-systems thinking because it fosters closure and greater control, and he associates secondary orality (or literate orality) with open closure. In primary oral culture, the oral performer and the live audience interact on occasions of public verbal performance because the performer responds presently to the audience, whereas the writer's audience (of readers, not auditors) is always absent at the moment of writing and is therefore a fiction in the imagination of the writer as he or she writes. In addition, the reader's enjoyment of the written text is retrospective rather than participatory. That is, the text comes out of the past, whereas the live oral performance is participated in at the present moment of the performance. Writing and print thus require separateness and invite closure. Such closure is assuredly desirable at times, particularly "at earlier stages of thought to rule out distractions and achieve control . . . for I can share only what I have control of" (1977a, pp. 340, 336).

However, "closure is not the only result of writing and print," Ong notes, "for writing and print also open and liberate. They give access not only to information otherwise inaccessible but also make possible new thought processes," eventually leading to our contemporary open-systems models for conceptual representation (1977a, p. 305). Openness paradoxically means strengthening closure itself in certain ways, for it means strengthening organization, principles, and resistance where needed. Consequently, the interactional, transactional, developmental, process-oriented thinking of recent open-systems models "appears to effect a change in external conditions far less surely than a change in consciousness. There had never been any closed systems anyhow," declares Ong (1977a, p. 329), because "life is openness" (1977a, p. 325).

The writing exemplified in his trilogy in the middle period of his scholarly career is nuanced and powerful in its sweep and penetration. Clearly the studies by Lord and Havelock profoundly encouraged Ong to further develop insights he had come to earlier in writing about Hopkins and Ramus. By developing some of the implications of Lord's and Havelock's work in a great variety of essays, he eventually articulated his fourfold model of culture. The four stages of culture identified by Ong—primary oral culture, manuscript culture, print culture, and secondary oral culture—are working hypotheses that take into account certain critical data, and yet they are open to further elaboration. In this respect Ong's formulation of the orality-literacy hypothesis resembles Darwin's evolutionary hypothesis. Moreover, Ong's hypothesis is sweeping in its implications because it is essentially heuristic in orientation; it orients the sensibilities of scholarly investigators to take a fresh look at well-known data to discover neglected relationships, interactions, and contrasts.

In the middle period of his career Ong became Professor of Humanities in Psychiatry at Saint Louis University (1970), where he had been Professor of English since 1959 (Lumpp, 1987a, p. 16). With the late Charles Hofling, M.D., he co-founded and co-directed a joint program both for M.D.s who were residents in psychiatry and for invited Ph.D. students in English. Ong's psychoanalytic orientation comes out most clearly in this period in his treatment of colonialism, racism, and male antifeminism in "Truth in Conrad's Darkness" (1977b), which he wrote after he had "delivered a series of 26 lectures, seminars, and videotapes in Zaire, Cameroon, and Senegal (in French) and in Nigeria (in English) on a tour sponsored by the United States Board of Foreign Scholarships (April-May 1974) to commemorate the 25th anniversary of the Fulbright academic foreign exchange program" (Lumpp, 1987a, p. 17). He subsequently elaborated some of the themes of the Conrad article in *Fighting for Life: Contest, Sexuality, and Consciousness* (1981a). Ong was an associate editor of the *Quarterly Journal of Speech* from 1960 to 1977, and in 1978, he served as president of the Modern Language Association of America, which led to his presidential address about the human nature of professionalism (Ong, 1979b). Also in this period he published "Literacy and Orality in Our Times" (1978b), which has been reprinted in 10 different publications since its original appearance. Prior to writing that article about the pedagogical needs of students from a residual form of primary oral culture, Ong had previously called attention to the need of "those dominated through adolescence by the functional orality of subcultures in our American cities or some of our rural districts" for the proper encouragement to learn "the analytic thinking processes which can be interiorized only by grappling with the written word" (1977a, pp. 257, 258). At this time, Randolph F. Lumpp reports, Ong had been "assisting in tutoring in inner-city University programs" (1987a, p. 17). However, Ong had never before elaborated the implications of his work for orienting pedagogy as fully as he did in "Literacy and Orality in Our Times." He continued to call attention to his concern about pedagogy in *Orality and Literacy.*

The Late Period

Just as Ong's achievement in his extensive study of Ramism enabled him to move on to discover the psychocultural relationships formulated in his trilogy, so too the insights developed in his trilogy enabled him to move on to write his three diverse, but more accessible, books of the 1980s.

Orality and Literacy (1982b) is summative. In it Ong discusses the basic orality of language, reviews the modern discovery of primary oral cultures, identifies certain psychodynamics of primary orality, notes how writing restructures consciousness, analyzes print with reference to space and closure, points out how oral memory influences story line and characterization, and proposes some theorems concerning the implications of orality-literacy studies for deepening our understanding of subjects of concern to scholarly investigators: literary history; New Criticism and Formalism; structuralism; deconstruction; speech-act and reader-response theory; social sciences, philosophy, and biblical studies; "media" versus human communication; the inward turn of consciousness and the text; and being human. Ong sums up not only his own work but also that of many other scholars, integrating their contributions within the heuristic model he himself had already developed, thereby adding greater particularity to his work. Conversely, especially in the last chapter, he challenges various other investigators to take into account the oral-aural dimension of communication.

Ong uses Havelock's (1982) work to call attention to the intersection of the technology of vowelized literacy and the human mind in the development of abstract thinking and discursive reasoning. Vowelized literacy is alphabetic writing with fully separate letters for vowels (Ong, 1982b, p. 89). The Greek alphabet added vowels, producing vowelized literacy (1982b, pp. 90, 91). Syllabic writing systems, such as the one used by the Vai people in Liberia, are not forms of fully vowelized literacy in the sense that they use no separate vowels (1982b, pp. 85, 88). Havelock (1982) suggests that vowelized literacy, as distinct from nonvowelized literacy and all other forms of writing (such as pictographs), is a necessary but not sufficient condition for the development of abstract thinking and discursive reasoning, because these intellectual developments emerged with the emergence of vowelized literacy in ancient Greece. In the evolution of human thought, the shift from primary orality to vowelized literacy involves the movement from an implicit sense of things in concrete operational thinking to explicit concepts articulated through abstract thinking. As Havelock (1978) argues, this movement is exemplified in Plato's explicit articulation of the abstract concept of justice that is only implicit in the Homeric poems. A similar movement occurs in the *Republic,* where Plato makes explicit in the theory of the Divided Line what was implicit in the Story of the Cave. In Ong's estimate, the field work of A. R. Luria (1976) supports Havelock's claims about the psychodynamics of orality and literacy (Ong, 1982b, pp. 47, 49-56).

In this book Ong surveys the orality-literacy polarity in antiquity, the Middle Ages, the Renaissance, the Romantic Movement, and the present, drawing on studies of Western and non-Western manifestations. The Bible is a massive instance of works composed according to principles of oral composition, just as the Homeric poems are. Ong uses both the Bible and the Homeric poems as touchstones to make several important points about oral composing practices in antiquity. He notes:

> Medieval literature is particularly intriguing in its relation to orality because of the greater pressures of literacy on the medieval psyche brought about not only by the centrality of the biblical text . . . but also by the strange new mixture of orality (disputations) and textuality (commentaries on written works) in medieval academia. (1982b, p. 157)

In the Renaissance the orality-literacy polarity was accentuated by the revival of classical rhetoric on the one hand, and the invention of letterpress printing on the other. "The Romantic Movement," he claims, "marks the beginning of the end of the old orality-grounded rhetoric" that was taught in school

(1982b, p. 158). Because "girls were not commonly subjected to the orally based rhetorical training that boys got in school," he points out that there is a need for major studies examining the style of women writers, who became more prevalent in the age of Romanticism (1982b, p. 159). The orality-literacy polarity at present is manifested in all our new electronic orality and computers and in the emergence of the "talked book."

As noted in passing earlier, he also maintains that electronics does more than create secondary orality: It also extends the visualist, spatializing drive to produce slightly later the computer, a new kind of inscription which brings with it its own form of consciousness (1982b, p. 136). The computer maneuvers words and, later, visual design in space with a sophistication far beyond that of writing and print. In the preface to the 1983 paperback edition of *Ramus, Method, and the Decay of Dialogue,* Ong calls attention to the resemblance between Ramus's binary dichotomized charts and digital computer programs (p. viii). Using Ong's work on Ramus, Philip Leith (1990), a computer scientist, has noted the further resemblance between the aspirations of Ramism and the hopes of those who think that artificial intelligence will ever be fully realizable. Leith sees Ramism as the most spectacular attempt in history to implement total formalism in knowledge and as evidence of the predictable failure of such attempted formalism. Ong discusses the effects of the computer more fully in his 1985 Wolfson College Lecture at Oxford University (1986b, pp. 23-50).

At no point does Ong's view foreclose history: No new stage brings everything full circle. Secondary orality, now more and more allied with the computer, does not complete or revalidate primary orality. It resembles but also differs from primary orality. History has an open front. Because television and the other electronic technologies of secondary oral culture affect what many people now interiorize through their senses, it would seem to follow that a new understanding of communication and thinking may eventually emerge. Ong views this prospect with equanimity, although he is critical of certain aspects of secondary oral culture (1971, pp. 284-303; 1977a, pp. 305-341; 1978a, pp. 100-121).

His equanimity about secondary orality is rooted in his basically positive regard for oral-aural phenomena. But his equanimity never leads him to express a simpleminded antiliteracy attitude. Ong never suggests that we should dispense with our efforts to teach people to read and write well. Ong does not say that orality is good and literacy bad, nor does he say that either orality or literacy is an unqualified good. However, he notes that no peoples who know of writing want to forego it. Writing is a more advanced form of verbalization. It is, Ong notes, consciousness-raising. But it is not without some shortcomings: It cannot produce a Homer. Finally, he insists that orality-literacy studies must not be reductionist but relationist. All changes in culture and consciousness are not due simply to orality-literacy shifts, but most, if not all, major changes in culture relate in myriads of ways to these shifts. (In a subsequent essay, Ong, 1988, suggests some differences between interpretation in a purely oral world and textual hermeneutics, and situates the recent rise of deconstruction and reader-response criticism in terms of a sensibility conditioned by secondary orality. He has also worked out some of the implications of his hermeneutics of communication for the study of the Gospels, 1987, and of Hopkins, 1990.)

In *Fighting for Life: Contest, Sexuality, and Consciousness* (1981a), Ong adroitly draws material together from a wide range of disciplines to elucidate the complex human phenomena connected with contest in such arenas of endeavor as spectator sports, business, academia, politics, and religion. Ong seeks to identify the common elements of contest. He argues that humans need adversativeness in order to grow, and he infers that the human psyche is agonistically structured. While this book can be classified as a work in sociobiology, Ong styles it a work in noobiology, "the study of the biological setting of mental activity (Greek *nous, noos,* mind)" (1981a, p. 11). The explicit use of biological data is new in Ong's writings, although attention to biological evolution can be found in his essays in *Frontiers in American Catholicism* (1957), *American Catholic Crossroads* (1959), *Darwin's Vision and Christian Perspectives* (1960a), *The Barbarian Within* (1962a), *In the Human Grain* (1967a), *Knowledge and the Future of Man* (1968), and in passing references in his trilogy.

However, attention to adversativeness in mental activity is not new to Ong's writings. Adversativeness was a major feature of the material Ong surveyed in order to write *Ramus, Method, and the Decay of Dialogue.* The standard practice of refuting the adversarial position in classical rhetoric was inherently adversative. In *The Presence of the Word* (1967b, pp. 192-286), Ong identifies a polemical orientation with orality and an irenic orientation with literacy. As yet another coordinate for developing the orality-literacy model, the polemic/irenic contrast is important.

However, it is likewise important to note that the interiorization of literacy did not mark the cessation of polemic, but the transformation of polemic into a more distanced and irenic procedure. Highly literate people today test hypotheses in a struggle to ascertain the probable truth insofar as it can be established with reasonable probability. This testing spirit is an example of what Ong refers to in *Fighting for Life* as an agonistic tendency or orientation. But Ong had been attending to agonistic behavior in the early period of his career in his work on Ramism and in the middle period in *The Presence of the Word,* as just mentioned, in "Latin Language Study as a Renaissance Puberty Rite" (1971, pp. 113-141), and in "Agonistic Structures in Academia: Past to Present" (1974a, pp. 1-12). Since Ong explicitly refers supportively to the black civil rights movement and the women's movement in *Fighting for Life,* however, it probably is fair to say that had these cultural movements not occurred, Ong most likely would not have written *Fighting for Life* as it is.

Ong argues that the psychological and cultural phenomena connected with contest are rooted in biology. Citing studies in ethology, Ong points out that agonistic display plays a more critical role in the lives of males than of females in higher animal species. He attributes this to the fact that, ontogenetically and phylogenetically, males are more insecure than females—an insight that makes much typical male behavior intelligible. Ong argues that males are more insecure than females because females are more important for the reproduction of the human race. To counterbalance this basic biological difference, males tend to be more agonistic than females. Ong carefully specifies that he is not denying female insecurity or agonistic behavior in females, both of which are real; however, by using the comparative terms *more* or *greater,* he is pointing to an asymmetrical relationship, he says. In other words, if insecurity of the kind he is referring to or agonistic tendencies could be quantified and measured, the mean scores of males on these two qualities would be greater than the mean scores of females. By contrast, a symmetrical relationship (i.e., no gender differences) would yield identical mean scores.

Hopkins, the Self, and God (1986a) is about Hopkins, the subject of Ong's Master's thesis who figures also in one of the essays in *In the Human Grain* (1967a, pp. 99-126). Hopkins thus was the subject of Ong's attention in the early, middle, and late periods of his scholarly career. This latest book is developed in four long chapters around four surprisingly interrelated themes: (a) the Victorian milieu conditioned Hopkins's fascination with particularity and the self; (b) the Jesuit ascetic tradition sharpened Hopkins's concern for the self; (c) moral and systematic theology and actual pastoral practice also conditioned Hopkins's concern for the self; and (d) Hopkins's concern for the self presages and helps make more understandable the central concerns of twentieth-century modernity, and especially personalism, with the self. These themes are so far removed from Ong's treatment of Hopkins in his Master's thesis (1949) and in *In the Human Grain* (1967a, pp. 99-126) that he does not cite either of those essays in this book.

But he does use insights developed through his other works to situate many of the phenomena treated in this study. Specifically, he relates the Victorian fascination with particularity to the gradual interiorization of literacy over the centuries, just as he associates the concern for the self with the inward turn and greater individuation of consciousness in print culture. Ong is here reconsidering Hopkins in the light of the heuristic model he more fully developed after his earlier essays on Hopkins. Ong in the early period calls attention to the oral-aural dimension of Hopkins's work. Ong in the middle period calls attention to Hopkins's evolutionary (i.e., noncyclic) sense of time. Ong in the late period sees Hopkins in relation to the interiorization of literacy and celebrates Hopkins's awareness of the uniqueness of each particular self. Ong's interest in the self grows out of his essays about personalism and about voice in *The Barbarian Within*.

In Chapter 1, Ong explains that Hopkins is concerned with the "interior, subjective self, which is not looked for or 'discovered' or constructed, but is simply present to each human person as taste is present, the confronting self, something given, simply there in the 'I' which each of us feels and utters" (1986a, p. 23). The self of concern for Hopkins is nameless in the sense that the "I" whereby each person refers immediately to himself or herself is not a name. It means something utterly different in the mouth of each different speaker. To this immediately accessible "I" names are given, applied, added externally—Gerard or Mary or whatever. "I" is a pronoun—from the Latin *pronomen,* something in place of (*pro*) a name (the Latin *nomen* means both "name" and "noun"). Ong considers Hopkins's concern for the self, this immediately accessible nameless "I," to be related to the Victorian fascination with particularity, which grows out of the gradual impact over the centuries of writing, and later of print, on the human psyche. Following the thirteenth-century scholastic, Duns Scotus, Hopkins considers each particular "I" to be dependent only upon the divine will for being the particular "I" it is. As Ong puts it, "I am I because God wants me to be me" (1986a, p. 107). Each "I" is idiosyncratically isolated or set apart from every other "I," and each "I" is the particular gift of God to the person and thus holy.

Jesuit spirituality also helped lay the ground for this attention to the particular. As Ong notes, Hopkins twice did a 30-day retreat following *The Spiritual Exercises* of St. Ignatius of Loyola. The culminating exercise, the Contemplation on Divine Love, asks one to consider the various particulars of creation as the gifts of God. In short, this Ignatian orientation is deeply consonant with the Scotist position adopted by Hopkins—that each created particular, including the "I," is something given by God.

In Chapter 2, Ong also explains that the famous Jesuit expression *Ad majorem Dei gloriam,* for the greater glory of God, is not a dedicatory motto that can be affixed to something already in existence. Rather it is a recipe for decision making, for choosing which possible alternative course of action one should undertake. Hence the comparative *majorem,* "greater," is used in the expression: Of the alternatives that confront me, I am to choose the one which is for the greater glory of God (not of myself or anyone else other than God). The self is shaped by such decisions. The decision making that fosters healthy self-growth involves "the loving encounter in faith of self with self, of the human being with God" (1986a, p. 82).

In Chapter 3, Ong discusses at length Hopkins's appropriation of the philosophy and theology of Duns Scotus and its implied break with the static cosmology of classic Greek writing. Hopkins found in Scotus the view that God's first intention in creation was the Incarnation of the Son and that God created the world so that the Incarnation could take place. The Incarnation was not added to history, but history followed on the Incarnation: "Christ is antecedent to history and, instead of Christ's being in history, all history is in Christ" (1986a, p. 109). Apparently Hopkins was so deeply influenced by the static cosmology of his seminary training, however, that he could not develop his Scotist premise into a fully developed dynamic cosmology.

Also in Chapter 4, Ong discusses the basic characteristics of twentieth-century modernity. He points out that to be modern is to be "at home in the real world, and certainly [at home] in its attentiveness to the self as self" (1986a, p. 134). In this deepest and most positive sense, Ong says, Hopkins is modern because of his profound concern with the nameless "I," the interior self.

Ong's interest in the self and modernism in *Hopkins, the Self, and God* grows out of his earlier interest in personalism and in voice, as found in the essays in *The Barbarian Within.* Hopkins, as Ong explains him, represents personalism at its best—subject-oriented, but not subjective; concerned with human individuation, but not committed to the ideology of egocentrism.

Conclusion

Whatever else might be said about Ong's work, it surely is not the product of egocentrism. Not only was he encouraged in much of his work by the work of others—notably Miller, Teilhard, Lord, and Havelock—but he also developed his own thought in response to the thought of others, most notably Ramus and Hopkins. Moreover, Ong came to formulate the insights in *Fighting for Life: Contest, Sexuality, and Consciousness* at least in part as a positive response to the black civil rights movement and the women's movement. That book readily illustrates that Ong is thoroughly at home in what McLuhan calls the global village, our secondary oral culture.

In addition to doing scholarly work, Father Ong has been active in the direct ministry of the Church. Until his health became a problem in recent years, he regularly offered daily early parish Mass, as well as early Sunday Mass and homilies, and gave two student retreats and other directed retreats each year, while also serving regularly for a limited time each week as a confessor in the College Church at Saint Louis University. Earlier he taught religion classes for boys in a correctional institution and to inner-city youngsters in St. Louis, and later he served as a part-time tutor in the Jesuits' North House, a residence in St. Louis's inner city. In addition, he taught regularly at Saint Louis University even after he had formally retired, never taking a sabbatical. Father Ong was a glorious teacher because he was so alive to ideas and scholarship and yet so deeply attuned to the concrete details of life. As a member of the Society of Jesus, he obviously has modeled himself after a teacher, and he lectures and writes as a teacher.

Ong's own words about what a teacher is, taken from his foreword to *Pius XII and Technology,* probably best sum up his own attitude about his work:

> [A] teacher is not one who merely passes on information to have it assented to and parroted. The mere passing on of information can be taken care of by electronic computers—and even rather better by them. . . . A real teacher plants truths in others' minds to have them grow and bear still further insights into truth. He wants his teachings to live, to be put to work by those to whom he addresses himself. (1962b, pp. ix-x)

Ong doubtlessly would desire to see others put his insights about communication, culture, and consciousness to work. While Ong did not introduce the vision of cosmopolis found in Doran (1990, pp. 355-386), he not only embodied but also admirably articulated the world-cultural consciousness Doran discusses (pp. 527-558). Ong's work is a step, and not a small one, toward building cosmopolis.

PART II

Rhetorical Studies

Introduction

BRUCE E. GRONBECK

Ong's lifelong interest in the history of rhetorical theory, visible from his doctoral dissertation on Peter Ramus to the present, operates at various levels of thought. His work on Ramus demonstrates a relatively specialized, technical expertise in rhetoric, as he exegetes an arcane theory of public discourse and finds in it a revolution in thought about communication. Yet, Ong's thoughts about rhetoric and psychoculture, especially in textual studies, show him off as a social epistemologist and linguistic anthropologist of the broadest vision. Further, his temporal sweep runs from characteristics of classical oral rhetoric to those of Renaissance-modern rhetoric and on to features of contemporary electronic communication; all the while he finds residues of past communicative practices that penetrate and enrich present modes of interaction. Ong thus is simultaneously the historian, critic, and theorist of rhetoric.

In Ong's hands, rhetoric is revalued. Too many in the academy relegate rhetorical studies to other areas, see in "mere rhetoric" the enemy of academic and civic thought, or think of it only as a way to inflate first-year composition's liberal values. Ong assures us that rhetorical studies has a power and importance reaching beyond its historical roots, its materialization of postmodern politics, or its status as a recoverable techne. In rhetoric—in the theorizing of modes of social influence, the investigation of discourse as sites for struggles to make sense of life, and ultimately the processes whereby individual character is integrated into the spirit of the collective—Ong finds the heart of sociality. Certainly ancient oral rhetoric illustrated all of these characteristics, but, to Ong's credit, he discovers them as well in Renaissance-modern written discourse and contemporary electronic messages.

Beyond revaluing rhetoric, he also expands its purview. Ong's major contributions to the study of rhetoric arguably are his orality-literacy

47

theorems. As he combines his own and Perry Miller's thinking on Ramus (1939, 1953) with Milman Parry's studies of oral structures in Homer (Parry, 1971), Eric Havelock's investigation of the collisions between orality and literacy in Greece (1963, 1986), Albert Lord's examination of oral literature (1960), and Jack Goody and Ian Watt's investigation of literacy (1968), he frames the dominant markers of orality and literacy in forceful ways. Further, he shows that by tracing relationships between modes of communication and both consciousness and culture, we are able to center rhetoricity squarely among the social-psychological forces of continuity and change.

The study of rhetoric for Ong becomes more than a dissection of communication in various epochs, more than a historical-hermeneutic study of the evolution of communicative practices, even more than an understanding of the civic roles of public talk down through time. Rather, rhetoric, broadly understood as a system of communicative practices situated in psychoculture, becomes the primary lens through which we can see the ways by which the individual is explored in itself, connected to others, and formed by and through collectivized others. Self, self in society, and self as a product of society are explored in rhetorical studies of discourse.

In the part of this book exploring Ongian understandings of rhetorical studies, Anthony Palmeri opens with an explanatory-critical look at Ramus and Ong's studies of Ramism. After laying out the tenets and moves of Ramistic rhetoric, Palmeri places Ong's work in historical and intellectual contexts, finishing the essay by reviewing Ramus/Ong's utilities for contemporary studies: They help us understand a key turning toward visualism in rhetorical theory, illustrate habits-of-mind that underlie twentieth-century perspectivism, and liberate the text-bound mind. A second essay working from sixteenth-century rhetorical doctrines is provided by David Heckel, who concentrates on Francis Bacon. He seeks to understand the epistemic functions of rhetoric as they develop in the new science of Bacon; he traces the mixing and matching of old rhetoric's inventional and stylistic machinery with the new science's understanding of investigative procedures, finding in Bacon's science a fusion of internal and external searching, an integration of *experientia literata* and *interpretatio naturae*.

If Palmeri and Heckel focus on the epistemic aspects of the orality-literacy theorems, the next two essays explore a more ontic issue in rhetoric: voice. Historically, "voice" was operationalized in the fifth canon or office of rhetoric, *pronunciatio,* and hence was explored in terms of technical proficiencies. Today, however, the term comprehends more than matters of oral delivery; theories of voice today treat an essential dimension of personhood

—being heard or listened to, comprehended, taken into account. Having "voice" is a precondition to being human. Contemporary rhetorical studies give new life to voice: What is voice? Who is and is not heard? What must one do to be heard, and with what consequences? These questions frame the essays by William Kennedy and Noël Valis.

Kennedy is interested in how our sense of voice can be framed or conceptualized at all, especially in view of deconstructionist thought. He starts his study with Longinus's *On the Sublime* in order to document how voice can emphasize one set of rhetorical meanings and suppress others—by stylistic choices. Kennedy then moves to Kant to find voice understood as a frame for or perspective on events. That view allows him, with Ong's help, to argue down the deconstructionists who raid Longinus and see voice as deviations from the norm; rather, we are asked to understand voice as dialogic and as the social dynamic vantage from which meanings are made and shared.

Valis approaches voice through concrete study of literature from French and Spanish Romanticism and realism. She finds in Flaubert's *Madame Bovary* a literary silencing of voice, and in Galdós's *Fortunata y Jacinta* an oral expression of voice. What seems to be a Spanish deviation from the norms of nineteenth-century European literature is explained through a look at the Romantic poets of Spain in the 1830s and 1840s, whose text-events were recitations. Oralisms became embedded in Spanish literature, Valis argues, and account for the strong presence of voice in later realistic novels.

Thus do Ong's orality-literacy theorems lead to fresh epistemic and ontic accounts of life and literature.

3

Ramism, Ong, and Modern Rhetoric

ANTHONY J. PALMERI

No contemporary treatment of the European Renaissance or Ramism is complete without reference to Walter J. Ong's *Ramus, Method, and the Decay of Dialogue* (1958a).[1] The reviews quoted on the back jacket of the 1983 paperback edition of *Ramus* clearly indicate the scope and stature of Ong's achievement. Wilbur Samuel Howell commends its "sound learning" to "Renaissance scholars in any subject." John E. Murdoch praises Ong's treatment of "the Renaissance as a whole"; while T. K. Scott, Jr., sees Ong's work as indispensable for understanding "where the modern mind came from." Neal W. Gilbert finds in Ong's work a "philosophical sophistication and historical insight seldom encountered." Wilhelm Risse sees Ong as providing "a model of in-depth humanistic understanding . . . of Ramism and of 16th century logic." "The most important book on the history of 16th century education which anyone has yet been able to write," declares R. R. Bolgar. Clearly these reviewers considered Ong's work one of supreme intellectual importance.

For Ong, Ramism is symptomatic of trends in pedagogical practice beginning in antiquity and continuing on through the Middle Ages and Renaissance, of the needs of a growing vernacular-speaking merchant class arising in the Renaissance, and of a general shift in Western consciousness regarding the nature of knowledge. In Ramus's day, the idea that knowledge is something visual, a notion that had been growing since antiquity and reinforced in the Middle Ages, reaches a new high point. Facilitating the visualizing tendency was the invention of typography, which committed words to space in a way not imaginable to pre-Socratic cultures and in a way more extensive than in the manuscript culture of the Middle Ages. The Ramist era begins the tendency to conceive habitually of words as twentieth-century culture commonly does: as "things on the page."

This essay has three major purposes. First, the various facets of Ramism, especially the reforms of dialectic and rhetoric, and Ramus's "method" of logical analysis will be explored. Second, Walter Ong's multifaceted interpretation of Ramism will be explained. Finally, the significance of Ong's work on Ramism for modern rhetorical study will be discussed.

Ramism

To say that Ramist works were popular is to understate the phenomenal appeal of these works throughout Europe and the English-speaking world, including the American colonies. Ong's companion piece to *Ramus, Method, and the Decay of Dialogue,* the *Ramus and Talon Inventory* (1958b), is a massive bibliography recording approximately 800 editions of works by Ramus and Talon (Omer Talon was Ramus's literary associate), and another 400 editions of works by Ramist educators. Since publication of the *Inventory,* more Ramist editions have been discovered in European libraries (Sharratt, 1987). This incredible dissemination of Ramist works led Perry Miller to speculate in *The New England Mind: The Seventeenth Century* (1939) that Ramist epistemology greatly facilitated the anti-iconographic mindset of the early Puritan settlers in New England. However, while Miller's study was and is an invaluable exploration of Ramism, it does not account for the development of Ramism within Ramus's own intellectual milieu. Such is the niche filled by Ong's work, a major portion of which was submitted in fulfillment of a doctoral degree at Harvard with Professor Miller serving as the project advisor.

Ramist Dialectic

Read from a twentieth-century perspective, Ramus's reform of dialectic appears to be an oversimplified revision of classical conceptions. Put in a proper historical context, however, Ramus's reform is seen as a further progression of mental habits arising in antiquity and continuing on through the European Middle Ages. A brief historical survey, highlighting the views of dialectic found in Plato, Aristotle, Peter of Spain, and Rudolf Agricola, will provide the context necessary for understanding Ramus's reform.

For Plato, dialectic was a method of reasoning about opinions. Platonic dialectic proceeds by question and answer in order to arrive chiefly at definitions. Serving pedagogical and philosophical purposes, dialectic became a way of training a young mind to refute theses and/or to secure the probable truth of a philosophical position in a debate. As the late neo-Platonist Richard M. Weaver phrased the issue: "What a successful dialectic secures for any position . . . is not actuality but possibility" (1953, p. 27). Later thinkers, equating dialectic with formal logic, would do away with probability as an end of dialectic. The trend probably reached an extreme with Ramus.

Aristotle retained the Platonic notion of dialectic as a question and answer dispute. As the art that preceded rhetoric, dialectic discovered the premises on which rhetorical discourse was based. Although dialectical reasoning and rhetorical reasoning were for Aristotle both concerned with probabilities, they were not the same because they were directed to different ends. The end of dialectical reasoning was arriving at probably true premises. The end of rhetorical reasoning was arriving at action. A separate class of logic, the logic of scientific (apodeictic) demonstration, had as its end the laying down of scientifically true premises. Only this last type of reasoning dealt with premises that were "certain."

Clearly, Aristotle did not equate formal logic and dialectic. The former is excused from the realm of dialogue and opinion and dwells in certainties, while the latter is embedded in opinion. With medieval scholastic Peter of Spain's *Summulae Logicales,* the distinction begins to crumble. Although Peter of Spain's definition of dialectic aligns itself with probable argumentation, Ong points out that the "*Summulae Logicales* actually treats dialectic as dealing with scientific certainties" (1958a, p. 60). The reason for this relates to the pedagogical constraints imposed on the medieval university teacher. Faced with the pragmatic need to educate young boys, the teacher simplifies by teaching everything as certain and is not able to make fine distinctions among logic, dialectic, rhetoric, and poetry. However, thinkers not faced with the demands of the arts curriculum, such as Thomas Aquinas, did not have the same set of pragmatic needs. William A. Wallace (1988) recently has shown how Aquinas developed theoretical distinctions between dialectic and rhetoric in the tradition of Aristotle.

The idea that there was only one logic, and that was dialectic, becomes amplified in the work of Rudolf Agricola (1444-1485). Arising in a pedagogical climate similar to Peter of Spain's, Agricola is also concerned with developing a dialectic comprehensible to young boys. Gone are Aristotle's and Aquinas's fine distinctions between the separate logics. More explicitly than Peter of Spain, Agricola contended that all discourse was directed toward the same end. That end was teaching (*doctrina*). Of Agricola's *Dialectical Invention,* Ong writes: "Indeed, today Agricola's book might well be headed, 'What Boys Should Know about Discourse,' or better, since it is addressed to teachers rather than pupils, 'Thoughts on Discourse and How to Teach It'" (1958a, p. 100).

Agricola's dialectic was highly amenable to the new Gutenberg technology, which favored a mindset conditioned to think of words as isolated "units" or "things" that are "clear and distinct." Riding on a crest of medieval thought that led Agricola to his conclusions, knowledge is something that can be seen on a page. Agricola's conception of knowledge as visual is his chief link to the Ramist dialectic. For Ramus, the dialectician communicated these "unit-pieces" in a clear way. It is a dialectic concerned not with resolving doubt, but with "discoursing well." It is a profoundly rhetorical dialectic, even though Agricolan/Ramist formulations have left rhetoric with a minor role in intellection. These dialecticians were concerned with clarity, an obsession that led to the development of Ramus's method.

Ramist Method

In contrast to modern conceptions of method, the Ramist version seeks to minimize interpretive power and contents itself with organizing discourse. This method of arrangement was a reinterpretation of the classical canon of "judgment." Traditional notions of judgment were conceived in terms of oral disputation: The whole act of "judging" presupposes someone saying something to someone else. Aristotle, for example, refers often to the audience as judges of what the orators say. For Ramus, the act of judging loses its oral status and instead becomes synonymous with a procedure more amenable to the printed page, organization or arrangement. Consequently, Ramist method becomes characterized by dichotomized tables representing general terms divided into twos until no more division was possible. In the preface to the 1983 paperback edition of *Ramus,* Ong suggested that Ramus had in the makings here what we would today call a flow chart for a computer program (p. viii).

Ramist method is in reality a way of defining terms in an easy to remember, genus-species relationship. Ramus never labeled his method a memory system, but that is essentially what it is. A young student could easily recall what dialectic, for example, was by simply recalling the bracketed dichotomy, which would divide dialectic into invention and judgment. This type of memory device had been in existence before Ramus, especially in more picturesque diagrams like the Porphyrian tree. Besides the fact that such picture-like diagrams were too difficult to reproduce in manuscript or print, Ramus objects to them on more fundamental grounds. Specifically, he is opposed to any type of iconology that portrays figures as representative of something in reality. The great irony here is that Ramus's method has in no way eliminated these "magical" mnemonic systems. Instead, he has turned words themselves into icons. Ong refers to this tendency as the Ramist "corpuscular epistemology" (1958a, p. 203) and, later, as the "inner iconoclasm" of Ramism (Ong, 1971, p. 111), as it is referred to by Frances Yates in *The Art of Memory* (1966, pp. 234-235).

Ramist Rhetoric

By Ramus's day it had become common to speak of rhetoric in terms of its five canons: invention, arrangement, style, delivery, and memory. Since antiquity, careful thinkers had distinguished between rhetorical and dialectical invention. Ramus was under the influence of the reformulations of these distinctions by Peter of Spain and Agricola, and he was held in the grip of his own dichotomous method. Consequently, Ramus thought it redundant to grant rhetoric those properties already granted dialectic. Thus, the province of rhetoric is reduced to style and delivery. In the dichotomous framework, memory is simply dropped from consideration.

Besides reinforcing historical misconceptions over the canons, Ramus distorted another staple of rhetoric, the enthymeme. Ramus took the medieval interpretations of Boethius and Peter of Spain, that the enthymeme was a "truncated syllogism," as the correct interpretation. Ong argues that such an interpretation is based on a fundamental misreading of Aristotle, who takes the enthymeme to mean "a syllogism defective in the sense that it moves from premises at least one of which is only probable, to a merely probable conclusion" (1958a, p. 187). Thinking of the enthymeme in purely quantitative terms—as lacking one premise—would seem congenial to a mindset conditioned to think of words as essentially "things" locked in space.

Ramistic rhetoric was popular across Europe and in New England through most of the seventeenth century. The popularity resulted less from the insight Ramism offered into communication theory and more from the fact that it was eminently teachable. In America, as Perry Miller has shown, Ramist rhetoric appealed to the Puritan desire for a "plain style" of preaching. In England, Ramist rhetoric led directly to the elocutionary movement, a reform that even further reduced rhetoric to a manual of style and delivery.

In academic circles, Ramist method lost favor much more quickly than Ramist rhetoric. Logicians could not take method seriously, and, as Ong points out, as a memory system it was not needed in an age that was seeing for the first time the massive accumulation of information in books. Rhetoric continued to suffer, however, becoming further silenced, as what Ong calls "print consciousness" began to take over the Western psyche. For a culture in which reasoning is strictly a private affair, rhetoric can only serve the role of making one's individualized thought more "clear" or "effective" to a public.

Such a consciousness was long coming in Western culture, and the Gutenberg printing press only enhanced habits of mind that had been around since antiquity and progressed steadily through the Middle Ages and early Renaissance. To understand more fully the shift in Western culture from a predominantly oral culture to a print culture, or from habits of mind favoring sound to habits of mind favoring sight, it is necessary to explore Walter Ong's insights about the significance of Ramism.

Ong on Ramism

Because Ong was a student of Marshall McLuhan at Saint Louis University in the late 1930s and early 1940s, and because McLuhan cites *Ramus, Method, and the Decay of Dialogue* in several parts of *The Gutenberg Galaxy,* Ong at times has been associated in academic circles with a McLuhanesque "technological determinism" approach to the history of culture and consciousness.[2] However, while Ong is interested in the effects of various media—or what he calls "transformations of the word"—on human sensibilities, he certainly does not see the transformations of the word in an exclusively deterministic sense and never at the expense of discerning other factors involved in human cognitive development. He states clearly in *Ramus* and other places that "printing is perhaps more symptom than cause" of the visualist emphasis that marks Ramism and much of the modern world.

For Ong, as already noted, Ramism as a phenomenon arises in a pedagogical tradition intensifying the worst habits of its predecessors in antiquity and the Middle Ages. Yet there remain two equally important elements of Ong's analysis to consider here: (a) Ramism as an appealing "account keeping" device of the new vernacular-speaking merchant classes arising in the Renaissance; and (b) Ramism as symptomatic of a shift in Western consciousness from habits of mind conceiving of knowledge as something essentially heard (a mindset favoring an animated cosmos and harmonious relationship with nature), to conceiving of knowledge as something essentially seen (a mindset favoring a silent, mechanistic universe and the control of nature).

Learned Latin, the Vernacular, and Commercialism

Upon the rediscovery of the classical authors during the Middle Ages, Latin became the "official" language of the universities. A schoolboy (the universities were exclusively male at the time) had to learn Latin before he could study any academic subject, including the natural sciences. So entrenched is modern education in the vernacular that few realize the relatively late date at which the vernacular was introduced into the classroom, around the middle to late eighteenth century. This issue should not be minimized: "Unless this linguistic situation is kept in mind the meaning of Ramism and its connection not only with a world of Latin humanists but with all of life cannot be appreciated" (Ong, 1958a, p. 13). In essence, Latin presents one more element of confusion in the Ramist scheme.

Learning Latin presented a serious paradox for Ramism. Ramus pictured himself as training orators in a male-dominated Ciceronian sense: His orators would represent a union of wisdom and eloquence, with the capacity to lead the masses to action in the academic and practical realms of experience. Yet with his studies steeped in Latinate expression, the student of the Renaissance humanist was really not equipped to do verbal battle in the vernacular-speaking practical world. The typical student of Ramus was not someone like Shakespeare, a product of Latin learning yet creator of classic vernacular works. Rather, the typical product of this education received his teaching degree, which allowed him to continue the tradition of Latin learning. Ong has argued (1962a, pp. 206-219; 1971, pp. 113-141) that Latin language study for this student took on the status of a "puberty rite" designed to reinforce the male-dominated academic setting and preserve vestiges of the rhetorical tradition inherited from antiquity, a tradition that had been gradually losing force for various reasons, yet retaining a powerful psychological hold over the Renaissance educator. The Latin language kept the student in touch with the real wisdom of the past, most of which was stored in books composed in Latin.

Ultimately, Ramism proved to be much more popular with the vernacular-speaking public, which is ironic considering Ramus's academic leanings. Ramus's dichotomous "credit/debit" method was eminently useful to the growing bourgeois merchant class arising in the Renaissance. In "Ramist Method and the Commercial Mind" (1971, pp. 165-189), Ong explored the relationship between the Ramist and commercial mentalities:

> There is an obvious relationship between this mentality and the mentality of a commercial, merchandising world, where goods had to be thought of in terms of operations with a view to possible users or consumers. Ramist "method" makes it possible to think of knowledge itself in terms of "intake" and "output" and "consumption"—terms which were not familiar to the commercial world in Ramus' day, of course, but which do refer to realities present within that world. (pp. 173-174)

Ramism favored an "accountant's approach to knowledge," concerned not so much with abstract understanding of the terms employed as with keeping everything in proper order (Ong, 1971, p. 189). Moreover, in reducing the aural component in communication to a new low, Ramist method fostered an irenicism congenial to the business world, where squabbling is rarely conducive to efficiency.

Noetic Shifts

A culture's noetic habits involve the characteristic perceptual and cognitive styles found within the culture. By far Ong's most penetrating insight about Ramism is the idea that it marks a change in Western sensibility, a shift from a pre-Socratic noetic that conceives of words as sounds, to a post-Gutenberg noetic that conceives of words as "things on the page." Typography is but a symptom of the shift, however; the shift developed in conjunction with a mindset that probably began developing when early peoples realized that pictures could represent things said. The alphabet then allowed for greater spatialization of sound, since it allowed for representation of words as individual units. The Gutenberg printing press, when introduced in the fifteenth century, only enhanced a long-standing approach to words as things "deployed," "maneuvered," and all other sight-oriented metaphors that further divorce words from their original habitat in the world of sound.

As a result, the tendency to think of words—and all knowledge—as something essentially seen does not begin with Ramus. Ong reports tracing the sound/sight distinction back to the ancient world: The Hebrew term *yadha* caught the personal, communal, hearing emphasis of that culture, while the Greek terms *gignosko* and *idea* caught the more impersonal, sight-oriented epistemology of that culture (Riemer, 1971, p. 152). For Ong, Plato's highly articulate criticisms of writing and his theory of forms could only arise in a culture that had been touched by literacy to the extent that reflection on such matters became possible. Words as sound exist only as they go out of existence. Words as things on the page allow for a type of reflection and abstraction not known to the pre-Socratics. To say this does not mean that pre-alphabetic cultures engage in "inferior" thought patterns, for their thought is quite complex indeed. However, it is a consciousness different from the one we know, one that structures knowledge in a way conducive to recalling the information that is remembered only in the human mind.

Printing allowed for a more efficient ordering of words in space than did manuscripts. Yet it was an invention late in coming because "it had to wait on a profound reorientation within the human spirit which made it possible to think of all the possessions of the mind, that is, of knowledge and expression, in terms more committed to space than those of earlier times" (Ong, 1958a, p. 308). Rhetoric, as an art formulated originally in the world of sound, becomes more and more "silenced" with each successive advance in spatialization. As words become more and more locked into space, the idea that writing governs what is said, and not vice versa, gains currency. Such is the birth of the "print-consciousness," which, though the twentieth century has witnessed a tremendous resurgence in sound, is still dominant in the Western world and governs the orality we hear spoken today over the mass media by and large. The orality of the electronic age has been styled by Ong as "secondary orality" (1982b) because it is an orality that is a product of a planned and self-conscious control of words and phrasings that was unknown to Homer and other strictly oral figures, although it may often be somewhat formulary, as Homeric and other primary oral forms of discourse were.

Howell's Objection and Ong's Response

At least one of Ong's early reviewers, Wilbur Samuel Howell, resisted the argument that rhetoric was left "muted and silent" as a result of Ramus's reforms. Howell's remarks will be summarized here since they represent a way of looking at the history of rhetoric that Ong is trying to correct by including parts of the historical puzzle that the more conventional view has missed. In his review of Ong's two-volume study of Ramism in the *Quarterly Journal of Speech* (1960, pp. 86-92), Howell cites examples of the seventeenth-century works of Louis Cresol and Michel LeFaucheur on voice and gesture, plus the entire eighteenth-century elocutionary movement, to demonstrate that Ong is mistaken about the silencing of rhetoric:

> The shift from the auditory to the visual was completely reversed, so far as rhetoric was concerned. It is hard to see how Ramist rhetoric could have caused oral delivery to perish of neglect, if even before the end of the Ramist era oral delivery suddenly begins to have more importance than it had ever enjoyed in the great classical rhetorics of Greece and Rome. (p. 91)

Howell generally viewed the aural-visual interpretation as vague, and he argued implicitly that more insight into the Ramist era is gained by studying the social forces at work in the Middle Ages and Renaissance. Taking a social forces approach, Howell concluded that the ecclesiastic controversies of Agricola's time necessitated a logic of controversies that Peter of Spain did not provide. Ramus then "tidied up" Agricola's system with his method, which out-popularized Agricola because of its simplification. Descartes then silenced Ramus because "of a growing dissatisfaction with the old learning and because of a summons by Descartes for a logic of inquiry to replace the Ramist logic of communication" (Howell, 1960, p. 90).

As evidenced by his remarks about the pedagogical and commercial connections with Ramism, Ong is surely not opposed to the study of social forces. Moreover, the emphasis on the sound-sight split does not necessitate a disagreement with any of Howell's arguments, but it does seem to shed additional light on most of these matters—especially the elocutionary movement. In his review of Howell's *Eighteenth Century British Logic and Rhetoric* in the *William and Mary Quarterly* (1972, pp. 637-643), Ong points out that the conventional view does not go far enough:

> One can discern additional patterns of development which he does not discuss and which carry the explanation even deeper. . . . These patterns show how elocutionism arose, paradoxically, out of the new subjugation of oral delivery to the inscribed word, a subjugation begun with writing but maximized with print. Elocutionism was a symptom of a major readjustment in the entire noetic economy. (p. 639)

Eighteenth-century elocutionists were concerned with oral delivery conceived of as reading from a text. Ancient orators, on the other hand, were concerned with the oral creation of a speech. Ancient orators typically wrote out a speech after its delivery, if it were written at all, and they relied on commonplaces or *topoi* in the oral creation of a speech.

In addition, the elocutionary movement's interpretation of the classical canon of memory differed from the ancients in a fundamental way. The ancient orators never thought of memory as the verbatim recall of a prior written text. Rather, memory was concerned with "rhapsodizing," with the thematic and formulaic recall of information. For the elocutionists, memory was concerned with verbatim recall of texts as when an actor memorizes his script. The elocutionary movement, though oral on the surface, was actually the product of a highly literate culture:

> The elocutionary movement, in short, shows in striking ways how the oral management of knowledge, threatened ever since the invention of writing, was by now thoroughly debilitated (Romanticism would mark its virtual demise). By the close of the 18th century orality as a way of life was in effect ended, and with it the old time world of oratory . . . or rhetoric. (Ong, 1972, p. 641)

Perhaps the elocutionary movement may profitably be viewed as a forerunne:
to the secondary orality of electronic culture. Notice also that when the study
of rhetoric undergoes a revival in the twentieth century, it does so not so much
because of a resurgence in oral ways of knowing as much as the growing
concern with the psychological dimensions of metaphor and a realization tha
many acts of communication beyond the public speech are "rhetorical." The
days of pure orality and the oratory associated with the rhetorical era are foreve:
gone, though it is true that some oratory in Third World countries is still close to
the old primary oral world of rhetoric. Yet rhetoric is subject to more
investigation now than ever before because, paradoxically, of the technological developments that contributed to the elimination of the tradition

Relation to Contemporary Rhetorical Study

What relevance does Ong's interpretation of Ramism have for today's
students of rhetoric? Three possibilities will be considered here: Ong's
analysis may (a) provide a fuller, more accurate portrayal of the dynamics
involved in the history of rhetoric, (b) help to put our modern perspectives
on rhetoric into larger frames, and (c) liberate us from our text-bound
consciousness. Each will be explored below.

On the History of Rhetoric

In *The Rhetoric of Western Thought* (1978), Goodwin F. Berquist, James
L. Golden, and William E. Coleman identify four myths regarding rhetoric,
the first and third of which reflect Ramus's reduction of rhetoric to style and
delivery. The four myths are the following:

1. Rhetoric deals with ornamental language rather than substantial ideas.

2. Rhetoric deals with appearances, not reality.

3. Rhetoric is a truncated art primarily concerned with style and/or delivery; or
   with limited aspects of invention.

4. The expansionist myth; the tendency to include all types of communication
   within the domain of rhetoric. (pp. 3-4)

The usual procedure for destroying any one of these myths is to show that
prior thinkers were somehow misled into their positions or simply inept in
their theorizing about rhetoric. Professor Richards, for example, in his
"Introductory Lecture" to *The Philosophy of Rhetoric,* noted that the sorry
state of rhetoric was due to the "traditional treatment" of the subject: "It

begins, of course, with Aristotle, and may perhaps be said to end with Archbishop Whately" (1936, p. 5). The consensus among moderns is that traditional thinking on the subject was, for the most part, too narrow to begin with and thus laid itself vulnerable to the quackery of a Ramus.

Nothing in Ong's *Ramus, Method, and the Decay of Dialogue* (1958a) tries to excuse the narrow thinking of the past (or of the present, for that matter). Indeed, Ong's explorations of Ramus's works at times approaches a scolding tone. Unlike most other writings on rhetoric, however, Ong's account of its history devotes substantial space to the particular intellectual and cultural milieu in which the narrow thinking takes place. In a later work, *Rhetoric, Romance, and Technology,* Ong argues for the necessity of studying rhetoric in a societal context:

> In the present world, the relationship of persuasion to the totality of human existence thus differs radically from what it was in the past. But only those who have no knowledge of the changes in culture itself think that the changes in the role of rhetoric have been chaotic. The history of rhetoric simply mirrors the evolution of society. (1971, p. 9)

Viewed in these terms, rhetoric can never be "restored" to a former place of dominance, and one might question whether the centuries-long dominance of oratory constituted a form of tyranny over the Western mind.

On Contemporary Perspectives

A major preoccupation of contemporary rhetoricians has been to reconcile the logical and rhetorical traditions of the West. Diverse thinkers such as Kenneth Burke, Richard Weaver, Chaim Perelman, Stephen Toulmin, the Frankfurt School critics, and many others have tried to show how Western standards of what constitutes knowledge have suffered from an addiction to a logical standard that denies any epistemic role for rhetoric. Most thinkers acknowledge the beginnings of the struggle in antiquity and then skip to Descartes as the turning point in the struggle—with logic emerging the victor.

As Ong has suggested in places, Ramism is essentially the turning point of these unresolved tensions between the logical and rhetorical traditions. Ramus succeeded in confusing the traditions more than any thinker before or since. Though not a direct influence on Descartes, in the sense that Descartes gives no explicit attention to Ramist method in the formulation of his own, Ramus nonetheless represents habits of mind manifested in a host of later thinkers right up until contemporary times. Discovering the nature of those mental habits makes the study of Ramism permanently indispensable.

One could argue that contemporary rhetorical theory is essentially an attempt to free the modern mind from the constraints imposed by Ramism. Is not the contemporary concern with the psychological impact of metaphor, symbolic action, rhetoric as epistemic, rhetoric as this and that, not simply assigning roles and possibilities for rhetoric that Ramism had shut out?

Liberating oneself from the habits of mind imposed by a long-standing tradition is never an easy thing to do, and rhetoricians need to be careful here. Ong shows in *Ramus* how even Ramus's critics fell into the same diagrammatic mental tendencies characteristic of pure Ramism, and our age has certainly not freed itself from this. The modern obsession with communication models falls prey to Ramist tendencies in trying to spatialize something that resists spatialization. Models are useful as long as their limitations are recognized and the user doesn't fall into the same "simplification" trap characteristic of Ramism.

The Liberation of the Text-Bound Mind

It is not the purpose of this essay to advise academicians to make *Ramus, Method, and the Decay of Dialogue* (1958a) required reading in their classes. However, if one were to advise this, it would be due to the book's liberating value. From what does Ong's work help liberate us? From habits of mind enforced by writing, enhanced by print, and now reinforced by the computer. We are all Ramists in the sense that all of us engage in the isolationist, reflective type of thinking that, for Ong at least, is characteristic of the mind conditioned by writing.

Yet the slavery enforced by Ramism is not reflective, private reasoning as such. The ability to engage in such thinking is indispensable for personal and social growth. The slavery of Ramism is the inability to get out of the isolationist stance, the inability to realize that true thought is ultimately a social affair granted truth value only in discourse with others. Since *Ramus,* Ong has devoted the better part of his writings to exploring the nature of the print consciousness that finds an early representative in Ramus and perhaps culminates in the New Criticism's reduction of all art to object (Ong, 1977a, pp. 213-229).

Ong's attempt to contribute to the liberation of the text-bound mind has come to be known as orality-literacy studies. To engage in such liberation is not to long for the oral past from which Ramus divorced himself and Western culture. The goal of such studies is not to seek a return to some idealized oral past, but to understand the relationships between the noetic styles arising out of each era of human development. Rhetoricians can least afford enslavement to a mentality favoring sight disproportionately to sound. Moreover, they can ill afford to ignore any work that explores that mentality and thus reminds them of the deep reasons for their historical and contemporary plight.

Notes

1. This is not to suggest that Ramus has gone unnoticed by others. As part of the twentieth-century academic revival of rhetoric as a discipline, scholars have shown how Ramus's misreading of classical texts led to a conviction that rhetoric's only true value could be ornamental—a way of dressing up the "truth" discovered through dialectic. Ramus's reduction of rhetoric to the Ciceronian canons of *elocutio* and *pronunciatio* was later recognized as a severe error in the academic world, at least in departments of speech communication and rhetoric. Yet many people today still perceive rhetoric in a negative light, as when an individual complains of the politician who "instead of deeds gave us rhetoric." (See Berquist, Golden, & Coleman, 1978; Howell, 1956; Murphy, 1981; Perelman & Olbrechts-Tyteca, 1958/1969; and Sharratt, 1987.)

2. Bruce Gronbeck has argued that McLuhan's supposed determinism was not characteristic of his later writings, which "advance a relational or phenomenological theory of communication, one wherein the 'mosaic' he discussed in the 1960s becomes operationalized as cross-sections of communication events" (1981, p. 123).

4

Francis Bacon's New Science: Print and the Transformation of Rhetoric

DAVID HECKEL

All science is only arrested dialogue.

—Walter J. Ong

It is commonly assumed that rhetoric has no epistemological dimension. Rather than a way of knowing, rhetoric is a way of speaking or of arranging what is already known for the purpose of persuading an audience. This argument is familiar and dates back to Plato's treatment of the Sophists in the context of which "he gives unmitigated preeminence to *episteme* over *doxa*" (Barilli, 1989, p. 6). In recent years the Platonic view of rhetoric has been challenged as rhetorical scholars have reasserted rhetoric's epistemological claims through an examination of the social bases of knowledge. These scholars have argued that if knowledge is socially constructed and if rhetoric is the art of obtaining consent, the rhetoric of any discourse is closely related to its knowledge claims, and in fact can govern the form and content of what is known (Bruffee, 1986; Olson, 1986). Rhetoric can be seen from this point of view as a way of constructing rather than simply a way of delivering knowledge.

Below I will examine the status of the figures and topics of Renaissance rhetoric in Francis Bacon's new science. I will discuss the manner in which they are transformed when language is objectified, as printed texts replace the hand-produced manuscript. My examination of Bacon's simultaneous rejection and adaptation of these rhetorical tools will draw upon the insights into textuality and the interplay of text and voice presented in the works of Walter Ong. I will argue that rhetoric is much more central to the epistemology of Bacon's new science than has been previously acknowledged (Jardine, 1974; Payne, 1983; Rossi, 1968; Stephens, 1975a, 1975b; Whitney, 1986). I will examine the significance of the fact that Bacon works at the interface between what Ong calls the residual orality of the Middle Ages and Renaissance and the fully interiorized print literacy of the modern age. I will examine what these concepts mean and how they relate to reading the Baconian transformation of rhetoric as its venue shifts from the residually oral world of the hand-produced manuscript to the silent, visual world of the printed text.

Ong has argued that the interiorization of the printed text as a conscious and unconscious model for noetic activity changed forever the way in which the world and language itself are conceptualized. The invention of letterpress printing "made possible the rise of modern science" (1982b, p. 118). Prior to the invention of the printing press, and for some time after it, intellectual attention had focused for the most part, Ong argues, on the preservation of knowledge or the reconciliation of new knowledge with old worldviews. Writing "served largely to recycle knowledge back into the oral world" (1982b, p. 119). The information storage and retrieval capabilities made available by the new technology of letterpress printing put increasing pressure on the operating procedures of the old intellectual traditions founded in the study of rhetoric and dialectic, largely oral in mode of presentation and habit of mind. In the process, rhetoric was moved to the margins of discourse as rationalists sought a language unencumbered by ambiguity and unaffected by the demands of public disputation. Ong seeks an explanation for these intellectual trends in the communication technologies in concert with which they emerge.

Rhetoric, Ong argues, existed first in the primary orality of cultures without writing. In Western culture, it was then codified and applied to the production of written texts tied very closely to oral reproduction through recitation and public dispute (1971, p. 4). When related to texts, rhetoric came increasingly to be seen as a way of varying or otherwise manipulating words in textual space; that is, words became objects in the space of the page, exchanging their acoustic existence for a physical one. This was the process of change the word was undergoing during the European Middle Ages and into the Renaissance, as first written and finally printed texts came to dominate and at last displace entirely the intellectual activities of oral disputation. Vocalized knowledge was replaced by visualized knowledge (1971).

During the European Renaissance, Ong maintains, the residual orality of manuscript culture was colliding with the literacy promoted by printed texts. By residual orality, Ong means "habits of thought and expression tracing back to preliterate situations or practice, or deriving from the dominance of the oral as a medium in a given culture, or indicating a reluctance or inability to dissociate the written medium from the spoken" (1971, pp. 25-26). Ong describes such residue:

> Habits of thought and expression inseparable from the older, more familiar medium are simply assumed to belong equally to the new until this is sufficiently "interiorized" for its own techniques to emerge from the chrysalis and for those more distinctive of the older medium to atrophy. (1971, p. 25)

What this means for the study of Bacon's use of rhetoric is that we might expect him to conflate unconsciously the older, more orally based practices of rhetoric and dialectic with the more recent visualist ways of knowing being promoted by the interiorization of print technology. We might also expect him to be applying these old practices to new purposes without being fully conscious of his doing so. Thus Bacon frequently asserts that he is employing a new way of examining nature when the evidence of his procedures reveals a heavy residue of rhetorical practice. While Bacon is contributing to the marginalization of rhetoric exemplified in the works of other visualist rhetoricians such as Peter Ramus (discussed below), he is also unconsciously transforming the rhetorical practices of figuration and topical arrangement into a typographic epistemology that "knows" the world as a printed text made up of discrete and repeatable units of information.

Much of Ong's work has centered on an examination of the displaced and marginalized art of rhetoric. He has sought to explain and reconstruct this process of marginalization by tracing its relation to the development of communication technologies and their effect on shifts in human consciousness (1971, pp. 1-22). Ong's work with the status of rhetoric in the shift from the manuscript culture of the European Middle Ages to print culture in the Renaissance is of particular relevance to the present study.

In his study of Ramus (1515-1572), for example, Ong illustrates an initial suppression of rhetoric in the Ramist move to cut discovery and arrangement from the rhetorical curriculum and traces this move to shifts in consciousness attributable in part to the growing interiorization of the printed text as a model for intellectual activity (1958b). Ong describes in detail the impact the static and spatialized word promoted by the printed text had upon the dialogical orientation of the logic and rhetoric of the Middle Ages. Ramus, according to Ong, replaced the fluid and agonistic world of the medieval disputation with graphically schematized lists of dichotomies, "Ramism in effect put all actuality into ledger books" and "foster[ed] a further move away from the orality of rhetorical culture to visualist scientism" (1971, p. 19). Ramism was typical, Ong argues, of a general cultural shift during which the dialogical, oral world of medieval disputation was being replaced by much more static and objectified representations of reality, "memorizable, flat statements that told straight forwardly and inclusively how matters stood in a given field" (Ong, 1982b, p. 134). Yet, Ong states, "it is a historical fact that Ramist method has its source in rhetoric" (1971, p. 177).

From the vantage point of Ong's theories concerning the effects of inter-iorized communication technologies, we begin to see that the notions of knowledge as finite and collectable are literate notions, informed by an association of knowledge with the printed book, the major means for the transmission of it after the invention of the printing press and prior to the invention of the various electronic media. Bacon's transformation of traditio-nal rhetoric, then, can be seen as a product of the way in which the internalized printed text replaces the residually oral manuscript with a more spatialized model of intellectual activity.

The mechanism of this transformation is suggested in George Kennedy's discussion of the concept of *letteraturizzazione,* which can be further refined by combining it with Ong's insights into the nature of textuality and the structures of consciousness. *Letteraturizzazione* is "the tendency of rhetoric to shift its focus from persuasion to narration, from civic to personal contexts, and from discourse to literature, including poetry" (Kennedy, 1980, p. 5). An Ongian application of *letteraturizzazione* would include the tendency of rhetoric to shift its focus from the aural-oral world of primary and residual orality to the increasingly graphically schematized world of the chirographic and printed texts. As the internalization of the printed text as a noetic model proceeds, the rhetoric of these texts is projected onto nature through the vehicle of the method of the new sciences.

As the technological and mechanical process of printing books replaces hand production, new habits of reading and writing nature also develop. The interiorized printed text becomes a noetic model for reading and writing about nature. While the residual orality of manuscript noetics reads nature with the desire to find concordance and harmony, Bacon's "sons of science" are instructed in the process of reading nature in new ways, ways that will add to the store of knowledge things and processes not before known, rather than reconcile the new with the old. In the process they will transform the older rhetoric of disputation into a rhetoric of experimental inquiry.

Such a transformation is implicit in the Renaissance understanding of the relationship between art and nature. The rhetorician, for example, sees rhetoric as a means for working upon the undifferentiated stuff of unadorned language to bring about an aesthetic or suasory effect. The shift in attention characteristic of Bacon's work from the stuff of language to the stuff of the natural world receives its major impetus from the objectification of the word by print and a projection of this objectification onto the phenomenal world. The medieval book of the divine *ordo* is transformed from a manuscript into a graphically organized printed text with a new set of print generated intellectual expectations.

Gellrich (1985) has documented the totalizing (Ong would say residually oral) habit of medieval intellectuals from Augustine forward as they attempted to read the phenomenal world, God's other writing or the veil of things themselves, as a meaningful part of the divine *ordo*. The book, Gellrich argues, becomes an imitation of the divine order of things and replicates it:

> In the progression from sign to sentence, page, chapter, book, Bible, nature, cosmos, the *manifestatio* of the summa does not validate articles of faith, but replicates in its style the divine *ordo*. . . . With regard to the medieval summa, paradigmatic structures are everywhere in evidence in the symmetrical subdivision, homologous interrelation of parts, patterned oppositions, parallel diction, syntax, rhyme and mnemonic devices; each part has the capacity to recall the larger system, and the style of the whole is the "Scholastic memory" of the vast classificatory network of the Book of Nature. (Gellrich, 1985, pp. 67, 69)

Though Gellrich does not use the term, I think this is a form of *letteraturizzazione*. Gellrich suggests that the rhetorical mechanisms of the manuscript book are projected onto the world of nature as it is read by the student of God's creation. This habit of projection is continued by the new scientists, but the content of the projection conforms to the demands of the new printed text. Nature is seen as a book to be read and recomposed as any text is read and recomposed by a Renaissance rhetorician. This process might include the identification and application of various figures of speech as well as the noting or writing down of various commonplaces to be saved for later use. (One should also note here Bacon's insistence on the importance of making notes, recording observations of the external world and the results of experiments.) A book might also be composed through the application of topics of inquiry, supported by commonplaces (discussed below), and amplified and made aesthetically pleasing through the application of the figures of speech.

Just as the medieval composer of texts saw a divine rhetoric in the natural world, so Bacon's sons of science are directed to pursue a natural rhetoric matched to the text of the cosmos. Traditional rhetoric, in turn, moves from the arena of discourse between speakers to the arena of inquiry into the nature of things through the creation of a system of experimental topics and figures. These topics and figures, originally used to manipulate language, are now by extension applied to the manipulation of nature and knowledge about nature, which they both organize and produce. Bacon's sons of science will inquire into the nature of things in a manner analogous to that recommended in the style books of Renaissance rhetoricians such as George Puttenham.

In his *The Arte of English Poesie,* Puttenham describes the manner in which the artist works in relation to nature. Puttenham's artists may operate in relation to nature in four ways: They may augment nature as do gardeners in making a fruit sweeter or a flower of a different color; they may imitate nature, as do painters or carvers; they may act upon the undifferentiated "stuff of nature in ways contrary to hers with results she could never achieve, as does the carpenter that builds a house, the joyner that makes a table or Bedstead"; they may enhance natural abilities through "study & discipline or exercise" as do dancers and musicians (1936, pp. 302-304). The analogies Puttenham uses here illustrate the relationship of linguistic operations to manipulation of the natural world. The rhetorical arts, particularly the use of the figures of speech, are compared to the manipulation of the stuff of nature. This comparison links the rhetorical life of texts with the natural world and defines the human relationship to it as people manipulate and transform the stuff of life into useful or aesthetically pleasing objects.

This unity between the textual world and nature is further expressed in Puttenham's description of how the poet works upon the real or natural stuff of language with his or her tools, the figures:

> The chief prayse of our Poet is in the discreet using of his figures, as the skilful painter's is in the good conveyance of his coulours and shadowing traits of his pensill, with delectable varietie, by all measure and just proportion, and in places most aptly to be bestowed. (1936, pp. 137-138)

Extending the analogy among nature, language, and text, we can see how Bacon carries this sense of an artificial and verbally based manipulation of natural language a step further by proposing in his theory of the scientific method the imitation of nature and the discovery of empirically verifiable knowledge. Much like Puttenham's poet, Bacon's scientist will strive to achieve a sort of natural/artificial eloquence that will imitate the methods of the figurist rhetorician and "make the mind of man by help of art a match for the nature of things" (1863, Vol. 9, p. 71). The goal of this method is to combine the natural and the artificial in a manner similar to that recommended by Puttenham and other rhetoricians concerned with the use of the figures of speech. Bacon conceptualizes his experimental method in terms similar to Puttenham's, as governed by some sort of natural instinct that distinguishes vain and artificial productions from those governed by the stuff itself. Language and art, Bacon feels, should assist in the discovery or manifestation of the stuff of nature, not hinder its revelations:

> For the wit and mind of man, if it work upon matter, which is the contemplation of the creatures of God, worketh according to the stuf [*sic*], and is limited thereby; but if it work upon itself, as the spider worketh his web, then it is endless, and brings forth instead cobwebs of learning, admirable for the fineness of thread and work, but of no substance or profit. (1863, Vol. 6, p. 122)

Bacon's ideal for the proper use of figuration is similar to Puttenham's inasmuch as he wants a style that does not interfere with nature, but rather uses language and art to assist in its proper expression. Bacon hopes to achieve a sort of natural eloquence in which the difference between the word and the thing or notion will disappear. Just as Puttenham's poet will be "more recommended for his natural eloquence than his artificial," the scientist of Bacon's New Organon will eventually abandon all ornaments of style and methods of discourse for a language perfectly in tune with nature:

> And for all that concerns ornaments of speech, similitudes, treasury of eloquence, and such like emptinesses, let it be utterly dismissed. Also let all those things which are admitted be themselves set down briefly and concisely, so that they may be nothing less than words. (1863, Vol. 4, p. 254)

I now will turn to an examination of Bacon's application of traditional rhetorical practices to the examination of nature. Throughout this discussion we will try to keep in mind Bacon's position as a transitional figure working at the interface between the residually oral world of the medieval manuscript culture and the fully interiorized print literacy of the modern world regarding the relation between language and nature.

In *The Advancement of Learning,* Bacon divides traditional invention into two parts. The first is that treated in traditional rhetoric, which, Bacon says, "is no *Invention,* but a *Remembrance* or *Suggestion,* with an application" (1863, Vol. 6, p. 269). The second type of invention involves the invention of sciences, and of this Bacon says:

> This part of invention, concerning the invention of sciences, I propose hereafter to propound; having digested it into two parts; whereof the one I term *Experientia literata,* and the other *Interpretatio naturae*: the former being a degree and a rudiment of the latter. (1863, Vol. 6, p. 268)

Though he accepts the traditional sense of invention because it is generally known and applied, Bacon refocuses the primary meaning by using it to refer to the acquisition of new knowledge, "for to invent is to discover that which we know not, and not to recover or resummon that which we already know" (1863, Vol. 6, p. 268).

Bacon's new manner of invention proceeds from two directions. One involves a new organization of and selection from the received tradition that will point out weaknesses and holes in this knowledge and will be described in *The Advancement* (1605) and the *De augumentis* (1620); the other will proceed by observation and the experimental application of the figures and tropes of *experientia literata* to an altogether new science of interpretation that will be the content of *Novum Organum*. In both *The Advancement* and *De augumentis,* his treatment of rhetoric is the measure of a shift in attention from the oral milieu of traditional rhetoric to the typographic milieu of science. The doctrine of *experientia literata* represents a midpoint in this shift in attention, and most of Bacon's discussion of rhetoric in the *De augumentis* turns upon putting it to new and more scientific uses.

Experientia literata is based upon a system of tropes and figures, which, when applied to natural phenomena and to the received texts of the tradition, begins to link rhetorical ornamentation and invention with method. Bacon connects literate experience (learned; i.e., textual) with direct experience of the natural world. For Bacon the natural world is a text and its qualities can be revealed through the application of figures and tropes of experiment similar to such traditional figures as *translatio* and *conjunctio*.

Experientia literata provides a series of figures for tropologically examining nature: "True experimentation proceeds principally either by the Variation, or the Production, or the Translation, or the Inversion, or the Compulsion, or the Application, or the Conjunction, or finally the Chances, of experiment" (1863, Vol. 9, p. 72). These figures function much as the tropes and figures do in rhetoric, only they are used to vary and embellish natural phenomena rather than natural language. As do the tropes and figures, they vary the matter but do not produce the axioms or formal causes that are the domain of logic and Bacon's New Organon:

> None of these [the experimental tropes] however extend so far as to the invention of any axiom. For all transitions from experiment to axioms, or from axioms to experiments, belong to that other part, relating to the New Organon. (1863, Vol. 9, p. 72)

Experientia literata will use the eight experimental tropes or figures (Variation, Production, Translation, Inversion, Compulsion, Application, Conduction, and Chance) to add to the philosopher's stock of knowledge by manipulating the matter of nature the same way the figurist rhetorician manipulates the matter of speech. For example:

> Inversion of experiment takes place when trial is made of the contrary of that which has been by the experiment proved. For instance, heat is increased by burning-glasses; is cold also? Again, heat spreads round, but with a tendency upwards; does cold spread round with a tendency downwards? For example: take an iron rod and heat it at one end; then raise it, with the heated part downwards and the hand above; it will burn the hand at once: hold it with the heated part upwards and the hand below, it will be much longer in doing so. (1863, Vol. 9, p. 79)

Bacon treats each of the experimental tropes in a similar fashion. Like most figurist rhetoricians, Bacon provides a definition of the figure and then provides examples of its use. In this regard his procedure is absolutely traditional. What distinguishes him most interestingly from the rhetoricians is the fact that he adds a currency of natural phenomena to the tradition's currency of words. Bacon's treatment of nature as object is tied to the manner in which the printed text encouraged the objectification of the word. In this dynamic relationship, the signified takes on many of the characteristics of the signifier. It is possible to collect and organize discrete bits of information about the behavior of heat and cold through experiment in a way analogous to the way a reader might collect bits of information, usually quotations, from a text. I will pick up this discussion as it relates to the tradition of collecting commonplaces following a discussion of Bacon's use of the topics.

Employing the procedure he used in his treatment of invention, Bacon divides arrangement into two parts: one totally deficient and rhetorical and the other useful to the new scientist. These two parts are Promptuary and Topics. Promptuary, or composition of arguments beforehand, a useful art for the orator, is dismissed as an art that "scarcely deserves to be spoken of as a part of knowledge, consisting rather of diligence than any artificial erudition" (1863, Vol. 9, p. 84). A Topic, on the other hand, is a place "where a thing is to be looked for, may be marked, and as it were indexed" (1863, Vol. 9, p. 84). This definition is highly typographical in its references to visual scanning and indexing but has its roots in late medieval traditions of text production. Indexes were a late development in manuscript traditions, where the labor of constructing them did not always pay dividends since no two manuscripts would be identical. Ong has suggested that "alphabetic indexes show strikingly the disengagement of words from discourse and their embedding in typographic space" (1982b, p. 124). Bacon's method of inner search is influenced by this interiorized model of the printed text. In Bacon's hands, topics and indexes are used not only as a means of organizing the contents of a book, but also as a means of organizing extratextual, phenomenal reality. With Bacon the book of God's work becomes more fully a printed book. Though this new printed book may be modeled on the sophisticated manuscript books created for royalty and aristocrats (Saenger, 1982), it will differ from them in its wide availability and its comprehensiveness. Ultimately all knowledge will be indexed and organized by topic.

Bacon follows Aristotle in dividing his topics into general and particular. He does not view the general topics as a "deficient" art and observes that they have "been sufficiently handled in logic" (1863, Vol. 9, p. 86). He does, however, include a typographically influenced amendment to the received tradition's sense of them:

> Only it may be observed by the way, that this kind is of use not only in argumentations, where we are disputing with another, but also in meditations, where we are considering and resolving anything with ourselves; neither does it serve only to prompt and suggest what we should affirm and assert, but also what we should inquire or ask. (1863, Vol. 9, p. 86)

In this manner, Bacon expands the use of the topics in a manner that indicates that he has internalized the printed page as a model for intellectual inquiry. He sees the topics as applicable to the inner space of the intellect, the outer space of the text, and the external phenomenal world as well:

> The same places therefore which will help us to shake out the folds of the intellect within us, and to draw forth the knowledge stored therein, will also help us to gain knowledge from without; so that if a man of learning and experience were before us, we should know how to question him wisely and to the purpose; and in like manner how to select and peruse with advantage those authors, books and parts of books, which may best instruct us concerning that which we seek. (1863, Vol. 9, p. 86)

Here we see a very interesting combining of the oral mode of questioning an individual and the literate mode of reading a book. But Bacon's method of reading is selective and not directed at reproducing speech, as reading in manuscript culture often was, but at gathering information imagined to exist in well defined bits and pieces. As Gilbert has suggested, Bacon turns "the debating procedure of the Topics into a transaction in which Nature replaced the respondent and the challenger became the scientist" (1960, p. 224). We also must note the typographically mediated sense of the word as objectified and finite, rather than voiced and social, that informs Bacon's ultimate goals. While there is an agonistic element to Bacon's project, he also rejects the old method of logical argumentation because those who have used it "have wronged, abused, and traduced nature" (1863, Vol. 3, p. 264-265).

The use of topics to objectively examine books and learned people is most clearly extended to include natural phenomena in Bacon's treatment of particular topics. The particular topics are "places of invention and inquiry appropriated to particular subjects and sciences" (1863, Vol. 9, p. 87). A particular topic is expanded through the application of specific articles of inquiry. The purpose of these articles is to accumulate knowledge about a particular topic. Through the articles of inquiry related to a particular topic and through the application of the experimental tropes, the new scientist can search the external world, both phenomenal and textual, to invent/discover arguments that clarify and reveal the nature of the particular topic under consideration. Thus the scientist proceeds much as the orator except that he examines the external world and not his own internal stock of commonplaces. Bacon intends to gradually replace the traditional stock of commonplaces ordered under a particular topic with a stock of experimentally derived facts. The ordering capabilities of the typographic text are essential to his plan and also demonstrate how he has internalized the printed text as a model for information management.

At the end of his discussion of the topics, Bacon provides as an example of his topological mode of inquiry "A Particular Topic, or Articles of Inquiry concerning Heavy and Light" (1863, Vol. 9, pp. 88-92). Bacon's sense of the use of the particular topics as sites for gathering information about a particular subject is clearly related to the rhetorical concept of *copia*. It is commonplace in the rhetorical tradition to refer to the orator's searching of his memory to secure *copia* as a gathering of flowers. Lechner describes the dynamic of this mental process "as 'hunting' for topics, identifying their location, and employing their 'contents'—previously stored in regions of the mind (or the pages of a book)" (1962, p. 232). As noted above, Bacon extends this search to the observable world of nature:

> For he that shall attentively observe how the mind doth gather this excellent dew of knowledge . . . distilling and contriving it out of particulars natural and artificial, as the flowers of the field and garden, shall find that the mind of

herself by nature doth manage and act an induction much better than they [the logicians] describe it. (1863, Vol. 6, p. 265)

He refers to the "particulars natural and artificial" as the "flowers of the field and garden," respectively. This parallelism combines a sense of literate or learned knowledge (the artfully tended garden) with a sense of natural or interpretive knowledge gained directly from nature (the untended field). Transforming the traditional rhetorical practice of an internal search for arguments, Bacon has his experimental rhetorician proceed through a series of specific inquiries to "gather" from texts and through experiment all the knowledge there is about Heavy and Light. The various articles of inquiry employ the experimental tropes described above, but the tropological procedure is secondary to the primary topical organization of the plan. For example, article 4 recommends the use of the experimental trope "compulsion," "when an experiment is urged and extended to the annihilation or deprivation of the power" (1863, Vol. 9, p. 79), and the researcher is urged to "inquire whether the quantity of a body can be so increased as to lose the notion of gravity; as the earth, which is pendulous, but falls not" (1863, Vol. 9, p. 88). This procedure follows the traditional model provided for the orator who would first use the general topics, then the particular topics, and then invent or hunt out the commonplaces with which to illustrate his argument. Furthermore, it is evident from this example that the experimental tropes were not intended exclusively for the manipulation of natural phenomena (such a manipulation of the earth would be impossible), but could be used to undertake an imaginary internal dialogue that could also produce satisfactory conclusions about natural phenomena.

Clearly the doctrine of *experientia literata* is an informal one and one to be used initially as a step towards the more formal logic of *interpretatio naturae*. But with the method of *experientia literata,* attention definitely shifts from the internal search of the traditional orator inventing arguments to the externally directed search of the literary seeker looking into the pages of a book, and by analogy, to the new scientist/philosopher seeking to unlock the secrets of nature that are "so much greater than the subtlety of words" (1863, Vol. 9, p. 69). It is also important to note that the limited goal of this method is a rhetorical one: to begin to find a light that will reveal hidden nature through a tropically based mode of inquiry. In the *De augumentis* Bacon refers to *experientia literata* as the "Hunt of Pan," a method that "must hardly be esteemed an art or a part of philosophy, but rather a kind of sagacity" (1863, Vol. 9, p. 71). The metaphor used to describe this method is also directly related to the hunt for commonplaces that Lechner (1962) describes (cf. Ong, 1967b, pp. 56-87; Payne, 1983, pp. 250-251). The use of these figures will train the mind and work toward the ultimate goal of an intellect as subtle as nature. Bacon will build on the textually mediated *experientia literata* a methodological edifice that will enable him to accomplish "the very thing which I am preparing and labouring at with all my might—to make the mind of man by help of art a match for the nature of things" (1863, Vol. 9, p. 71).

The experimental tropes, figures of speech, and topics serve the double purpose outlined above of providing an orientation in the textual and in the con-textual material world. Ong's observation concerning the Renaissance collector, Zwinger, is true also of Bacon: "The original 'places' in the mind, a highly metaphorical conception, have here been transmuted into physical places on the printed page" (1977a, pp. 174-175). Using a topological model similar to that used in the commonplace books and other medieval and Renaissance collections of traditional materials, Bacon proposes a re-search and reorganization of the material they contain that will be supplemented and expanded through experiment. The particular topics and the experimental figures will be two tools that will effect this reorganization.

Though Bacon joins in the movement to reject rhetoric's epistemological functions, I believe the preceding analysis suggests that his method suppresses more than it rejects. Habits of mind shaped by rhetorical practice and transformed by the internalization of the printed text as an epistemological model persist at the very core of his project. As a transitional figure occupying a significant position at the juncture between the rhetorical and the modern worlds, Bacon may be accepted as an "impure scientist." Yet, as I hope this study begins to demonstrate, our understanding of the epistemological claims of rhetoric in modern discourses might well begin with him.

5

Voice as Frame: Longinus, Kant, Ong, and Deconstruction in Literary Studies

WILLIAM J. KENNEDY

As this volume shows, Walter Ong has raised profound questions about the nature of literacy and orality, rhetoric and communication, culture and consciousness, literary voice and the personal human voice. Among these topics I would like to press further our current concept of literary voice. Modern critical theory sometimes takes that concept for granted. Practical literary criticism has long discussed voice in lyric poetry, prose narrative, and dramatic characterization without fully defining the term or exploring its implications. Walter Ong's work, however, provides valuable insight into the nature of that phenomenon and nudges us toward a clear definition. It does so because it assimilates the entire history of classical rhetoric and modern aesthetics with a deep awareness of their ramifications in contemporary culture. Using Ong's work and referring to its concern with current theory, I will propose that voice is a rhetorically constructed frame for a potentially indeterminate discourse, and I am going to argue that we can find fertile grounds for interrogating this idea in Longinus's *On the Sublime* (*Peri Hupsous,* A.D. 80) (1927) and in Kant's *Critique of Judgment* (1951). Both of these treatises posit voice as a frame of reference that emphasizes some dimensions of rhetorical meaning and suppresses others. It acts upon language to clarify unruly meanings that otherwise resist conscious classification.

A great deal of modern critical theory—including such variants in literary theory as formalism, structuralism, and deconstruction—has tried to reify the concept of voice in a play of verbal signs. For deconstruction in particular, the play of signs is endless and it figures a radical loss of "the present voice" in its material infinity. For Walter Ong, on the other hand, words are always more than things, and no voice, not even a materially written voice, ever submits wholly to reification. Voice is dialogic and therefore a social event even when the speaker speaks only to himself or herself:

> In the human situation . . . the center of emission is a kind of receiving center, too, and cannot emit its words properly unless it is at the same time receiving them. Similarly the receiving center has to be a kind of center of emission, for it receives its words by imagining them as emitted. One consequence of this is that it is fallacious to imagine that words are capable of being reduced to impulses. (Ong, 1962a, p. 52)

Here Ong describes a dialogic quality of the human voice that pertains to literary voice as well and that should be of interest not only to literary scholars but also to students of communication, psychoanalysis, semiotics, and ideological critique, and indeed to all who reflect seriously on various kinds of rhetorical performance.

Walter Ong's own studies in literary criticism have shown that poetic voice achieves its effects in contradictory, oxymoronic ways, and for that reason it notoriously resists simple, methodological analysis (1977a, pp. 272-302). Voice offers semantic stability by implying a bond between the speaker's meaning and intention. At the same time it disrupts that stability by making linguistic usage distinctive, personal, idiosyncratic. Figurative language, too, nourishes semantic instability. Figures, however, differ from voice in at least one fundamental way. Whereas figures breach the relationship between signifiers and signifieds, voice heals the breach. In a linguistic universe of semantic instability, readers and hearers perceive intended meanings in figurative language because rhetorical voice makes them understood. It works to control the spread of meaning, heightening some of its rhetorical dimensions while suppressing others.

In this sense voice is not an essentialized figure but a supplement or accompaniment to figures that directs, channels, and clarifies figurative meaning. Voice is a multifarious event, and as an event it lies open to instability. It requires performance for completion, but infinitely variable conditions of performance guarantee that any completion will be only provisional. Individual performances frame voice. Enclosed within this double framing of voice and performance, then, the focus of discourse comes into shape with a host of rhetorical clues. Longinus's *On the Sublime* describes some of these clues. By interpreting them the reader assigns meaning to the text, but judiciously, based on a keen sense of how a text might call for a certain kind of frame. Kant's aesthetics articulated in the *Critique of Judgment* describe this process for art in general.

One might imagine that process as a dialectical interaction. Focus and frame interact to produce intelligible meaning. Especially when the focus itself may be figural, as in poetic utterances, the text requires a frame to be understood. If the frame were also figural, its figuralism would only compound the text's unintelligibility. That condition may occur in literary texts when the speaker assumes an ironic voice in order to mislead a naive audience. Even then voice is not wholly figural, no matter how much it dissociates signifiers from their expected signifieds. Separated from the focus of the text, the frame has no meaning of its own and serves no purpose. Without the frame of voice, on the other hand, the focus of the text amounts to a purely formal structure of meaning that lacks semantic depth and intellectual complexity. A system of intelligible exchange governs the audience's movement from focus to frame and back again, and it evokes the model of the hermeneutic circle. Frame and focus restrict and define one another by agreement and contrast, convergence and divergence, similarity and difference. One gauges the meaning by balancing part against whole.

Speakers and writers shape their personal voices, whether fictive or not, by lexical choices, syntactic combinations, features of repressed utterance (e.g., transference into metaphor or other figures of speech, displacement into stylized or conventional language), and devices of rhythm, tone, and pacing. The voice that emerges gives the audience a context to judge shades of meaning, filtering out some dimensions of meaning and admitting others. It organizes meaning more efficiently than impersonal utterance. It also limits a proliferation of meaning. By highlighting linguistic traits uniquely associated with the character of the speaker or writer, voice establishes a real or imagined center of gravity that defines tone or point of view (Kennedy, 1978, 1987).

Among various modern approaches to literary analysis, deconstruction continually insists that the meaning of any literary text is fundamentally undecidable. In its quest for concrete empirical grounds to understand a text's multiple meanings, deconstruction finds few satisfactory ones for defining voice. The scandal of voice is that it eludes descriptive labels. Voice is no more or no less than idiosyncratic utterance. The scandal of literary voice is that it eludes even the authority of sensory experience that belongs to spoken voice. It is the impalpable product of a rhetoric that expresses intentional states of mind. Even though it issues from rhetoric, it nonetheless submits to no class or category of rhetorical figure, scheme, or trope.

For such a mental state as intentionality to be known, it must partake of some phenomenalization. Language and other semiotic systems express personal intentions in fits and starts. They no sooner reify ideas than they insist on their metaphysical mode of existence. Jacques Derrida, on the other hand, emphasizes the primary materiality of language. This materiality disequilibrates all relationships between words and things, signifiers and signifieds. Extending Saussure's principle that each sign acquires meaning only through its difference from other signs, Derrida asserts that "there are only everywhere differences and traces of traces" (1981, p. 26). Words convey no stable meanings of their own, but rather multiple, polysemous, unstable other meanings; and allegory, taken as "other speech," defines their material mode of existence.

This material view of language conspires against the concept of voice. Unmoored from any ground of essentialized meaning, language functions as common coin, public property, changeable merchandise that belongs alike to all. To the degree that the human psyche is predicated upon language and the human subject depends upon a stable language to articulate its own core of being, the disappearance of voice portends a disappearance of the subject. This disappearance moreover signals the absolute impossibility of any intentionality. Throw out the subject and one throws out the interiorized mental states that constitute intention. Even if one allowed the fiction of a personal voice to inscribe intentions within a text, we would have no stable reading subjects able to decode it.

American deconstruction restates the problem with yet a new version of the difficulty. It pursues a radically ahistorical approach that denies language a specific field of meaning at any given moment in time. For its most eloquent proponent, Paul de Man, "the historical nature of literary discourse is by no means an a priori established fact" (1979, p. 79). The eclipse of historical specificity synchronizes all intertextual possibilities. This synchrony exerts strong pressure on language's figurative capabilities. Since "other" meanings always fray out from any linguistic expression and language lacks the means to control their spread, every perceived meaning deviates from other perceived meanings in a given expression. Language is inherently tropological, full of dead metaphors and sedimented figures of speech.

Voice undergoes its own tropic turn in this scheme. Even though voice lacks the certainty of an essentialized sense perception, it still constitutes a fundamental aspect of all written texts, and perhaps the fundamental aspect of lyric texts. Linguistic slippage ensures that every voice will deviate in some way from the intention of its speaking subject. The specific trope that expresses this deviation in lyric texts is prosopopoeia, a figure that Quintilian defines as one in which "we lend a voice to things to which nature has denied it" (1920-1922, chap. 9.2.29). To designate voice as a figural deviation inherent in poetry lends materiality to the idea of voice in lyric. Paul de Man concludes that:

> the text is therefore not a mimesis of a signifier, but of a specific figure, prosopopoeia. And since mimesis itself is a figure, it is the figure of a figure (the prosopopoeia of a prosopopoeia) and not in any respect, neither in appearance nor in reality, a description. (1985, p. 61)

To the degree that it is then a form of figural substitution exemplified by prosopopoeia, voice becomes available as an actual sensory experience in poetry, embedded in the material inscription of the text.

This conception of voice is unabashedly circular. Because all language is figural, so too must voice be figural. The problem begins with the conception of figure itself when it is defined as deviation. One will find this definition to be incomplete the more one traces its roots in classical rhetoric as Walter Ong has in his study of Ramus (1958a, pp. 277-281). Classical rhetoric depicts figure as a heightened form of expression. If it begins as a deviation from a code, it requires the dialectical intervention of its opposite, a return to the code, in order to be intelligible. Only this complementary action can give form to the deviation itself. Without this action, deviated meanings will drift unintelligibly away from the grasp of understanding. With it, however, the referent emerges reconstituted on a higher level (Ricoeur, 1977, pp. 149-157). The startling effect of a momentary deviation gives way to fuller, richer meaning. In this sense tropology entails not deviation but intensification.

Voice achieves this effect in classical rhetoric precisely because it functions as a frame that throws into relief some dimensions of meaning and obscures others. It clarifies the focus of figural discourse by providing a point of reference. Since discourse is a social event whose speakers belong to a linguistic community, one might reasonably expect the rules of that community to illuminate the idea of voice. Longinus's *On the Sublime* provides a *locus classicus* for a discussion of voice and rhetorical figures in ancient rhetoric as well as for a discussion of rhetoric in the context of literary theory. Its insights proved especially significant for Kant and his contemporaries because Longinus's idea of the sublime as a standard for literary excellence incorporates the ideas of freedom and democracy as its social concomitant. Thus in Longinus's Chapter 44, sublime eloquence guarantees the freedom of a republic and the banishment of slavish customs.

Longinus's discussion nonetheless presents enormous problems. Not only does it come to us incomplete and in mutilated form, but it also lacks internal organization and system. Terms slide into one another, definitions blur at the edges, and conclusions go begging for resolution. For some, internal inconsistencies tear at the heart of Longinus's theory (Wimsatt & Brooks, 1957, pp. 97-111). For others, however, Longinus's subversion of methodological rigor confers great benefits (Fry, 1983, pp. 47-86). It frees Longinus's theory from an impossible effort to systematize rhetoric and it permits far-ranging observations on linguistic functions outside of limiting contexts.

Longinus's discussion of voice is an important by-product of this freedom. Without the constraints of a formal or closed system, Longinus need not attach the concept of voice to any single class or category. Its instability allows him to exploit the metonymic character of voice as a sign for the speaking subject's ethos. In one example voice occurs as a function of question and answer with "their appeal to the imagination" (Longinus, 1927, chap. 18.1). In another it occurs as a function of word order that "bears, so to speak, the genuine stamp of vehement emotion" (chap. 22.1). Still other examples refer to grammatical and syntactical forms of language that "serve to lend emotion and excitement to the style" (chap. 29.2).

In each of these examples voice is figural, but figural in a very special way. Here Longinus appropriates conventions of classical rhetoric that sharply discriminate among different types of figure. Schemes, or figures of words, refer to grammatical and syntactic arrangements that implicitly heighten or intensify meaning. Tropes, or figures of thought, refer to semantic displacements or substitutions of thought in ways that explicitly change meaning. The former encompass figurations as parts or units of a sentence whose meaning would prevail without those figurations, while the latter encompass shifts and turns of meaning in its deviation from common usage. True, any schematic shift in word order will entail some readjustment of emphasis, but its primary effect is to focus meaning rather than to change or dissipate it; any shift of meaning is momentary and reversible, a simply perceived by-product of verbal arrangement.

Longinus nonetheless blurs the distinction between schematic and tropological figures by discussing two types of *schemata*. He designates them as schemes of word (*lexeos*) and schemes of idea (*noeseos*) (chap. 8). All the examples that he adduces for these *schemata* in chapters 16 to 29 concern syntactic patterning. In each of these functions, voice mitigates the shiftiness of figural and tropological discourse. Intensified speech and/or unusual arrangement provoke suspicion. They alert us to fraud, hidden traps, plots, deception, fallacies. A skillful use of voice may temper this scandal by associating the speaker's discourse with his or her subjective *ethos*:

The sublimity and effect on the emotions are a wonderfully helpful antidote against the suspicion that accompanies the use of figures. The effrontery of the artifice is somehow lost in its brilliant setting of beauty and grandeur: it is no longer obvious, and thus avoids all suspicion. (chap. 17.2)

Longinus compares its effect to that of painting where a play of shadow and light belies the two-dimensional nature of the painted surface: "Though the high lights and shadows lie side by side in the same plane, yet the high lights spring to the eye and seem not only to stand out but to be actually much nearer" (chap. 17.3). Here the status of voice as an illusion constitutes a lid or cover that extends over figurative errancy, contains and protects it, and thus frames the discourse of which it is part.

The illusion falls into discredit, however, when figurative schemes mask a disjunction between expression and idea, signifiers and their signifieds, words and things. Longinus perceives a dialectical exchange between these terms when the force of the signifier contributes to the meaning of the signified and vice versa: "Thought and diction often explain each other" (chap. 30.1). The bond between signifier (*phraxis*) and signified (*tou logou noesis*) confers upon the speaker a sense of illuminating presence: "It endues the fact as it were with a living voice" (chap. 30.1). It nonetheless risks disruption at moments of high emotion when metaphor dissociates the signifier from its usual signified. Metaphor incurs a violence that figurative schemes only help to contain:

The proper antidote for a multitude of daring metaphors is strong and timely emotion and genuine sublimity. These by their nature sweep everything along in the forward surge of their current, or rather they positively demand bold imagery as essential to their effect, and do not give the hearer time to examine how many metaphors there are, because he shares the excitement of the speaker. (chap. 32.4)

By the efficacy of its framing power, voice subdues the uncontrollable spread of meaning in metaphor and opens it to precise understanding.

Longinus's idea of voice as a frame for discourse might raise problems if one regards the subject as an unchanging monolithic entity. If one regards the subject as a historical being in process, however, the problems resolve themselves, as Ong has shown (1977a, pp. 17-22, 41-49). The speaking or writing subject as a subject-in-process shifts, changes, and transforms, and so does his or her thought. Rhetorical voice dramatizes the transformation itself.

Longinus cites various figures that intensify voice, and all involve temporal process (chaps. 16-29). They all disrupt the continuity of speech and the
temper of the speaker. Acknowledging the speaker's or writer's subjectivity
and instability, they allow voice to emerge as an event. They include *syncope*
(omission of a syllable from the middle of a word), *apocope* (omission of a
syllable from the end of a word), *epenthesis* (addition of a syllable to a word),
hyperbaton (disruption of normal word order), *ellipsis* (omission of words
understood in context), *parenthesis* (interpolation of authorial comment), and
antithesis (juxtaposition of contrasts). In this context, then, voice is a powerful result of figurally intensified speech. It frames the entire discourse of
which figures are a part.

To say that voice is a frame prompts an important question in aesthetics:
Is a frame part of its picture or not? Where does the one begin and the other
end? Derrida asks this question when he deconstructs Kant's aesthetics and
the notion of mimesis in the visual arts in *The Truth in Painting* (1987). Kant
considers the frame of a painting as an "ornament" or *parergon* that
supplements the painting with its own formal qualities:

> Even what we call "ornaments" (*parerga*) [*Zierathen (Parerga)*], i.e. those things
> which do not belong to the complete representation of the object internally as
> elements, but only externally as complements [*als Zutat*], and which augment
> the satisfaction of taste, do so only by their form; as for example, (the frames of
> pictures [*wie Einfassungen der Gemälde*] or) the draperies of statues or the
> colonnades of palaces. But if the ornament does not itself consist in beautiful
> form, and if it is used as a golden frame is used, [*wie der goldene Rahmen*]
> merely to recommend the painting by its charm, it is then called finery and
> injures genuine beauty. (1908, p. 226; 1951, pp. 61-62)

For Kant the frame constitutes a buffer between the painting and the viewer,
between the work of art and society. It affords a common ground between art
and society and thus emblematizes the social dimension of the work of art.
This dimension is as crucial in Kant's aesthetics as it is in Walter Ong's:
"Empirically the beautiful interests only in *society*" (Kant, 1908, p. 296;
1951, p. 139). It is also crucial in Derrida's deconstruction of Kant's
aesthetics.

Derrida begins his deconstruction by focusing on the Greek word that Kant
uses for "ornament": *parergon*. It refers to a supplemental *hors d'oeuvre* that
functions not only side-by-side (*par*) with the work (*ergon*), but also contrary
to it. Kant's example of a picture frame conceals an ambiguity. As a border
that frames the picture, it accompanies the picture; as an ornamental work of

art in its own right, it competes with the picture. As a supplement to the picture, it can be detached and transported to a second picture without detracting from the first. Or, Derrida asks, can it? The problem is to determine where the frame begins and ends, where it belongs to the picture and where it doesn't: "Where does the frame take place?" (Derrida, 1987, p. 63). For Derrida there is no natural, transcendent frame; there is only the activity of framing: "There is frame, but the frame does not exist" (1987, p. 81). Frame is a metaphysical abstraction rather than a common ground that invites the viewer and the object to interact.

Derrida expands upon his idea of the frame's autonomy. As ornament, *parergon,* the frame virtually embodies free form. As pure supplement, the ornament discloses free form in tension with purposiveness. The frame of a painting, for example, is a nonreferential, nonrepresentational play of line and form, a margin of absolute liberty that participates in what it frames. "The *parergon* constitutes the place and the structure of free beauty" (p. 97). It in fact exemplifies Kant's very ideal of free, detached, indefinite beauty. It embodies, too, Derrida's own substantial concept of a beauty that originates in absence. It reconciles brute matter with pure form and thus resolves the tension between them that hobbles classical aesthetics. According to Derrida, however, Kant fails to recognize the productive possibilities of understanding the frame as an emblem of art itself. Even as he espouses free form, Kant devalues the *parergon.* His pervasive effort to keep the frame in its place unmasks anxieties about his own unstable philosophical system.

American deconstruction extends Derrida's insight. According to de Man (1981), Kant's anxieties betray his blindness about figurality. Kant's aesthetic valorizes architectonic construction rather than figural or symbolical texture, and it illuminates structural relationships as a ground where artist and audience share attitudes toward form. It views language not as a system of tropes but as an activity of performance. A general consequence is that Kant occludes the tropological dimension of his own discourse as narrative. Without knowing it, he has constructed "a story, a dramatized scene of the mind in action . . . determined by linguistic structures" (de Man, 1981, pp. 140-141). A particular consequence is that Kant also occludes the figures of voice and address in his own writing: There is "no room for address in Kant's flat, third-person world" (de Man, 1981, p. 135). Its aesthetic is "purely formal, devoid of semantic depth" (p. 136).

Even if we can agree that Kant subverts figures and that he articulates an antirhetorical stance, we can do so only in a highly qualified way. Walter Ong has remarked that Kant's views about language maximize a closed-system paradigm (1977a, p. 332). Kant asserts that a rhetorician shapes discourse in order to coerce an audience. The orator attempts "to win minds . . . before they have formed a judgment and to deprive them of their freedom" (Kant, 1908, p. 327; 1951, p. 171). As a rhetorical frame, voice controls the audience's response by exciting affections. In a critical mind it arouses the charge implicit even in Longinus about "the secret suspicion that one is being artfully overreached" (Kant, 1908, p. 327; 1951, p. 172). Just as Longinus qualifies the degree of suspicion by evoking the power of voice, so does Kant. Poetic discourse offers an effective counterpart against rhetorical overreaching: "It plays with illusion, which it produces at pleasure, but without deceiving by it; for it declares its exercise to be mere play [*für blosses Spiel*], which however can be purposively [*zweckmässig*] used by the understanding" (Kant, 1908, p. 327; 1951, p. 171). Poetic voice frames the illusion by representing the speaker's affections and reproducing them for the audience.

To construe voice as a material figure, however, is to defer its mimetic powers. Can voice admit any openness to change that nonetheless accommodates some form of closure as a guide to meaning and intention? Walter Ong's concept of orality certainly implies that personal voices can be active and free, yet also prompt to decidable meaning through accent, intonation, pitch, stress, and juncture. Literary voices can be likewise because they are never alone to themselves, but are always part of a social dialogue. The individuality of any voice, personal or literary, is not mere idiosyncrasy, eccentricity, or uniqueness, but is rather a sharing in the speech of others through customs, conventions, traditions, and ritual. Openness to others permits not only an assimilation of individual consciousness and collective culture but also the very distinctiveness of self that an individual voice projects (Ong, 1981a, pp. 193-199). Kant himself regards such openness as the basis of enlightenment and progress, the product of a free and flexible competition of ideas framed by individual voices in responsible discourse.

Like Kant and Longinus, Walter Ong reminds us that responsible discourse is a critical event. It entails a continual questioning of tradition rather than any blind conservation of it for its own sake. With literary imitation, for example, the responsible text does not copy earlier texts slavishly. It projects its own voice. Longinus explicitly challenges the notion that canonical rules determine artistry. In a reference to Polycleitus's canonical statue, the *doryphorus,* Longinus asserts that a text's highest linguistic potential exceeds the mere correctness of rules. Norms provide guides that the individual writer must overgo: "Distinction of style, however unevenly sustained, is due to genius" (chap. 36.3). In his own reference to the same canonical statute, Kant likewise challenges the notion of standard correctness: "Its presentation pleases, not by its beauty, but merely because it contradicts no condition, under which a thing of this kind can be beautiful. The presentation is merely correct" (1908, p. 235; 1951, p. 72). Correctness does not necessarily subvert voice, but it does institutionalize and therefore limit the ways a writer can achieve voice. Neither Longinus nor Kant, however, wishes to curb any possibilities of developing a voice that expresses the sublime.

Significantly, one of Kant's examples of the sublime involves the distortion of a human voice. The example contrasts the sound of a bird in nature with the voice of a boy who imitates that sound. The boy's voice casts a spell over his auditors as long as they think they hear a bird. Any sudden recognition of the truth breaks the illusion and defers the audience's interest. This recognition, however, clears the ground for a different sort of satisfaction:

> We have a faculty of mere aesthetical judgment by which we judge forms without the aid of concepts and find a satisfaction [*ein Wohlgefallen*] in this mere act of judgment; this we make into a rule for everyone, without this judgment either being based on or producing any interest [*Interesse*]. (Kant, 1908, p. 300; 1951, p. 142)

The voice itself is no illusion, but it sustains an illusion—the sound of the bird that it represents. The audience now can shift its interest from the object represented (the sound of a bird) to the frame around it (the boy's voice). As long as the boy's voice projects the sound of a bird, its auditors take an immediate interest in that illusion:

> It must be nature or be regarded as nature if we are to take an immediate interest [*ein unmittelbares Interesse*] in the beautiful as such, and still more is this the case if we can require that others should take an interest in it too. (Kant, 1908, p. 302; 1951, p. 145)

The moment the boy steps outside of his projection, the illusion ceases. The auditors' interest is now mediated by their awareness of the boy's voice as a fashioning frame for the sound of the bird. That voice defines the terms of its own performance, maps its territories, establishes its conventions, and constitutes the ground for its own articulation. It is both background and foreground for the sound that issues forth.

The audience's interest in the artful voice is formal, then, as if the represented object were autonomous, self-sufficient, and independent of the producing artist. Whether that object exists outside its artistic representation (a real bird outside the sound of a bird represented by the boy's voice) becomes unimportant. Its existence as a fiction suffices to compel our attention to its transcendent otherness. It is worth noting, too, that the concept of disinterested pleasure (*interesseloses Wohlgefallen*), subtending these remarks but explained elsewhere (Kant, 1908, pp. 209-211; 1951, pp. 43-54), implies anything but aesthetic indifference or the neutrality of art for art's sake. It implies, in fact, the opposite: an involvement through dialogic interaction. *Interesselos* suggests "immediate" and "fully participatory" in the sense that nothing exists or intervenes between (*inter esse*) the subject and the object of the artistic experience (see Wellek, 1955, Vol. 1, pp. 229-230).

Involvement through the action of a heightened awareness is in fact the result of a disinterested pleasure. In *Foundations of the Metaphysics of Morals* (1909), Kant asserts as a moral imperative that good for one person can be good only in so far as it may be good for all. An analogous principle in the *Critique of Judgment* asserts that beauty for one person is beauty only in so far as it can be beauty for all. Aesthetic value is social and communal, a matter of common sense or feeling available to everyone. Kant nonetheless insists that this value cannot be prescribed according to a set of rules. It emerges only through the audience's capacity for "enlarged thought," the capacity "to put ourselves in thought in the place of everyone else" (Kant, 1908, p. 294; 1951, p. 136). The capacity to understand difference and otherness, indeed to experience them indirectly and vicariously, makes the writer's voice responsible to the audience and to the world. An individual's consciousness is what it is because of how it relates to others.

Voice in this scheme goes far beyond registering a figural deviation from some norm of expression, as deconstruction would have it. It is instead a social, historical event. Because voice is an event, it is itself unstable and indeterminate. Its instability and indeterminacy impel you to question the limits of voice: Where does it begin? where end? These questions frame the speaker's discourse and establish the limits of its otherness. At the same time they prompt the audience's creative participation with the speaker as though in dialogue. Like Longinus, Kant is aware of rhetorical means that voice uses to stimulate dialogue—question and answer, ellipsis, parenthesis, hyperbaton, and so on. The dramatic illusion of voice achieved by these means limns the humanity of the speaking subject and inscribes it in a social context. Voice enables the speaker and the audience to share attitudes towards possible meanings in the words that they use and in the things that those words refer to. The frame of voice situates material *logos* in the fully human field of *ethos*.

Longinus's rhetoric and Kant's aesthetics, then, offer a basis for this view of voice as a dynamic frame around shared meanings. Deconstruction, on the other hand, regards voice as a reified figure that forever defers meaning. For J. Hillis Miller (1987) its arch figure takes the form of a narrative that is undecidable in meaning. The action of Kant's "enlarged thought" might prompt us, in Miller's terms, to "perform a little experiment, enter in imagination into a little fiction, an 'as if' or '*als so*' " (German for "as so" or "as such"; 1987, p. 28). For de Man the arch figure is allegory, a form of "other speech" in which signifier is radically dissociated from signified.

I am not sure, however, that an implied narrative is necessarily undecidable or that "other speech" as a synonym for "allegory" adequately translates the etymological roots of *allos agorein*. As Walter Ong has recalled in his study of Renaissance place logic (1958a, pp. 106-107), *agorein* derives from *agora,* the public marketplace. *Agorein* means to speak openly in the marketplace, to project one's voice into the public arena. To speak *allos* in the public arena is to say something in another register that the audience nonetheless comprehends clearly. In this sense allegory signals the capacity of language to do two things at once by uniting open and closed meanings, public and private voice, strange and familiar discourse. It appears as a subspecies of oxymoron, the bringing together of two terms that are usually contradictory. Voice functions as a frame precisely to reconcile these opposites and allow language to do two things at once. Human language distinguishes itself from artificial intelligence, cybernetic language, and the sign systems of lesser animals by its power to sustain these opposites as "both/and."

If I were pressed to designate one figure as emblematic of voice, I would select oxymoron. It seems the quintessential figure animating human discourse because it epitomizes an embrace of stark opposites within the frame of a single voice. Ong's work everywhere evinces the paradoxical containment of opposites within the compass of human voice. Not the least merit of Ong's concept of rhetoric is its power to summon a historical poetics in the tradition of Longinus and Kant, one that is cognizant of language's social function to reconcile opposites through voice. That function, as Ong's writing continually reminds us, is inherently dialogic, a foundation that allows humankind to enter upon a new and advanced stage in the evolution of consciousness. To situate voice in the arena of that evolution is to demonstrate its power to frame human discourse.

6

Romanticism, Realism, and the Presence of the Word

NOËL VALIS

I

Walter J. Ong, SJ, has suggested that "all human intellectual activity implies belief because it implies faith in the possibility of communication and faith in someone with whom we can communicate" (1962a, p. 55). Certainly this holds true of our relationship with literature. Ong reminds his readers that in reading a literary work, we enter into that work as into another person's interiority. This is because we "hear" as we read another person's voice and we are moved to respond. "Literature," he concludes, "exists in a context of one presence calling to another" (1962a, p. 59).

I wish to explore how what Ong calls the "presence of the word" manifests itself in written literature and what that vestige of orality signifies as communication. The Spanish philosopher Miguel de Unamuno wrote in 1924 that "any written style that does not come from a spoken style, any writing that does not have its roots in voice, in the word, is not style, it isn't anything" (1954a, p. 592). Indeed, that is true of all writing, not just of imaginative literature. Thus, the concern of this essay with voice is a concern that should guide our understanding of all writing. Ong's own work, especially from *The Presence of the Word* (1967b) on, is a beautiful example of that communicative joy of the human voice.

In this essay, I show that performance-oriented texts in nineteenth-century Spanish literature did not disappear with the historically short-lived Romantic movement in Spain. I will argue that certain realist novels like Benito Pérez Galdós's *Fortunata y Jacinta* should not be joined with texts like Gustave Flaubert's *Madame Bovary* that arise out of Romantic subjectivity as pure interiority. Rather, the deep underlying link between Spanish Romantic writers (Zorrilla, for example) and realists like Galdós remains oral and communal in nature, although sifted through a particular kind of Romantic consciousness.

In the traditional schema of Spanish literary histories, Romanticism and realism are conveniently seen as opposing movements or tendencies, even though most critics recognize that Romantic (and melodramatic) elements still cling to realist fiction (Ciplijauskaité, 1988). I would suggest that a significant link between Romanticism and realism in Spain lies precisely in the oral trace of shared knowledge and values expressed through voice. Not all realist texts demonstrate this trace. To see just how "voice" functions within two different literate contexts, how it can be silenced in one and soar in another, I will lay out those differences in two masterpieces of the realist tradition, Flaubert's *Madame Bovary* (1857/1965)—often taken as the classic proof-text for the norms of realism—and Galdós's *Fortunata y Jacinta* (1886-1887/1986).

Fortunata y Jacinta is structured around the conflictive interweaving between "two stories of married women," as the subtitle reads. One, Fortunata, is of lower-class origins; the other, Jacinta, is upper middle-class. Fortunata's adulterous liaison with Jacinta's husband, Juanito, provides a thematic parallel with the better-known Madame Bovary. But the two novels are otherwise poles apart, representing as they do two realist models that incorporate Romantic consciousness in different ways. In *Fortunata y Jacinta,* "voice" speaks as the symbolic ordering of communal experience, with the same emotional bonding that inspired Spain's performance-oriented Romanticism. In *Madame Bovary,* "voice" is silenced, because it originates in Romantic subjectivity as pure interiority.

II

In a remarkable chapter about "the art of listening" to *Fortunata y Jacinta,* critic Stephen Gilman once said that even the most passionately devoted of Galdós's readers could not ignore the translating difficulties of the novelist's "oral hermeticism" (1981, p. 252). Yet he also says that to read *Fortunata y Jacinta* is really to practice a form of listening. Gilman's advice on reading, however, poses an intrinsic problem: If reading *Fortunata y Jacinta* means to catch the winged word of spoken speech, then how do we read oral intentions? To put it another way, because we no longer know how to listen to human sound without thinking of it in written terms (Ong, 1967b, p. 19), our own deafness has sealed us in silence.

Erich Kahler has spoken of the "inward turn of narrative" that modern fiction has taken in delving deeper and deeper into human consciousness. Such an inward turn of narrative suggests a parallel process in the inward turn of reading. Silence and interiorization seem to pair off naturally, slipping away off-side as voice and exteriorization are paradoxically exiled to a lonely, unwanted center. The postmodern critique of the centrality of speech in Western tradition logically extends the prevailing notion that thinking— and therefore, all human endeavor—is a curious form of inner isolationism in which we break down the external categories of authority by consigning them to the void.

Unfortunately, this consequent loss of voice, which brings with it the intriguing self-referentiality of writing as *écriture,* has also ultimately impoverished our understanding of a large body of writings—among them, *Fortunata y Jacinta*—that are predicated on the presence of the word, or the sound of writing. Of course the process of silencing writing has been going on for a long time, but the "technologizing of the word," as Ong (1982b) puts it, has certainly speeded up that process. In shifting from a primarily oral-aural culture to the visual field of print, we as readers find ourselves caught like the two lovers, Emma and Rodolphe, during Flaubert's country fair scene of *Madame Bovary,* in a verbal cross fire as highly literary and self-consciously romanticized lovemaking is forced to compete with the lowing and bellowing of cows and country speakers at an agricultural fair. Flaubert resolves the split between speech and writing (or hearing and reading) in an uneasy privileging of writing over the spoken word. "Uneasy," because Flaubert's contempt for the bourgeois order of things can also be seen as a Dickensian "attraction of repulsion."

Viewed this way, *Madame Bovary* becomes the ultimate novel of humiliation as in scene after scene Flaubert silences—that is, writes out—the speech of authority, even as he brilliantly exemplifies one of those pioneer "auditory explorers" that Stephen Gilman spoke about (1981, p. 259). At this point, I would like to discuss a scene from *Madame Bovary* before turning to *Fortunata y Jacinta* and the presence of the word. How Flaubert uses words illuminates the radically different approach Galdós takes in his masterpiece.

I take Charles Bovary's entrance into the schoolroom, which also happens to be his entrance into the novel and ours as well. Charles is asked a simple question.

"What is your name?" queries the master.

The new boy articulated in a stammering voice an unintelligible name.

"Again!"

The same sputtering of syllables was heard, drowned by the tittering of the class.

"Louder!" cried the master; "louder!"

The new boy then took a supreme resolution, opened an inordinately large mouth, and shouted at the top of his voice as if calling some one, the word "Charbovari."

A hubbub broke out, rose in crescendo with bursts of shrill voices (they yelled, barked, stamped, repeated "Charbovari! Charbovari!"). . . .

However, amid a rain of penalties, order was gradually reestablished in the class; and the master having succeeded in catching the name of "Charles Bovary," having had it dictated to him, spelt out, and re-read, at once ordered the poor devil to go and sit down on the punishment form. (1965, pp. 2-3)

This wonderfully comic, yet supremely cruel, scene at first reading suggests that it is built entirely on mimesis, the imaginative reproduction of human speech. Moreover, the setting is a classic one, the schoolboy's ritual initiation into manhood as he passes through the academic rigors of oral contest (Ong, 1981a, pp. 125-39). Traditional performance-oriented educational structures, in which the mastery of verbal eloquence through Latin, declamation, and oratory was considered essential, persisted well into the nineteenth century. Flaubert's scene first of all punctures that tradition by recreating it through the parodic model of unintelligibility. Charles Bovary not only lacks eloquence, he lacks speech. The raucous symphony of animal sounds expressively accompanying his clumsy stammerings merely heightens the helpless sense of inarticulateness he feels. Speech is power. Without it, Charles is powerless—and subsequently humiliated.

The instrument of his humiliation is not, however, as might be expected, the master's show of eloquence. Instead, Flaubert's character is demolished by the use of two devices. The first is the explicit degradation of speech itself through the barbaric mimicry of the phrase *Charbovari*. But the most daring and radical deployment of this Flaubertian attack on language comes about through writing itself, when the master "seizes" (*saisir* in the original) the name of Charles Bovary, has it "dictated to him, spelt out, and re-read" in front of the class. Charles's effacement as a linguistic presence is now practically complete. His name is torn apart, and he is later made to copy the phrase "ridiculus sum" 20 times. In exercising his own savagely comic aggression against the aggression of language itself, Flaubert in effect takes on the entire tradition of Western logocentrism, that is, the primacy of the spoken word, as illustrated in this scene of agonistic academic shenanigans.

By depicting here and throughout *Madame Bovary* a pervasive meanness of spirit through linguistic (and other) devices, the novelist, it would appear, has doubly triumphed. He has managed to seem morally strong by distancing his narrating self from the petty miseries of his characters' bourgeois manners. And he has stripped away the very heart of society by starting with the centrality of speech itself and thus undermining the authority of character as voice within the text. Simply put, Flaubert makes language do his dirty work for him, thus ensuring that his own remote position within the novel remains untouchable.

But does it? As in all operations of decentering, this one holds the risk of bringing down the ax on the executioner's head. If there is meanness of spirit in *Madame Bovary,* it is at least in part because the letter kills. When writing is used against *spiritus,* the "breath" of life, then the voice or "spoken word [that] is inseparable from the breath" fades away (Ong, 1967b, p. 188). There is a strange irony of effacement here, which seems to work against both narrator and characters on the principle of humiliation as the ultimate silencer. For me, this shaming of his characters (think, for example, of the debt-ridden Emma's desperate last-minute efforts to find money) also functions as a barrier to our fully communing with them as presences; for shame makes the human character close inward in self-defense and move a little closer toward death.

That Flaubert should be continually cited as the model for psychological realism in the novel strikes me, in the context of these remarks, as ironic. Galdós and other Spanish realists of the period often have been unfavorably weighed on an invisible and unstated scale measuring standards of novelistic interiority. For example, E. Inman Fox observes that Galdós's

> models are Balzac and Dickens, not the psychological novel of Flaubert and Dostoievski. Galdós's principal technique is to carefully interconnect the private history of his characters with the public history of Spain. Thus, the psychology of character is not interiorized, but is projected outward. (1986, p. 349)

The question is, what constitutes interiority? As Ong notes, concepts like interior and exterior cannot be adequately dealt with as abstractions, and dictionary definitions of this sort "tend to be . . . relentlessly circular." These are notions that are "existential or historically grounded," in the intimate and changing conditions between the self and the other, the self and the outer world (1967b, p. 119). But literary historians and critics have tended to canonize such concepts as interiority in accordance with particular literary models (see Scholes & Kellogg, 1966, p. 4). In so doing, the definition of interiority turns even more circular, referring merely to other interiorities, in this case, literary ones. In a word, one must also attend to the *history* of interiority, within the literary context (see Kahler, 1973; and Ong, 1971). The Flaubertian sense of the inner issues out of Romantic notions, the creative thrust of imagination that as pure interiority expresses itself through *écriture,* through writing as imagined void or silence. Romantic alienation, which still retained its echo in Romantic poets, dives deeper into the wreck with Flaubert, submerging the word as event or sound and making it appear increasingly voiceless.

III

In turning to the Romantic poets in Spain of the 1830s and 1840s, readers are often disturbed by a singular absence of interiority (Fox, 1986, p. 345). Inman Fox suggests that because the Spanish writer lacked intellectual distance between himself and reality, world and subject became hopelessly confused (1986, pp. 344-345, 347). If this is so, then we need to approach such writings in a different way, not simply as writing or "reified textuality" (Kennedy, 1987, p. 214), but as voice.

Take the example of José Zorrilla. Ortega y Gasset once wrote that the most popular play in Spain, José Zorrilla's highly Romantic version of Don Juan (1844), lived inside every Spaniard, "like one more ingredient, acting as a permanent presence, an energetic dynamo" (1958, p. 246). He attributes a large part of that popularity to the magical properties of Zorrilla's verses. Unamuno as well was fascinated by the perennial attraction Don Juan Tenorio has exercised on Spain. In an essay from 1917, he spoke harshly of the mellifluous superficiality and triteness of the playwright's verses. Zorrilla, he said, was an inveterate improviser, a poet of *copia,* of natural—and irritating—abundance (1950, pp. 80-81). He excelled, alas, in the commonplace, in worn-out epithets. How could he be Spain's premier poet? But seven years later, Unamuno found himself remembering how, as a young boy in the 1870s, he delighted in memorizing and declaiming under a quince tree those same verses he thought he despised. What was poetic or memorable in lines like these, he asked?

> *A day passed and another day,*
> *a month and another month passed,*
> *and a year passed too;*
> *but from Flanders Diego did not return*
> *though to Flanders he had gone.*
> *(quoted in Unamuno, 1954b, pp. 575-576)*

Finally one day, a friend said to Unamuno: If you really dislike Zorrilla, why is it you still remember his poetry? And Unamuno thought, of course, he is right. "Those verses put down roots in my memory" (1954b, p. 576). The paratactical structure of the lines (from Zorrilla's ballad, "*A buen juez, mejor testigo*"), in which language is "additive," points to a "performative" syntax, as Eric A. Havelock has remarked about oral tradition in general (1986, p. 76). The elements that make up Zorrilla's literary Romanticism—*parataxis, abundantia,* a profusion of commonplaces and epithets, and incantatory rhythms—are oral techniques adapted to a literate tradition. Zorrilla's dynamic presence, of which Ortega y Gasset eloquently speaks, first of all possesses a voice.

But the popularity of Zorrilla's poetry cannot be attributed solely to its oral character or to the mnemonic ease with which his verse can be recited by heart (see Alberich, 1982, pp. 13-24; and Mitchell, 1988, pp. 169-189). Ortega observes that there is nothing at all problematic about Zorrilla's Don Juan. His work is pure *convencionalismo*; and it is this conventional quality that makes him the accepted symbol of the national poet for the general public: "He sings to us and tells us of the already known . . . the accumulation of commonly shared experiences" (Ortega y Gasset , 1958, p. 250). Here, the commonplaces of discourse and the commonplace things of life converge in Zorrilla, revealing the close and complex relationship between Romanticism and the commonplace tradition (Ong, 1967b, pp. 79-87; 1971, p. 257).

The commonplace in both senses of the word is rooted in oral tradition and shared values. The way Zorrilla became the collective voice of Spain illuminates how Spanish Romanticism and a sense of national identity became symbolically fused at a certain moment in time through the agency of the human voice. That moment was February 15, 1837, the day of essayist Mariano José de Larra's funeral, when a young man publicly read a hurriedly written elegy before the suicide's grave. Another poet, Nicomedes Pastor Díaz, remembered the intense impression caused by Zorrilla's reading:

> It was a composition right then and there, by that poet, in that moment, in that setting, for us, in our language, in our poetry, in poetry that stirred us

passionately, that electrified us . . . . If he had been alone and read the poem individually to each one of his listeners, would he have produced the same effect? . . . Surely not. (1943, p. 15)

Larra's grieving friends, as they stood before the brilliant but tormented "Fígaro"'s grave, wrote Pastor Díaz, were looking for "an interpreter of our affliction . . . a voice through which the individual notes of all our sighs would harmonize in common concert" (1943, p. 14). When Larra killed himself, his peers were devastated. When Zorrilla read aloud for the first time before the essayist's grave, writers then and since saw in those particular circumstances a moment of high cultural significance. As Pastor Díaz's words reveal, there was a forging of Romantic and national identities.

Most extraordinarily, Zorrilla himself, as he was reciting, was acutely aware of the effect he was making on his listeners:

The silence was absolute; the public, most fitting and ready; the scene, solemn, and the occasion unequalled. I had a young, fresh and silvery timbred voice then, and a way of reciting never heard before, and I began to read . . . but as I was reading . . . I was [also] reading in the absorbed faces surrounding me the astonishment that my appearance and my voice were causing them. (1961, pp. 35-36)

The significance of this scene has been commented on many times since then. Undoubtedly, as Russell Sebold has observed, the event was flawed by self-glorification and a kind of individual and collective egotism (1983, pp. 176, 179; see also Dowling, 1989), but the intense emotional bonding that occurred between Zorrilla the public reader and his audience marked a scene that was to be repeated over and over in the past century not only by Zorrilla himself, but by other poet-reciters like Antonio Grilo and Emilio Ferrari, and by scores of middle-class readers who saw in public reciting a form of creative self-identification (see Alcalá Galiano, 1877; Martínez Cachero, 1959, pp. 112-115; Moral, 1943; and Valis, 1986).

Zorrilla's act of homage to Larra was really a text-event, a performance of historical significance in which the human voice becomes a vital "dimension of the poetic text" (Zumthor, 1984, pp. 67, 71). Zorrilla's voice acted upon his listeners as pure revelation. We don't really know exactly how Zorrilla sounded in his public readings, only that he had "a way of reciting never heard before." One writer, Emilia Pardo Bazán, complained his voice was like monotonous singing, while Zorrilla himself said that he could read without taking audible breaths and that the public hung on his very words, following the movements of his mouth (Ramírez Angel, 1915 [?], pp. 159, 186). Certainly, the poet's remarks demonstrate a heightened self-awareness of a histrionic nature. Yet Zorrilla put Romantic subjectivity and a modern self-consciousness at the service of collective ideals. And he did so through his "voice." "Voice" meant not only his actual bodily and acoustic presence but also the written voice he quickly learned to incorporate into his poetic texts. As Kessel Schwartz (1988) shows, even in the early poetry Zorrilla used repetitive auditory patterns.

I suspect that Zorrilla learned what his poetic voice was during his first public performance at Larra's funeral. Havelock notes that within an oral tradition "relationships are governed exclusively by acoustics" (1986, p. 65). An "echoic memory system" in primary, or preliterate, oral cultures expresses through devices of repetition the collective voice as a ritualized recollection of communality (Havelock, 1986, p. 70; see also Kiparsky, 1976, p. 91). It is evident, however, that written cultures also function through repetition, as Zorrilla's poetry reveals, thus suggesting first of all that the oral technique is never lost, as Albert Lord maintained (1960, p. 129), but fused into certain types of writing as part of a text-voice.

Proposing Zorrilla as a modern-day Homeric bard is not my intention. To begin with, he was far too immersed in written culture to be anything but a product of nineteenth-century values, as a poem like the posthumously published "La ignorancia" ("Ignorance") clearly shows:

> We are twelve million Spaniards
> who don't know how to read. Incredible fact! (1925, p. 278)

Zorrilla's amazement and dismay at the high level of illiteracy in Spain—the manuscript is dated 1892—place him squarely within his own time and culture.

Moreover, his self-conscious pose as a latter-day bard precludes any consideration of Zorrilla as an atavistic throwback. In the late twentieth century he is no longer regarded as Spain's premier poet, thus further promoting the point that his national prominence was historically grounded in a specific cultural context of an orally constituted Romanticism. In this respect, Zorrilla—and I would suggest Spanish Romanticism in general—contradicts to some extent Romantic devaluation of "oral recitation in favor of private epiphanies achieved alone" (Ong, 1967b, p. 253). His use of commonplaces based on oral tradition also runs counter to Romantic exaltation of strange and unique imagery. Zorrilla's hybrid stance as a Romantic poet, in which Romantic subjectivity and self-consciousness promoted a collective identity, suggests not only a striking divergence from other European Romanticisms but a different agenda as well. In this agenda, the presence of the word resides in a halfway house, somewhere between Romantic interiority and oral communication with the other.

IV

Looking backward, then, we can see how Romanticism in Spain was in truth a performance of Romanticism, in which a poet like José Zorrilla, blessed with an extraordinary talent for oral recitation, could act out as voice and as text the play of Romanticism. But what Zorrilla as an acting-poet heard was the sound of his own voice, that "harmonious and soft" voice possessing "something of all the echoes that fill the empty spaces of air" (1943, p. 655), as he puts it in one of his most successful and self-serving poems, "Recuerdo del tiempo viejo" ("Old Times Remembered"). The failure to reach that most essential of interiorities—the echo produced when we hear within ourselves the presence of the other—would in the end reduce Spanish Romanticism to mere sound effects. Yet the performance-oriented text did not disappear with the short-lived Romantic movement in Spain. Indeed I would argue that in *Fortunata y Jacinta,* the voice lessons Galdós had taken not only in the streets and houses of Madrid but in the repercussive pages of Zorrilla and his peers, were literally to be in-corporated as bodily presences within the novel and thus interiorized in a way that neither the Spanish Romantic poets nor writers like Flaubert had envisioned.

To view the art of Galdós as lacking interiorization because it is projected outward represents a profound—and I believe, pervasive—misunderstanding of the novelist's extraordinary intuition of presence, of the cohesion between voice and human personality, which marks *Fortunata y Jacinta* as a culminating point in the fusion between the oral and the written. In this sense, the significance of Fortunata's name is more than symbolic, that is, metaphoric or textual. It is also heard. When that terrible and anonymous voice first yells out, "Fortunaaa!" and Juanito Santa Cruz hears it, we hear it, too. When Jacinta hears that "murderous voice say clearly, 'I am Fortunata' " (1986, pp. 571-72), we are listening, too. And what we hear is not simply reproduced speech or cultural codes imprinted linguistically, significant as they are (Andreu, 1986; Gilman, 1981), but the "word as event," as a powerful presence (Ong, 1967b, pp. 111-112). "One cannot have voice without presence," observes Ong, "at least suggested presence. . . . Voice is not inhabited by presence as by something added: it simply conveys presence as nothing else does" (1967b, p. 114). And he goes on to say: "*Sound is a special sensory key to interiority.* Sound has to do with interiors as such, which means with interiors as manifesting themselves, not as withdrawn into themselves, for true interiority is communicative" (117). This inward locus of communication means not only that voice moves from one interior to another, but that in rhetorical terms, a speaker "has a kind of otherness within himself or herself" (Kennedy, 1987, p. 227; Ong, 1962a, p. 52). Thus in fiction voice points to both presence and absence, habitations of the word that are both real and unreal. So Fortunata can feel the charity of activist Doña Guillermina inside her, "as if she had swallowed her or taken her like a Communion wafer. The saint's eyes and voice stuck to her insides like perfectly assimilated substances" (1986, p. 594).

This fullness of being—as opposed to the radical insufficiency of life that Madame Bovary feels—can be seen as a gift. Rather than Emma's poison, Fortunata takes the communion of life. So too, in the end, as Gilman notes (1981, pp. 287-288), Fortunata's final speech before she becomes an "angel," that is, dies, represents the ultimate *rasgo* or act of generosity when she gives her son, the fruit of her love affair with Juanito, to his childless wife Jacinta. The term *rasgo* brims with rhetorical and historical implications as well. The historical reference is to Spanish orator-statesman Emilio Castelar's 1865 article, "*El rasgo,*" in which he criticizes Queen Isabel II's pecuniary back-handedness. But *el rasgo*—the queen's questionable generosity—is also Castelar's written exercise of rhetorical bravura. Now both Queen Isabel and the famed orator's acts take place in what could be called a market economy. Neither act is gratuitous. Fortunata's, on the other hand, partakes of gift economy, when the gift—here, the child—leaves her hands forever, without question, without exchange. The gift of the child arises, as all gifts do, out of *eros* (Hyde, 1983, p. 22).

How Fortunata gives away her child is, I believe, crucial to an understanding of Galdós's celebration of the word as event, as an acting out of communal significance, in which the voice surges out of writing and fills us with its soaring presence. Fortunata, we recall, dictates to Plácido Estupiñá a letter for Jacinta:

> "I don't want to die without doing you a kind deed, and I'm sending you . . . the little 'angel face' that your husband gave me by mistake." No, cross out "by mistake" and put "that he gave me, stealing him from you." But no, Don Plácido, not like that; it sounds awful . . . because it was me who had him, me, and nobody took anything away from her. What I mean is that I want to give

him to her because I know she'll love him and because she's my friend. (1986, p. 802)

Fortunata's search for the right words to express the true meaning of her act reveals an eloquent consciousness of significance. The child, she says correcting herself, was not given to her by accident nor was he stolen from Jacinta. Thus there is no transaction going on here, and certainly no restitution. Like giving food over the coffin (Hyde, 1983, pp. 40-41), the child is a threshold gift, indicating passage or transition. And like all real gifts, this one creates a lasting bond between giver and recipient, one that Jacinta, too, recognizes as a strange form of "companionship founded on their mutual suffering" (1986, p. 810). That mysterious nature of the gift to which Lewis Hyde refers has much to do with the inner pools of human personality. In literally dictating that the child be given away as a gift, the "letter" is made spirit and gives life in Fortunata's dying words. The fact that she dictates and does not write the letter herself underscores of course her bodily weakness and perhaps, too, an unconscious resistance to writing itself, an art of which she is but a clumsy practitioner at best.

In this scene, the close connections Galdós establishes between the gift and orality suggest first of all the survival of a deep underlying oral culture of communal ways—not surprising, given the high rate of illiteracy in Restoration society (López, 1981; see also Botrel, 1987; Guzmán Reina, 1955; and Marrast, 1974) and Spain's long-standing oral traditions, traces of which persist in Spanish Romanticism, as we have already seen. Most significantly, when he makes voice the carrier or bringer of the gift, Galdós brings with it the larger gift of the human personality itself, thus far surpassing Zorrilla's echo of himself. Fortunata's literal words are not important; what is remembered is an inner text or subtext of "gestures, sounds, inner or outer movements, auditory or tactile sensations that lie behind and beneath the words of a text" (Kennedy, 1987, pp. 215-216). Thus the subterranean flow of Fortunata's inner experience trickles slowly upward and finally penetrates the surface of the text as the sound of consciousness.

In this we see how the radically different economies of words in Flaubert and Galdós construe interiority along divergent paths as well. In the end there is no gift in *Madame Bovary,* except the cruelly ironic one of a packet of love letters Charles Bovary finds months after Emma's death. Once again, as in that first scene of the novel, writing—here, in the proof of infidelity—functions as the ultimate act of betrayal and humiliation. Charles's death—his silencing—is a foregone conclusion. His inarticulateness, like Emma's feelings of insufficiency, points to loss, the loss of voice itself. For Flaubert, "the human tongue is like a cracked cauldron" (1965, p. 138).

But a "cracked cauldron" does not resonate. How silent our reading world has become! Then I open wide the covers of this book—*Fortunata y Jacinta*—to large and uninhibited pleasure, wherein a joyous performance is heard, and the inner reach of experience meets the outbound stretch of imagination. And I am in the resounding presence of the word.

PART III

Media Studies

Introduction

BRUCE E. GRONBECK

To focus on media, in the Ongian view of the world, is to focus on the least studied yet perhaps most important aspect of the psychoculture. Ong even has been tempted by the deterministic view that changes in channels or media of communication produce or cause alterations in cultural systems and in psychological operations or consciousness (Gronbeck, 1990). For example, a chapter in *Orality and Literacy* (1982b) asserts that "writing restructures consciousness," and the end of *Ramus, Method and the Decay of Dialogue* (1958a) comes close to positing the move to visualist discourse as a vehicle for cultural transformations of the first order.

However often he has flirted with media determinism of the type that afflicted Harold Adams Innis (1972), Ong never became a thoroughgoing determinist. To Ong, as to Innis, media studies ought to be historically grounded examinations of the interrelationships among media, culture, and consciousness. But those relationships are not causal. Rather, media, culture, and consciousness are materialized or variably structured at particular points in time and space; and in different situations one or another of them may seem to be "the cause" for alterations in the other two. James Carey's (1989) analysis of the telegraph is a case in point: On the one hand a growing market economy demanded the kind of quick point-to-point communication technology that the telegraph represented, and the desire for speed created mindsets ready to accept and process telegraphic messages; on the other, the telegraph in turn prepared the way for newer and faster electronic communication media, altered consciousness with its emphasis on shortened and commodified knowledge, and changed social structure forever with its separation of communication from transportation. Similarly, communication media, cultural orientations, and states of consciousness are hopelessly intertwined in the Ongian view.

105

More important than the intertwining of influences, however, is the interplay of defining features that weld communication, culture, and consciousness into particular relationships. Orality as a medium, for example, is defined by Ong (1982b) partially in terms of the mental habits it plays off and partially in light of the social organization it operates well within. When mental habit and social structure become integral to the very definition of a medium, then of course it is impossible to treat media of communication, culture, and consciousness as independent entities.

If these terms threaten to collapse into one another, how are we to study aspects of mediation? The essays in this section offer some intriguing answers to that question. Richard Enos and John Ackerman seek to ground communicative practice among the Sophists not only in a conceptual definition of orality, that is, within a certain tradition of rhetorical theory, but also in characteristics of Athenian geography and culture. The authors see echoed in sophistic discursive practice, therefore, not only remnants of thought processes but also the tailings of extrarhetorical features of life. The result is an archaeological approach to media studies.

Dennis Seniff's translation of Pedro de Navarra's *Dialogues on the Differences Between Speaking and Writing* (c. 1560) is revelatory for what it tells us about sixteenth-century thought. In the aftermath of the Council of Trent, Navarra's distinctions between speech and writing carry not only the expected sociolinguistic but also sociopolitical implications. Seniff suggests their presence, but leaves it to his readers to pursue more fully the politics of Peninsular Spain. He likewise sets up distinctions between oral and literate mindsets or voices that will allow others to fit Navarra's early modern thought into the historical record. His is a historical investigation of media.

Concrete in its study of discursive oral, written, and televisual practice is Annabelle Sreberny-Mohammadi's look at contemporary Iran. She posits near-isomorphic relationships between cultural structures (especially distinctions among the clergy, clerisy, and masses) and habitual communication media. Her study is strongly sociological in its orientation to social structure and media use. This allows her to respecify the operations of "stages" of media and cultural evolution, because, of course, she is working with a country wherein oral, written, and electronic media all operate together to reflect a particular sociopolitical orientation.

Roger Silverstone, known to most for his cultural studies of electronic media, writes on the relationships between television and consciousness, particularly the unconscious. His view of consciousness allows him to integrate the psychoculture—to collapse distinctions between ontogenesis and phylogenesis, between self-development and cultural evolution. The technology that television represents is a narrative machine to Silverstone, one that allows viewers to be both passive (receptacles of formulary stories) and active (creators and recreators of themselves as psychosocial beings). His, thus, is a critical-cultural study of mediated mind and life.

Finally, philosopher and computer scientist Philip Leith offers a telling analog between the Ramistic machinery of knowledge—of analysis and synthesis processes—and binary computing systems. He characterizes Ramism as well as computer storage and retrieval systems in terms of formalist thought, finding that Ramism not only anticipates computer science but also illustrates the shortcomings that plague systems with similar epistemological assumptions.

Ong's sweep across time, space—and intellectual vantages on both—results in a rich conception of mediation. His views on the evolution of media, his characterization of electronic media as kinds of "secondary orality," and his hope to integrate culture/consciousness/communication creates agenda for these and numerous other scholars of media studies.

7

Walter J. Ong and the Archaeology of Orality and Literacy: A Theoretical Model for Historical Rhetoric

RICHARD LEO ENOS
JOHN M. ACKERMAN

> Works of literature, works composed in writing, can no longer be studied seriously simply in themselves without cognizance of the fact that literature has a vast prehistory in highly self-conscious oral verbalization, which works quite differently from composition in writing.
>
> —*Ong (1977a, p. 275)*

Introduction

A. D. Leeman characterizes ancient rhetoric as a "manifold notion" and oratory as "one of the three major prose genres . . . the other two being historiography and philosophical writing" (1982, pp. 41, 43). As the epigraph illustrates, Walter J. Ong, SJ, recognizes with Leeman the close relationship between oratory and literature, a relationship not without profound impact in antiquity. Hellenic oratory was irrevocably altered by the inscribing of a phonetic alphabet, and its subsequent integration into a sophisticated Greek culture resulted in what I. J. Gelb called "the last important step in the history of writing" (1974, p. 184). The alphabet not only gave written form to speech, but also inaugurated the shift from orality to literacy. Several scholars, seeing fifth-century BCE Greece as the origin of the Western literate revolution, capture the linguistic dynamism of the period and its powerful influence on later cultures. Ong's *Orality and Literacy* provides dramatic illustrations of the reciprocal influences of oral and written discourse with his discussion of "primary and secondary orality" (1982b, p. 11, passim), and Eric A. Havelock led a scholarly onslaught against what he termed the "cultural arrogance which presumes to identify human intelligence with literacy"

108

(1982, p. 44, passim). George A. Kennedy's notion of *letteraturizzazione* (1980, pp. 4-6) further reveals the relationship between orality and literacy by drawing clear distinctions between "primary" rhetoric, which is characterized as oral, persuasive, and pragmatic, and "secondary" rhetoric, which is written, artistic, and enduring.

These and other scholars argue that relationships between oral and literate expression exist and, more important, that understanding the nature of these relationships will help us to better understand the specific discourse under examination. With few exceptions, (e.g., Enos, 1988; Ong, 1990) such arguments are advanced from generalizations about cultures and periods, not from specific studies. Yet specific observations can be advanced only upon a descriptive framework that accurately maps the relationship between orality and literacy, a framework presently unconstructed. The sophists of classical Greece are excellent subjects to study to build such a framework. Beneficiaries of a tradition of oral composition, they were familiar with writing and widely influential; in fact, the nature and extent of their influence are best realized by an analysis based on the relationship of orality and literacy. Building on the general observations of Ong and others, this essay provides a descriptive framework detailing the relationship of orality and literacy and then specifies that relationship by discussing features not readily apparent in literary artifacts but nonetheless instrumental in rhetorical composition. The subject of inquiry for this study is Gorgias of Leontini, commonly regarded as the father of sophistic rhetoric (Philostratus) and an enduring paradigm in the history of rhetoric.

Constructing a Framework for Analysis: An Archaeological Motif

The contributions of Ong and other oralists provide the foundation for a descriptive framework for understanding sophistic expression. Such an effort is akin to the objectives of the archaeologist; that is, using and developing equipment that will help to reconstruct the past. Rather than unearthing physical artifacts, however, our intent is to provide the most precise conceptual tools for reconstructing past phenomena. Such a mapping should provide a representation of those features of Gorgias's rhetoric that reveal composing processes not well understood, processes that ultimately make apparent not only persistent surface characteristics but also provide a window for viewing the formulation of sophistic discourse. The following table (Enos & Ackerman, 1987), based upon the general chronology and terms of Ong,

TABLE 7.1 The Literate Evolution of Hellenic Discourse

(Based on the Terms and Chronology of Eric Havelock, George Kennedy, and Walter Ong)

1100-700 BCE	700 – 400 BCE	400 BCE ff.
Primary Orality	Primary Rhetoric	Secondary Rhetoric
Nonliteracy	Preliteracy	Literacy
Oral, conservative, formulary discourse	Oral, civic, persuasive discourse	Literate, personal, narrative discourse

Kennedy, and Havelock, aligns temporally the major classifications of Hellenic discourse. These classifications offer both a context and a frame of reference necessary for subsequent discussion on the features and forces influencing Gorgias's rhetoric.

As Table 7.1 illustrates, the period of "Primary Orality" encompasses the natural development of languages and the correspondingly natural systems used to express thoughts and sentiments; that is, the various ways individuals learn to speak as they develop from infancy. The observation and systematization of speech characteristics nurture the development of a "Primary Rhetoric." While maintaining the dominance of orality, a primary rhetoric introduces a self-consciousness of language and the institution of the *techne,* or an artificial system abstracted from natural language processes, which is usually studied and acquired for specific objectives. Last, the third period, "Secondary Rhetoric," represents the widespread integration of reading and writing into the society. The systematization of literacy is often accomplished by applying relevant oratorical principles to writing systems. That is, principles of oral expression that are effective in learning literate skills are adapted to reading and writing.

The utility of Table 7.1 is realized only with specific qualifications. As beneficiaries of a tradition stressing oral composition, sophists such as Gorgias did not stress an abstract system of heuristics characteristic of Aristotle's *Rhetoric,* but gave preeminence to oral, poetic composition for the culmination of *krisis* or judgment and knowledge indirectly manifested through style and arrangement. Pre-sophistic notions of eloquent expression were believed to be grounded in divine inspiration and were modified over centuries by generations of rhapsodes who developed stylistic and formulaic constructions to compose, preserve, and transmit heroic tales (Enos, 1978, pp. 134-143; Kirk, 1976, pp. 124-128). We know that early Greek literature was oral and that disciplines that emerged to better express ideas grew out of this oral environment. Yet classical Athens is acknowledged as a literate society, one in which reading and writing were widely known and practiced (Havelock, 1982). Our understanding of the evolutionary period, the oral-literate transition phase, is limited. There is little doubt, however, that sophists made an enormous impact on Hellenic thought, particularly in the area of rhetoric. Although sophists came out of an oral tradition, many were known to have used writing to facilitate their expression (Enos, 1990, pp. 46-64). The practice of logography, or speech composition, was prevalent during this period but by no means the sole illustration of composition wedding orality and literacy (Enos, 1974).

Other intellectual enterprises that evolved out of the oral tradition of Homeric discourse also provided a foundation for sophistic thought. Both the efforts of the rhapsodes to utilize writing as a way of preserving the phonetic features of Homeric discourse and the evolution of history from chronicles to reasoned probability benefited from writing, but grew out of an oral tradition of "tale-telling" or *logoi* (Enos, 1978, 1976). These earlier efforts reveal a more complete context of the richness of the climate for oral composition and its relationship to writing than can be realized from the remarks of Plato and Aristotle or than would be available by examining the sophists in isolation. An understanding of the factors present in how sophists such as Gorgias composed discourse, particularly their notions of speaking and writing, can provide invaluable information about the connecting links of orality and literacy during this medial period. In essence, Gorgias and his fellow sophists of the classical period were not, as Plato encouraged us to believe, deterrents to knowledge and expression, but rather precursors to the literate period, one which would build upon an oral tradition a system that would promote literacy.

In the generation of text, *letteraturizzazione* reveals techniques abstracted from the dynamics of oral communication situations and reapplied in a static form, emphasizing not an acoustic but a visual sense to unlock meaning. In short, sound is replaced by scrawl. If, as Ong and Kennedy urge, historians of rhetoric view the relationship sequentially, in its natural order of oral to literate discourse, an understanding of features becomes apparent. Explicitly literate features assist a reader toward an author's intention partly because of the absence of oral textual cues (Enos & Odoroff, 1985). In this respect, the *presence* of oral discourse is far from silent in *letteraturizzazione*. For example, euphony, the juxtaposition of words to evoke a pleasing sound, did not disappear with the invention of the alphabet. So, Dionysius of Halicarnassus studied literary composition partially to investigate the emotional power of the sound elements in writing (*De Compositione Verborum,* sec. 13, passim).

Even though writing fostered a separation of author and text, the voice as the shaper of emotive meaning remained at the center of classical rhetoric, despite Aristotle's laments throughout his *Rhetoric*. Ong's expression of early writing's "heavy oral residue" recurs throughout his works (1977a, 1982b), for it characterizes well the dominant oral features that shape developing writing systems. The following diagram (Enos, 1990, pp. 46-64) posits the shift to literary forms.

As Figure 7.1 indicates, language initiates as uttered thoughts and sentiments a state of "primary orality." The introduction of the *techne* abstracts and categorizes oral discourse into an artificial system creating a "primary rhetoric." Orality continues to dominate under primary rhetoric, but writing is introduced as an instrument permitting words to be "frozen" and thus removing the dependence on individual memory and, indirectly, facilitating abstract thinking. *Letteraturizzazione,* represented as the ring in the figure, is the process that applies orally based heuristics to writing and fosters literacy. Eventually, as the benefits and functions of writing become increasingly obvious and pervasive, writing as an instrumental aid to memory is conjoined with writing as an inherently artistic effort or a "secondary rhetoric." This evolution to a secondary rhetoric stresses writing as *ars gratia artis*. Moreover, as technology dominates discourse, what is here styled a "secondary orality" emerges. The connecting lines at each phase of the model underscore the point that at each phase a change in technology is a change in epistemology: Thought and the technological methods that facilitate thinking interact with and germinate each other.

Placing the sophistic tradition of composition within the diachronic process of *letteraturizzazione* plots its evolution into three periods: Pre-Sophistic, Classical Sophistic, and Second Sophistic. In the Pre-Sophistic period (that is, prior to the fifth century BCE) emerging notions of discourse grew out of oral compositional techniques and fostered the development of epic poetry, philosophy, and drama. The Classical Sophistic flowered during the fifth century BCE and raised a consciousness about the processes of discourse, resulting in *technai* that facilitated an understanding of the nature of expression and how it could be produced. While oral expression continued to dominate the modes of public discourse, the development of literacy evolved as a facilitating tool for speech and thus was highly interactive and often overlapped with techniques of oral composition. The Second Sophistic (occurring here as early as the Hellenistic Age) witnessed the development of sophistic writing for its own sake; that is, writing not exclusively as an

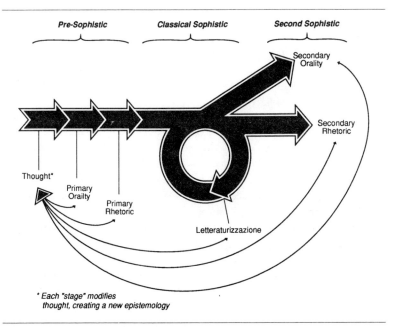

Figure 7.1. Periods of Sophistic Composition

instrument to aid orality, but also writing as an artful form of expression in its own right.

The harmony of the three sophistic periods with the three stages of orality and literacy offers an opportunity for learning much about composition, particularly during the Classical Sophistic period, for it is within this period that Gorgias and other sophists developed *technai* that would be the basis for the modes of literary expression that would subsequently emerge. Reconstructing sophistic composition from such a framework offers four important possibilities for insights. First, a more precise accounting of the methods by which sophists thought and composed thought into discourse will be offered. Such an accounting should replace earlier efforts and remove the incompatibilities that plague competing theories. Second, reconstructing the composing process of the sophists enables us to analyze a phenomenon that was a major intellectual force in rhetoric's history. Third, a study of individuals who composed out of the oral tradition will provide an example of the impact on writing both in its use and in its shaping of thought. Fourth, such a study will reveal new dimensions and insights into composing discourse.

The contribution is historical and in that sense is different from current work that seeks understanding through current practice. If historians of rhetoric view the relationship in reverse order, we can use the literary artifact as the route to reconstruct the oral features of the discourse. That is, as Ong explains in his discussion of "exterior retrospectivity," a conscious "association of literature with the remote past" prompts an awareness of "the old oral culture of humankind" (1977a, p. 243). In a similar respect to Havelock's discussion of the "echo-principle" (1982, pp. 177-178), the artifacts of writing, viewed as the remnants of the culture's discourse, can provide valuable insights for reconstructing its most elemental, primitive features. Yet efforts to understand thought processes shaping discourse are indigenous to their context, and much of that context is developed from features that do not echo clearly in the fragments of discourse or artifacts of theories. Isolating and identifying such "unechoed" features, however, is necessary for a reconstruction of sophistic rhetoric, if we are to understand those forces that shaped its processes.

The approach recommended here is in harmony with the observations of Gelb, who argues that "very little work has been done in the field of relations of writing to language" and that what work has been done has often been limited to the study of "living written languages, neglecting the rich sources of information which can be culled from ancient written languages, especially ones with pre-alphabetic systems" (1975, p. 64). Applying the principles presented here to a study of the traits, habits, and context of an individual sophist will help to reveal the notions, presumptions, and predispositions driving the composition of discourse. Thus, in both the theory and production of discourse, a study of Gorgias of Leontini provides the opportunity to capture features of composition not apparent in the extant fragments while mapping the route of primary rhetoric through the derivative secondary rhetoric that was its echo.

Gorgias and the Grounding of Sophistic Rhetoric: A Study of Extra-Rhetorical Features

Reconstructing the processes of sophistic composition is, in many respects, much more difficult than the initial goal of refuting Plato's caricature of sophistic rhetoric. Although we know that Plato's parody of Gorgias (Enos, 1987) does not provide an accurate representation of sophistic composition, it nonetheless reveals certain traits and, in that respect, provides important historical information. The challenge of reconstructing a theory of sophistic composition by sifting fact from opinion in such historical sources as Plato's dialogues is further directed toward constituents of discourse evident in the fragments of sophists. That is, in an effort to examine primary evidence, scholars instinctively direct attention to the extant fragments of sophistic discourse and the commentary on specific stylistic features evident in those fragments. Yet to examine only literary artifacts as evidence for understanding sophistic rhetoric is to retrieve only part of the facts.

We know, for example, much about the stylistic patterns of Gorgias's rhetoric from earlier studies (Enos, 1987; J. Poulakos, 1983, 1984; T. Poulakos, in press). Not all features echoed in the fragments, however, capture the features that influenced their composition. Unlike other phenomena in the history of rhetoric, sophistic composition carries with it contextual features that are here termed extra-rhetorical because they do not directly manifest themselves in the discourse, but nonetheless are an instrumental force in shaping sophistic thought and expression. Isolating and discussing some of these more tacit but salient factors in composing sophistic discourse should establish the point that such features must be researched in detail and accurately accounted for in theory if we are to acquire the most sensitive reconstruction of sophistic composition possible.

In short, the intent here is in large part a jurisprudential one; that is, an effort to justify subsequent research into factors that are indirect but essential to understanding sophistic composition. Realizing the nature and processes of Gorgias's rhetoric beyond his stylistic patterns, however, should provide the justification to amend such views as well as advance new areas for inquiry. The task here is to provide an illustration of such factors, through a study of Gorgias of Leontini, commonly regarded as one of the most prominent sophists of the classical period, that reveal a relationship of oral and literate processes more specific than earlier, exploratory work offers.

Topography and Travel

The topography of Greece strongly influenced the social and intellectual climate of Hellenic culture. The hilly terrain and numerous islands made Pan-Hellenism more of an ideal than a practical goal. Travel was seasonal and, at its best, difficult over land and often risky at sea. These geographical conditions nurtured autonomy among city states in dialect, politics, and social custom (Enos, 1990, pp. 46-64). Yet the notion of Hellenism was a bonding influence, and the sophists provided both a thesaurus of Greek culture and alternative perspectives that were attractive throughout the

Hellenic world. Philostratus's writings, for example, not only make apparent the practices of sophists such as Gorgias during the classical period but also illustrate (in some instances) their near-nomadic existence.

Thus, by design, inclination, or calling, sophists were an itinerant group and, as such, spent a considerable amount of time on the road. Sophists traveled for several reasons. Frequently, their compositions were viewed as entertainment and they regularly participated in literary and rhetorical contests (Enos, 1986). Patronage was also a common feature and sophists— particularly during the later periods—were often either commissioned for specific events or sustained under the beneficiation of a wealthy patron for the enrichment and glory of the city (Enos, 1977). Eventually, Greek cities formalized such arrangements and, during the Roman Empire, regularly offered and established municipal chairs of rhetoric for sophists (Avotins, 1975). In addition to such performance aspects, sophists were often attracted to cities that claimed to be intellectual centers. It is this phenomenon that is well captured in Plato's dialogues, for Socrates was frequently in competition with prominent sophists for distinguished students. In short, travel became a natural condition of their livelihood, and sophists' attraction to various cities was frequently a function of municipal attention in the form of patronage, festivals, and intellectual centers. It is reasonable to assume that sophists used the considerable amount of travel time available to them to compose and polish their favorite pieces, ingrain commonplaces, and hone their style. The constant exposure to new ideas, themes, and expression, conjoined with the opportunity to polish and thus internalize their repertoire provided by countless hours of travel, meant that their memories could constantly be kept keen and their conceptual thesaurus of *logoi* active and full.

Mentor-Apprentice Relationships

The importance of this phenomenon is made apparent by the frequent practice of mentor-apprentice relationships that appear throughout Greek education, but are particularly characteristic among the sophists. Both the *Gorgias* and the *Phaedrus* illustrate how sophists constantly performed before, and were accompanied by, youth. The didactic advantage of such a relationship is obvious, but, in addition, the opportunity to constantly have a dialogue partner and a candid critic would insure motivation for keeping skills sharp. In addition, the ability to teach youths the techniques of sophistic composition reveals that it was anything but a craft literacy; that is, being able to teach the principles of sophistic composition to youths reveals its accessibility to the public and, most likely, its public appeal.

Given such relationships, there should be little wonder why the study of models would be so important. The value of a living paradigm would enable the developing youth to experience all the nuances of sophistic composition—only some of which were words. The parallels with youthful and mature composers among Yugoslavian bards (Lord, 1960, pp. 22-31) and Hellenic sophists is striking in its uniformity, particularly when one notes Lord's claim that "the oral singer thinks in terms of . . . formulas and formula patterns" (p. 130). Sophists often taught principles of rhetoric directly through practice, and this paradigmatic act complements the understanding and application of abstract notions, since each apprentice was, by definition, committed to the sophistic mentor as the living embodiment of proficient discourse, a model to emulate.

Age and Memory

It should be noted that sophists are characteristically seen at their peak, and correspondingly accorded deference even by their opponents, quite late in life. The *Gorgias* is a good illustration of how age is an index of both maturation and development of sophistic skills, with the presumption that years of practice are required to have mastered ability in skills of expression and accumulated topics to expound. Certainly, the relationship of bards out of oral traditions is a complementary phenomenon. The years of experience in acquiring a full and supple memory, of honing performance skills, and of mastering techniques of euphony are products of time as well as nature.

A phenomenal memory, as Eunapius illustrates (*Vitae Sophistarum,* sec. 488-490), was a subject for bragging rights; sophists could have ample opportunity to practice memory training and thus keep their memories active. Simonides, by comparison, is an oral poet who provides the best example of such an ability; that is, memory can be the storehouse of creativity through analogical experience (Yates, 1966, pp. 1-2). Memories not only kept an agenda of possible strategies available to the sophist but also provided a conglomeration of themes to draw upon. Such a perspective would give the memory a newly defined role as not only the preserver of wisdom but also the storehouse of creative ideas.

Agonistic Production Before Real Audiences

Another extra-rhetorical feature, one mentioned earlier, has to do with the pragmatics of real, as opposed to abstracted, audiences; that is, abstracted audiences are the fictions that a writer constructs mentally. Sophists attracted crowds. Their tenure in a city was often highlighted by not only pedagogical skills but also public performances of rhetorical contests in which listeners would gather to hear the rendering of themes. Oratorical and literary contests, sponsored at regional and Pan-Hellenic games, were frequently held in conjunction with music and athletic events, fostering excellence through honor and fame (Enos, 1986). Since a sophist's ability was judged by effect before real audiences, it is understandable why *kairos* or the situation would be so central to their discourse. Sophists were composing for the pragmatic concerns of situations that involved real audiences. Popular techniques of style would naturally emerge and these abstract concepts, such as *dissoi logoi* or metaphor, would be the principles for effective oral discourse and, eventually, the standard for written rhetorical composition. Even our contemporary principles of "voice" and "tone"—long removed from their original antecedents—still have a persisting oral quality (Ong, 1982b, p. 69).

Physiology and Natural Selection

The variations of audiences from city and dialect, audiences with different values and priorities, would provide a sort of natural selection principle whereby those sophists who could best adapt to the changing environments in which their discourse was composed would thrive while others, who could not adapt to the immediacy of the theme and opportunities of the situation, would fail. Several physical attributes essential to sophistic composition do not operate today, for much of our refinements in technology have minimized the physical attributes necessary for excellence in composition. The robustness necessary to travel to various centers, the vocal attributes required to speak to large crowds without assistance of amplification instruments, and, of course, the primitive and often nonexistent technology of scripts to record, preserve, and create discourse necessitated a well-developed and well-practiced memory, a euphonic voice, and physical prowess. Isocrates, by counter-example, is the best illustration of a sophist whose personal weaknesses in oral delivery necessitated his stress on logography and (eventually) rhetorical education.

Initially and primarily an oral phenomenon, sophistic composition orchestrated rather than severed the senses. The only sense necessary for reading today (noting the distinctiveness of Braille) is sight; the only senses necessary for writing today are touch and sight. Since reading and writing were commonly not performed in isolation or in silence in ancient Greece (Stanford, 1967), it is clear that all the senses that normally come to bear in the shaping of meaning would be apparent in sophistic composition. Sophists were often criticized for their histrionics, for their excessive display or "performances" of compositions. Body-rocking, so popular in oral cultures for establishing a rhythm to their oral compositions (Ong, 1982b, p. 67), was evident in sophistic composition. Similarly, various features of phonology were important: diction, volume, and prose-rhythm through tonal quality. This holistic approach to composition provided an orchestration of senses that were not seen in abstract isolation until the literate period.

In short, all features of the presentation, visual and verbal, were necessary in sophistic composition, so those individuals who were able to develop their physical robustness and voice training, could expose themselves to well-traveled journeys in which they could sharpen such skills against the elements and the ears of listeners. While such physical characteristics are minimized today, it is necessary to account for such extra-rhetorical features if we are to account accurately for the composition and production of sophistic discourse.

Conclusion

These physical skills and social conditions bear directly on the cognitive skills necessary for sophistic composition. Features of composition as discussed here, while rightly labeled extra-rhetorical, nonetheless were dominant in the lifestyle and processes of sophistic composition and, correspondingly, must be adequately and accurately reflected in our theories of sophistic composition. To do so, however, will require historians of rhetoric to extend their inquiry from the literary artifacts and account for those social and cultural conditions that influenced the shaping of discourse. While comparative field study akin to the Parry/Lord icon is an admirable model, our objective of accounting for contextual conditions likewise should motivate us to new ways of retrieving and synthesizing factors that shaped discourse. It is an undeniable fact that these features of composition were not only the precursors to written composition but also its basis, and understanding the evolution of the composition process cognitively and historically will reveal insights that will enhance our understanding of one of the most complex things people do: express themselves. Inquiry into such processes can doubtlessly inform us not only about oral composition but also about the strong bonding of orality and literacy that was welded during this period. Intimate knowledge of such a joining will make apparent not only connecting links between our two dominant modes of expression but also those conceptual processes that are involved in the making of meaning itself.

Gelb once claimed that "we can only deal with the language within our sight" (I. J. Gelb, personal communication, November 2, 1984). The observations of Ong and others have been an invaluable aid in providing an expansive window to viewing ancient rhetoric, a path leading to a better understanding of the relationship of orality and literacy and, eventually, our understanding of their processes. Since the NCTE in 1963 called for inquiry into the relationships between spoken and written language, several researchers of contemporary composition have studied orality and literacy (Kroll & Vann, 1981, p. vii). Yet current efforts in rhetoric, lacking a descriptive framework to model the transformations of thought and discourse, have neglected rich sources of historical evidence that could yield information enormously beneficial to contemporary research. Supplied with such wisdom, current concepts such as "voice" and "tone" may once again come to life when the echo of their oral genesis is made apparent, revealing an epistemology ever in operation but never fully understood.

8

Ong, Ramism, and Spain:
The Case of Pedro de Navarra's
Dialogues on the Differences Between
Speaking and Writing

DENNIS P. SENIFF

Background

In recognition of Walter J. Ong's contributions to communication studies, I wish to present here for the first time in English a translation of the watershed document by Pedro de Navarra, the *Dialogues on the Differences Between Speaking and Writing* (c. 1560). But first I will situate it with reference to Ong's work and current scholarship on Ramism in Spain.

The title of one of Ong's most important essays suggests that voice is a summons to belief, a crying out to be listened to, to be given credence, to be believed in ("Voice as a Summons to Belief," in 1962a, pp. 49-67). Voice is the primordial medium of communication, the basis of all dialogue. The inherently dialogic qualities of voice, the self-conscious awareness of one person crying out to be heard and responded to by another, can be carried over into writing and print, or silenced, because a written register develops that is different from the oral register of speech. Plato's *Dialogues,* Thomas More's *Utopia,* and Erasmus's *Praise of Folly* are famous efforts to embody the qualities of voice in writing through the use of dialogue as a literary form, and orations in the tradition of classical rhetoric were structured in principle on dialogue inasmuch as they built in not only a presentation of one's own position but also a response (*refutatio*) to the adversarial position. The adversarial position involved the negation of one's thesis. The orator was expected to present arguments for the antithetical position and then respond

121

to them point by point. But as Ong indicates in the title of his masterwork, *Ramus, Method, and the Decay of Dialogue* (1958a), Peter Ramus (1515-1572) eschewed dialogue in principle by dispensing with the *refutatio* as a standard part of a presentation. Moreover, Ong suggests that Ramism resented virtually all aspects of human speech:

> Speech is no longer a medium in which the human mind and sensibility lives. It is resented, rather, as an accretion to thought, hereupon imagined as ranging noiseless concepts or "ideas" in a silent field of mental space. Here the perfect rhetoric would be to have no rhetoric at all. Thought becomes a private, or even an antisocial enterprise. (1958a, p. 291)

Thus the spread of literacy after the advent of printing undermined in Ramist quarters the power of classical rhetorical dialogue, just as the interiorization of writing and the development of the Socratic dialogic process of abstract reasoning had unseated traditional formulaic thought patterns characteristic of earlier Homeric oral culture (see Havelock, 1963, p. 49). Truly, another plateau in the history of human communication had been reached.

In Spain, however, the *agonia* between speech and written text was not resolved so easily as Ramism would have it, because the Spanish Inquisition, fierce in its suppression of Ramism, however, effectively limited its diffusion. While Ong sees the Hispanic Schoolman, Peter of Spain (1210/20-1277; later Pope John XXI), author of *Summulae Logicales,* as an intellectual ancestor of Ramus (1958a, pp. 55-65), he is quick to point out that "except for sallies into Basle, and into Spain under the aegis of Francisco Sánchez de las Brozas ['the Brocense'], the Ramist movement as it is represented by printed works is restricted to France up to Ramus' own death in 1572" (1958a, p. 295).

What Ong (1971, pp. 25-26) calls oral residue characterized much of the literature of the Iberian Peninsula—the oral subtext of Hispanic writers for more than seven centuries. The following titles indicate the persistence of a strong Peninsular dialogic tradition—one that was not easily displaced by Gallic influence: Pedro Alfonsus, *Disciplina Clericalis* (ca. 1100); the anonymous debate poems *Elena and María, Discourse of Love* (or *April's Repose*), and *Dispute Between the Body and the Soul* (all thirteenth century, see Menéndez Pidal, 1900, 1905, 1914); Sancho IV, the *Elucidarium* (late thirteenth century); Juan Manuel, *The Book of the Knight and the Squire, The Book of Count Lucanor* (1326/1982, 1335/1983); the anonymous mid-fifteenth century *Dance of Death* (Solà-Solé, 1981); Fernando de Rojas, *Celestina* (1499-1502/1982); Alfonso de Valdés, *Dialogue about the*

Things that Happened in Rome (1529/1928); João de Barros, *Spiritual Merchandise* (1531/1983); Juan de Valdés, *Dialogue of Language* (c. 1535, but not printed until 1736/1928); Pedro de Navarra, *Dialogues on the Differences Between Speaking and Writing* (c. 1560/1968; 1985); Miguel de Cervantes, *Don Quixote, The Colloquy of the Dogs* (1605-1615, 1613/1914-1917); and Francisco Javier de Santiago y Palomares, *The Master of Reading: Orthological Conversations* (1786). This, it must be emphasized, is just a minimal list whose sole purpose is to reflect the strongly oral character of the Hispanic text, be it prose, poetry, or drama, in script and in print.

The *Dialogues*: Study and Translation

In his article "Recent Work on Peter Ramus (1970-1986)," Peter Sharratt provides a reasonably accurate overview of scholarship on Ramus's influence in Spain, noting that "Not much has been written on the presence of Ramism in Spain [during 1970-1986], and this corresponds fairly accurately with what existed" (1987, p. 52). Sharratt, while closely following Ong's lead in *Ramus* (1958a, p. 295), appears not to have been familiar with the extremely important issue of *Dispositio: Revista hispánica de semiótica literaria,* nos. 22-23, 8 (1983), which contains the section "Hispanic Rhetoric," featuring the fundamental articles "Introduction to the Study of Rhetoric in Sixteenth-Century Spain" by Luisa López-Grigera (pp. 1-18) and "Data Format-Bibliography" by members of a University of Michigan graduate seminar on Spanish Renaissance rhetoric (pp. 19-64). López-Grigera goes beyond Ong's reference to "the Brocense" by including among Spanish Ramists Pedro Juan Núñez, Luis de Verga, Veruete, and Miró (1983, pp. 7-8).

Pedro de Navarra, one of Spain's first modern linguists, wrote in a manner that was doctrinally acceptable. Although his work might be considered a foreshadowing of the stylistically oriented studies on *langue* and *parole* that were espoused by Charles Bally (1909/1963) and others some four centuries later, it is clear that a primary issue for him was the peril of communication. Indeed, the author of the *Dialogues,* who knew that in the Rome of 1555-1557 certain things could not be said or written under punishment of execution or confiscation of property, indicates through one of his protagonists that it is best "not to write anything at all so as to avoid calumny" (Navarra, c. 1560, fol. 11rv). No Ramist don Pedro!

Curiously, scholars have all but ignored Pedro's treatise. Published in Toulouse, in about 1560, by Jacob Colomerio, "University Printer," exemplars of the *Dialogues* are now housed in Madrid's Royal Spanish Academy

Library (R-78) and in New York's Hispanic Society of America (two copies); several other copies are given in the above-mentioned Rhetorical Seminar bibliography ("R18. Navarra, Pedro de" 31). The work receives short shrift by the nineteenth-century bibliophiles Pedro Salvá (1872, p. 283) and Cipriano Muñoz y Manzano, Count of La Viñaza (1893, col. 906). In the twentieth century, Juana de José Prades has offered a physical description of an exemplar (1954, p. 11, no. 18), whereas D. O. Chambers has provided the first diplomatic edition (1968). Chambers' contribution also lies in his recognition of the generally fragmented nature of Spanish literary preceptive theory (Navarra, 1968, p. i).

The best critical study of the *Dialogues* to date is that by Elias L. Rivers (1984). Extremely brief, this masterful piece compresses in fewer than five pages commentary on the phenomenon of diglossia (the coexistence of oral and written registers in a given language and its literary tradition), a brief biography of the illegitimate Pedro de Navarra (or Pierre d'Albret), an evaluation of the ambience in which the *Dialogues* was written, and a summary of the principal ideas of the text itself:

> The two personages of the work, which is divided into five brief dialogues, are called "Duke" and "Bastard" [the latter doubtless representing the illegitimate Pedro]. . . . They express an attitude of admiration before the marvel of language, but they also seek authentically scientific precision in discussing it: while speech is a gift of God, [it is also how man] "declares the concepts of his mind and makes himself understood in every way, according to the will of his spirit." (Rivers, 1984, pp. 309-310; my translation)

Rivers also notes Pedro's contention that writing is "more difficult to compose, but semiotically more useful" (p. 311), marveling too at how the *Dialogues,* with its exposition of the evident formal advantages of writing, has been ignored by modern scholars, just as F. W. Householder's important essay "The Primacy of Writing" (1971) has been. For Rivers, the importance of such studies needs to be emphasized for a fuller understanding of the phenomenon of diglossia. (For a discussion of diglossia and monoglossia in English, see Rivers, 1987.)

The edition of the *Dialogues* by Pedro Cátedra (1985), a precious little book 11.5 x 8.5 cm., provides a fine essay on the life and works of Pedro de Navarra in the introductory "Noticias de Pedro de Navarra" (pp. 9-57), which contains extensive historical and textual documentation in footnotes in an amazingly small space. Cátedra mentions the existence of five exemplars of the *Dialogues* in the Madrid National Library, the British Library, and the Hispanic Society (p. 32, note 23), but curiously does not include the Toulouse (c. 1560) text of the Royal Spanish Academy used by Chambers in his 1968 edition; indeed, he appears not to be aware of the existence of Chambers's work at all, for he nowhere describes it. Rivers's 1984 study appeared too late to be cited in the Cátedra introduction, one would assume.

But these omissions in no way affect the significance of this little edition, which places in the hands of scholars a text that, while orthographically modernized, is quite faithful to the Toulouse *editio princeps.* Cátedra emphasizes the notion of the danger of the written word that pervades the *Dialogues* in light of the "canonical dispositions of the Council of Trent regarding books and any expression of thought at the time" (p. 56; my translation). Are the issues posed by the Counterreformationist author appropriate for other cultural issues as well? Cátedra believes this to be so, citing the fact that the *Dialogues* appeared right before another text by Pedro did, the *Dialogues on the Immortality of the Soul,* which is concerned with "religious libertinism caused by excessive freedom of expression" (p. 57). Interestingly, no mention is made of Ramus or Ramism, whose influence was diffused primarily through printed books. But concerns about the printed word no doubt grew out of the longstanding association of speech and power, and Kathleen Kemp Forrest (1976) shows that in Shakespeare's England freedom of oral expression was just as sensitive an issue for the civil authorities as was freedom of written expression for ecclesiastical authorities in Spain and Italy.

Pedro de Navarra's *Dialogues on the Differences Between Speaking and Writing,* then, appears to be a sociolinguistic phenomenon, a theoretical *tour de force* to be examined at several levels. I here offer an English translation based on the 1968 edition of D. O. Chambers, made from the Madrid Royal Spanish Academy exemplar R-78 (Toulouse: Jacobo Colomerio, c. 1560); however, obvious errors in the Chambers text have been rectified on the basis of that of Pedro Cátedra (1985). I omit the introductory "Letter of Dedication" and a few repetitive passages, shown by ellipses, but otherwise adhere closely to the original Spanish.

[f. 3r] **About the Differences There Are Between Speaking and Writing**

Dialogue I

Duke: Peace to the people, and freedom for you.

Bastard: These two things you request now are so necessary for our uneasy lives! But war is so extreme in this land and liberty so scarce for individuals, that in Rome they permit us neither to travel around freely nor to write.

Duke: This is a clear punishment for our faults, since we always are disregarding God's Will to satisfy our own vices. Consequently, we shouldn't complain about our prince, if the war he makes is so dreadful, but our damned consciences, which have exiled peace. But enough of affairs of state; let's deal with your concerns. Tell me. Why . . . What are you doing transfixed before the Holy Crucifix? Even now I am the object of your vision, and you act as if you've never met me!

Bastard: In my blessed boyhood this was shown to me: that before going to bed I should examine [f. 3v] my conscience regarding the good and evil I had done that day, and that I should thank God for the good things and repent of the evil things, and sleep thereafter with the goal of never sinning again. And the next morning before performing my duties, that I should pray with a clear conscience, with the necessary auricular confession, begging God that He should keep me in His grace, and keeping His people free from His wrath. But as you know, human inconstancy is considerable, especially in mental acts of divine character; and all the more because I've been involved with the hardships that this war has caused the Roman people—as well as the Christians. Consequently, my body is exhausted and my soul transfixed, so I haven't paid close attention to you.

Duke: I praise your efforts; surely by doing what you say, you won't die in sin. I go around so preoccupied with the business of this world that soon I'll have to have it out with the Devil so as not to die in sin. Soon I'll have to repent and ask forgiveness, [f. 4r] mentally and verbally, sobbing and promising not to sin any more, and giving alms, and (when possible) receiving the sacraments of Holy Church, which purify the conscience of contrite and humble hearts. You know all this. Let's go out to the mezzanine, where it's cooler.

Bastard: Just as you like.

[Duke]: Well, we've discussed issues regarding the safety of our good conscience in the midst of so much war. Let's discuss how we should write and speak without incurring the law that our prince has made that no one should speak nor write to anyone else inside or outside Rome.

Bastard: The new prince's law should be closely considered before being disobeyed, especially during such dangerous times as we live in now. Given that in general this law prohibits us from speaking and writing and encompasses all forms of these activities, it is more than appropriate to discuss which areas should be free from this prohibition, and to know in general what speaking is, and what writing is, and what the differences are [f. 4v] between them. . . .

End of Dialogue I

Dialogue II: What Thing Speech Is

Duke: Tell me, oh discreet Bastard! What is this thing called speech?

Bastard: It is a gift and grace that God gave, among all the animals, only to man; so that David could praise and worship Him as his Creator; and so that men could understand each other and communicate in all their actions, absent and present, past and future, to the honor and glory of God.

Duke: What is speech in itself? [f. 5r]

Bastard: It is a spirit, or wind, or breath, governed by the tongue, measured by the teeth, and pronounced with the lips (like artificial music), by means of which it pronounces and declares the concepts of the soul, according to the meanings that Adam gave to things or that each nation has assigned to them in its own tongue.

Duke: So speech is nothing more than an interpretation of the concepts of the soul, and all things are understood by the interpretation or meaning and name that Adam gave them, or that his successors have assigned to them?

Bastard: Yes.

Duke: Then man, if he is born normally, naturally has the ability to speak and to pronounce, but is not born with the knowledge of the meaning of things, rather learning them later through usage and art; and, through the teaching of his parents or schoolmasters, learns to apply to each one its name, and to order these as necessary. Through art, custom, and discretion or memory, his speech proceeds to order all these words, by means of which he declares the concepts of his mind and makes himself understood in every way, according to the will of his spirit, in his own way to suit himself, and for his own contentment?

Bastard: Yes.

Duke: So I can conclude [f. 5v] that a word is an exhalation or breathing by man, administered with the tongue, measured by the teeth, pronounced with the lips, and formed in the mouth with the tongue, and that with this are pronounced and interpreted all words and meanings and concepts so ordered by our minds, as in the music of an organ, which by means of the wind of its bellows, and the pipes, and the movement of the fingers on the keyboard plays do, re, and mi, thereby forming music which all understand without difficulty?

Bastard: Yes!

Duke: To what end was speech created?

Bastard: You yourself have just said it: for the understanding of our actions, if not to understand each other. Otherwise we wouldn't be different from wild beasts, or we would live in confusion, as did those who built the Tower of Babylon [sic].

Duke: So if I am asking what thing speech is, you would respond that it is an interpretation or declaration or demonstration of the concepts of the mind, by means of which I gain intelligence, and I understand everything I ask about or say.

Bastard: Yes.

Duke: What a marvelous and eternal gift! It gives an animal grace, so that [f. 6r] it can understand and make understood that which is in its mind with just its tongue! Truly it is a thing of God, and an almost divine act.

Bastard: It is divine, primarily because God conceded it so we could praise His divinity in all our undertakings; and although not to the same degree, He also gave it to other animals and plants, since they all praise God in their own ways at every moment. Could you wish for greater grace and virtue than that which God provides through language, providing knowledge about all things on earth and in heaven, as well as about the essential virtues and sciences and arts? Even to the point of knowledge of divine essence, inasmuch as our human nature can know about it, such that we praise God and find eternal dwelling with Him and in Him?

End of Dialogue II

Dialogue III: What Thing Writing Is

[f. 6v]

Duke: Well, you have told me about speaking. Tell me about this thing called writing.

Bastard: It's a memorial or perpetuation of speech, or a cipher and sign of the concepts of the soul, or a painting and stamp of words that the tongue pronounces and the mind conceives. Such that just as you have a clear idea of the countenance of the duke, your father, when you look at his portrait, you will also know through this writing that which you spoke and wrote in the past, or [what] someone else writes or speaks to you [now]. Because writing is a portrait of the act of speech, and a form of words that remains after you've spoken; or an image or life that facilitates your seeing speech, it will bring to your memory what speech represents, just as the painter creates the figure which is easily recognizable. And although a word can't really be seen [when spoken] nor perceived with sight . . . because it is breath, it can still be printed and painted . . . with visible characters that, even though it is unspoken, I can understand.

Duke: So the difference between speaking and writing is that a word endures no longer than the length of its pronunciation, whereas writing does for as long as it is preserved. And a word, if it is heard, isn't seen, but writing is seen as being written and is heard if read. Too, a word can only be understood [f. 7r] while one is nearby; but writing can be diffused throughout the world.

Bastard: You speak the truth, for when I'm absent from your presence, and I want to talk to you, the distance is so great that you can't hear me or understand me; but as soon as I write you in characters that we both understand, you can grasp all my concepts. And if you write me back, I'll understand yours.

Duke: Glory to God for such a gift, for it really seems to be something He would reserve for Himself! Is there anything like it in the world? Imagine a person in the Orient speaking and being understood by someone in the West, or a Westerner by a Northerner; imagine someone who had died a thousand years ago speaking with me every day, or me, alive today, communicating with people two thousand years hence! And lastly, imagine me being able to understand through writing or words the concepts of every foreign mind, being an act belonging to God alone inasmuch as only He knows the hearts and intentions of men!

Bastard: You know how long it has been since Moses, David, Solomon, Alexander the Great, Julius Caesar, and Christ died? But you also know how, through their writing they speak to us every hour, just as if they were alive. Similarly, you are familiar with the actions, lives, customs, etc., of all the generations of man since the beginning of time until now, [f. 7v] as well as their appearance, dispositions, qualities, good or bad fortunes, and thoughts.

Duke: Truly this is a gift that God gives us; a divine one, too, for just as He knows all things past and future right now, without the need for writing or anything else, he teaches us through writing how to know this past, and part of what is to come.

End of Dialogue III

Dialogue IV: What Difference There Is Between Speech and Writing

Duke: What other difference is there between writing and speech?

Bastard: Speech and writing both proceed from concepts of the soul, but the difference is like that between painted fire and real fire. Physical writing is seen, whereas a word that is spoken is just an audible breath. Consequently, writing is more easily understood than is speech; [f. 8r] for when one speaks, even though he might make his concepts clear, they can't be perceived so clearly than if he had written them. The reason? When I read, my understanding has time to absorb it all and to distinguish the good parts of a particular writer's work. This doesn't happen during speaking, because our souls just aren't that efficient, and I can't pay total attention to everything that is said—especially if it is elegant, too arranged, sententious, or frivolous.

Duke: So speech is not as difficult or efficacious as writing?

Bastard: No, and all the more because it suffers from overuse of extraneous words and impertinent things that are said. People don't keep this in mind when they speak like they do when they write . . . nor is speech efficacious or perpetual, for it dies out after signifying the desired concepts of the speaker. But writing remains, and always "speaks." Item: a word, when spoken, cannot be captured, but writing can be, to the point of being perfected and published. Finally, speech only serves him who is present and hears it; whereas writing serves the absent, the present, and the future individual, as well as the deaf and dumb.

Duke: Isn't [f. 8v] the living word that I hear more efficacious than the dead writing that I read?

Bastard: For the ignorant, yes; but for the wise man, no. What is read can be pondered better than what is heard.

Duke: On the basis of what's been said, I now understand what speech is, how it is engendered and formed; and what writing is, and how much it differs from speech. This is a considerable difference, for speaking admits carelessness that is not tolerated in writing, for writing measures words, submitting them to the judgment of the reader, who regards them prudently. . .

End of Dialogue IV

Dialogue V: How One Should Prepare Oneself for Speaking Well and for Oratory; and for Writing and Dictating

Bastard: Speech is licit for everyone, but not everyone knows how to use it correctly, such that you'll find wise men in the sciences who are foolish in their speech[!]. [f. 9r] Even though they are excellent writers and are full of learned concepts, they don't know how to express themselves well. Truly, they are "diamonds in the rough"! There are other excellent writers who are awkward and confusing in their teaching and speaking. The latter include our courtiers, who while esteeming beautiful speech only know how to malign others. How can they be considered learned if they speak in a gross, ignorant manner? The offshoot of all this is twofold. Firstly, in order to speak well, one mustn't follow extremes: evil speech, or the use of strange or unusual words, must be avoided. I'm saying that you should choose the most commonplace, [f. 9v] clear, proper, honest, modest, and weighty terms for your speech. Avoid those that are satirical, curious, unknown, dishonest, or impertinent; these mordant ones offend, and, indeed, are prohibited in this court by the prince.

If you want to speak like a wise man, adorn your language in a clear manner with the terms I've mentioned, and think about what you want to say—have it fixed in your memory—before you form your sentences. Because if it's not clear before you say it, there is no way that you as a speaker can save yourself and continue your speech so as to make your listeners attentive, happy, content, and wise. That is the way to speak well.

Duke: You presuppose that one must be a wise man to speak well. For if he's a fool, he won't understand wise concepts. So, he must be prudent, because if he's thick-headed, he will lack too many things [f.10r] to be considered well-spoken. He must be an elegant person by nature, because if he's stupid he will be lost. He must be studious and curious, because if he's lazy he will speak badly. His method of speaking must be relaxed, with modest gestures, so he won't seem too audacious. His voice must be forceful and spirited, for if he's timid he'll be lost. He must have a great memory, otherwise he won't be able to speak perfectly. He must use proper language and lead an upright life; otherwise, he will be discredited. His speech must be graceful and witty so as to be agreeable for his audience.

Bastard: Too, it is useful that it be a person who would wish to become a professional speaker, just as he ought to, with this greatness enhanced by the following: a good mind, one that is clear, strong, and profound; a solid, useful, and notable education; a sharp, clear memory; distinct, modest, and diligent in his conversation; clear, sonorous, and suave in his speech; and finally, artistry in knowing oratory, using clear, proper words that show perfectly the meaning of his intentions. Here he should know how to [f. 10v] exaggerate, encumber, abate, measure, repart, pronounce, and to speak with such an elegant style so as to enhance his address. This is the excellence of the orator, his speech, and his writer. . . .

Duke: Thus, he who uses writing will be obliged to follow these precepts so as to make his work wise, eloquent, weighty, and useful?

Bastard: Just as you see it, for if more profit is expected from it, it is just that it exceed speech in greatness.

Duke: What authors should I imitate in writing?

Bastard: There are so many to choose from! But if you want to be considered a serious writer, follow the serious ones, etc.

Duke: What did you do in your case?

Bastard: I've always tried to read them all, and be eclectic. As it stands now, many of the ancient writings contain words no longer acceptable, and there are many neologisms being invented today. So on the advice of many people I've taken prudent liberty (as should be done) in my speaking and writing so as to seem agreeable to my listeners and more easily understood by them.

Duke: You talk [f. 11r] like an expert, and a discreet one at that. Is this because the judgment and understanding of the people of this day are so delicate that writers must avoid making mistakes? Well, now I know how I must speak and write in general, at least in theory. Better we should now discuss how to govern ourselves in this Republic so as not to incur the wrath of the prince's law, since that was the basic reason we undertook this discussion.

Bastard: Just as you like: necessity compels us to do so.

Duke: How should we deal with a discussion of our own Rome?

Bastard: Well you know, illustrious duke, that because of our past liberty and present subjection and danger, it would be convenient to make use of our time as we see fit, on whose behalf—as I see it—we should "occupy ourselves with blessing God in every act," as Saint Paul puts it, so as to extricate ourselves from the present perils, and even acquire a good name and heaven. Keeping this as our main goal, and only dealing with sciences and writing on an ancillary basis, we will be free from evil people who can't accuse us for our speech nor calumniate us with evil works.

Duke: And with regard to writing, what should we do?

Bastard: [f. 11v] The best and wisest treatment would be not to write anything at all so as to avoid calumny, right?

Duke: No doubt it's the safest thing to do, since there will be nothing to fear from spies who are within, nor guards who are outside, nor judges who surround the streets, nor princes who easily lend their ears. Farewell!

9

Media Integration in the Third World:
An Ongian Look at Iran

ANNABELLE SREBERNY-MOHAMMADI

The dynamics of communications development in the Third World have not been an independent and natural unfurling of media, but have been closely linked with the broader processes of socioeconomic development and political struggle, themselves intricately entwined with international relations. As different media are taken up by different interests in the competition for social authority and power, the four stages of communication and culture identified by Walter J. Ong (1967b)—orality, chirography, typography, and electronic orality—overlap, contaminate, and compete with one another, as they did in Western cultures. Nevertheless, a case study of Iran in Ongian terms raises issues in international communications that are pertinent to analyzing transitional societies in the Third World. The "thick description" of Iran's media ecology presented here focuses on the interaction of communication media with preexisting relations of power and influence (Geertz, 1973).

James W. Chesebro has suggested that many Third World countries have proceeded from primary orality to "mass electronic culture," skipping the writing/print stages of communication and culture (1986). For Iran today, identification as a mass electronic culture does little justice to the long and rich literate traditions of panegyric poetry and religious hermeneutics that play a central role in cultural life. Nor does it help to elucidate the complex themes of political repression and cultural identity that helped shape the communications environment of Iran.

The clergy and the clerisy are the two major groups competing as alternate sources of social authority for the masses in Iran today. These three social groups—the clergy, the clerisy, and the masses—lie at the heart of current cultural and ideological politics in Iran. Their media involvements, especially their literacy levels, and their cultural developments have taken different trajectories. In Iran today, print appears to be the preferred mode of secularizing elites, while traditional religious authorities use both primary and secondary orality to maintain influence.

To understand the Iranian media system, one has to understand the Iranian state under monarchical dictatorship and its particular pattern of dependent development. Despite an early constitutional revolution at the turn of the century (1905-1911), which codified a written constitution limiting the power of the shahs, and despite a mass movement under Mossadegh in the 1950s, which also demanded democratic rights and separation of the three branches of government, in the 1970s the second Pahlavi Shah was a preeminent royal dictator. He had developed one of the largest armed forces in the world, possessed a security system called SAVAK, which appeared omnipresent, and was following a mimetic rather than an indigenous pattern of development. Thus life in Tehran came rapidly to resemble life in New York, with high-rise apartment buildings, traffic jams and pollution, Western-style clothing, food, and increasing amounts of Western cultural products. State-owned radio-television—the most extensive system in Asia after the Japanese—offered a diet heavy with American television, interlaced with home-made soap operas and traditional music. More foreign than domestic films were shown because many of the domestic products never survived the gaze of the censor. Print media, although ostensibly independent and privately owned, were heavily monitored and directed by the state.

Despite this ideological apparatus, the dictatorial state was coercively powerful but lacked social legitimacy; it possessed power without authority. Critiques of its political repression and massive abrogation of human rights, of its economic inequality, and of its cultural intoxification with the West grew. These served to precipitate the revolutionary mobilization and the crisis of 1979.

The Nonclerical Clergy

Islam was brought to Iran by Arab conquest in the seventh century. However, Shi'ism was developed as a state religion, different from the Sunni version of Islam as practiced by the Arabs of the Ottoman Empire, under the expansionist period of the Safavid dynasty (1501-1722), particularly during the rule of Shah Isma'il (1501-1524). Despite a rhetoric hostile to secular rule and despite frequently severe repression by royal dictatorships, much of the religious establishment had accommodated to the last Shah. The religious establishment still possessed a substantial nationwide network of ayatollah, clergymen, prayer-leaders, theology students, low-ranking mullah, preachers, traditional school teachers, and procession organizers, who maintained extensive holdings of mosques, seminaries, meeting halls, and endowed lands (Abrahamian, 1982).

Religious and spiritual affairs overlapped with civic and public involvements. Every bazaar, the traditional hub of economic life, possessed its own mosque with meeting rooms, library, and educational facilities; the traditional *bazaari* merchants financially supported the religious establishment and organized pilgrimages and community associations. Also there were (and are) a variety of informal religiously oriented community gatherings such as religious dramas, *ta'aziyeh,* and the reading of homilies (the Greek root of which means the crowd, reinforcing the idea that such gatherings were not only opportunities for moral preaching but also expressions of collective identity and public communication). This sphere of activity was comparatively free of state interference and provided forms of civic participation with a strongly religious underpinning.

The clergy constituted a religious sodality within the state whose public authority, while periodically challenged, had never been socially undermined. A traditional religious education in a *maktab* has always included texts—the Koran, the Sharia, their interpretations—and involved exegesis and hermeneutic debate, part of a long tradition of Islamic scholarship. This was, of course, particularly powerful during the tenth to fourteenth centuries when Islamic architecture, scientific and medical scholarship, libraries, and calligraphy were second to none. The rich development of Islamic culture from the seventh to thirteenth centuries, with its populous cities, paper-making techniques, scientific discourse, and well-endowed libraries is often overlooked. When paper-making finally arrived in Northern Europe and printing was developed, that region took over the cultural dynamism that Islam had enjoyed. Now much of the population in the Islamic World remains illiterate, and only recently has a new self-consciousness and cultural renaissance reasserted itself.

However, the central texts and rituals of religious life—the Koran itself, the *namaz* prayers that should be repeated five times daily, and much religious exegesis—are conducted in Arabic, not in Persian. Thus not only is much religious ritual highly formulaic but it is also conducted in a foreign language not comprehensible to the Iranian masses. In this respect Arabic in Iran today is much like Learned Latin was for centuries in Europe (cf. Ong 1967b, pp. 63, 65, 76-79, 87, 208, 250-252).

Perhaps in recognition of their need to maintain a social as well as an explicitly religious role in Iranian life, the clergy has invoked the power of the spoken word. A central element of religious education is the study of oral rhetoric, known in Persian as *ma'ani bayan*. The practice and maintenance of oral address occur regularly through sermons and the preaching of homilies, *rowzeh,* to the masses from the pulpit, *minbar,* during Friday prayers at the mosque, and through a variety of other religious rituals of social life. Thus for the religious professionals a powerful literate/literary tradition coexists with a recognition of the need for regular oral address of the masses in accessible language with socially valued references.

A recent and dramatic illustration of the clergy's social legitimacy and communicative effectiveness was the mass mobilization of the Iranian revolution of 1977-1979, which resulted in the overthrow of the Shah and the establishment of an Islamic republic. During this period, Khomeini's physical absence in exile, in Iraq and later Paris, was overcome through the construction of a powerful international "electronic *minbar*" of cassettes of his speeches, sometimes recorded over international telephone links and almost instantly available on the streets of Tehran (Sreberny-Mohammadi, 1985, 1990). Not only did the special timbre of his voice echo in private houses, mosques, and lecture rooms, but the well-known tropes of Islamic rebellion came to be the slogans of a growing political movement.

Perhaps no moment better reveals the power of formulaic phrases than a burgeoning social movement. While there were many slogans that commented on unfolding events, the key slogans of the Iranian movement were *Allah hu akkbar,* God is great, and *Marg bar Shah,* Death to the Shah. Islam provided a simple preexisting polarity of values, *ra-ye khoda,* the way of God, versus *taghout,* the demonic. It also utilized a simple dichotomous class analysis for easy identification and comprehension, Iranian society being divided between the *mostakbarin,* the oppressors, and the *moztazzafin,* the oppressed. And to maintain solidarity and prevent factionalism, which was never far from the surface, Khomeini continually stressed *vahdat-e kalame,* unity of the word—a play on the word of God, on the language of Islam, and on the need for ideological oneness. Thus Islam was an integrated, well known frame of social life that lent itself to mass mobilization when perfected through the oral techniques of the religious leaders.

Iranian Shi'ism is the faith of 98% of the population and remains unchallenged despite an internal reformation process most often associated with Ali Shariati. Within Shi'ism, the high clergy, or *mojtahed,* are considered the intercessors between the masses and God and the source of revelation and interpretation that demands a following. Religious knowledge that is the possession of a few requires the following of the masses, another very potent example of active mimesis that Ong suggests is such a central part of orally dominated societies. Thus, the religious establishment's knowledge is not only received and therefore indisputable, but it is also community-binding, a "tribal possession" that carries authority and is of necessity authoritarian. Ong calls attention to some pertinent connections:

> An oral-aural economy of knowledge is necessarily authoritarian to an extent intolerable in a more visualist culture. . . . A personality structure built up in an oral society, feeling knowledge as essentially something communicated, will be relatively more concerned that this knowledge ties in with what others say and relatively less concerned with its relationship to observation. (1967b, pp. 231-236)

But beyond the overtly political elements of Khomeinist rhetoric, the concern for economic egalitarianism, and the lack of political freedoms lies a much deeper clash that Ongian analysis helps to elucidate. It is the long-brewing struggle between two fundamentally different and competing forms of authority, the religious and the rational/scientific. In the West, a rational scientific outlook radically questioned and undermined religious authority, a process only possible with and set in motion by the development of print and the growth of ideological struggle. Thus, Alvin W. Gouldner (1976) compares the relatively fixed and limited claims to be made in traditional, religious societies, when the justification was authorized usually by the authority or social position of the speaker, with the more complex and abstract claims and identities that writing and ideology conjured up. Ong also describes how the authoritarianism of oral-aural culture inhibits "solitary original speculation" so that "even the most intellectually venturesome individual simply cannot detach himself from the tribal thought, from what 'people say' " (1967b, p. 230). The break from tradition was fostered by print, although it took time to develop, and the challenge to received wisdom and the carriers of that wisdom was felt most powerfully by the church.

In Europe the competition between religious and secular authority was set in motion by the Enlightenment and scientific challenges to received religious wisdom and was accelerated by the growth of mass literacy, the development of a public sphere, and the advent of capitalist relations with the Industrial Revolution (Habermas, 1974; Horkheimer & Adorno, 1972). These conflicts fueled the French Revolution and were fought out variously across nineteenth-century Europe and the United States in the spheres of politics, particularly mass enfranchisement, education, and law.

In Iran, a form of advanced capitalism was rapidly laid over a semi-feudal, still illiterate population, a veneer of super-modernity pasted on top of a highly traditional society. This precipitated the revolutionary/reactionary backlash, because at least for the religious leadership that mobilized the masses, this was a retraditionalizing movement, a last-ditch stand by these aging authority figures to protect a way of life and mode of thought that was in potential deep decline. These forces underlay the deeply bitter antagonism between the two key symbolic figures, the Ayatollah and the Shah, whom Khomeini came to see as the embodiment of all "devilish" impulses.

While the religious orientations are by no means homogeneous politically, much of the religious rhetoric underscored certain recurring themes, central to which was the undermining of Islamic faith and Iranian identity under the Pahlavi dynasty. This was said to have happened through a mimetic adoption of modernizing lifestyles from the West, from the unveiling of women in the 1930s to the changing of clocks for summertime in the 1970s (to which a sizeable segment of the community refused to adhere, creating a astonishing degree of social confusion!). Electronic media, which were given high developmental priority in the 1970s under the last Shah, were treated with scorn by the clergy. Television in particular was vilified both as a carrier of decadent Western culture and as a tool of a repressive monarchy. During the popular movement in 1977-1978, cinemas were burnt along with liquor shops as repositories of devilish culture.

Thus the clergy was able to mobilize the masses by making political involvement a religious duty, by skillfully wielding its well-established community authority, and by developing a clear and simple activist ideology that every Iranian could not only understand but also identify with. After the establishment of the Islamic Republic, its oral rhetoric was transposed into electronic secondary orality.

With the establishment of the Islamic Republic, radio and television have become major tools of internal and external propaganda, utilized in very particular ways. In the West strict temporal divisions of broadcasting with tight and regular television schedules act as an important social and economic timekeeper. By contrast, Islamic broadcasting has fitted in to the rhythms and tempo of primary oral communication. When Khomeini spoke for three hours without a break, that was the length of the television program. When news of special importance breaks, the news program continues as long as is felt necessary. When a mullah demonstrates the proof of the existence of God by writing on a blackboard simultaneously with both hands, the single camera records his presentation in long-shot much as a member of a live audience would view it.

The Clerisy

The main grouping in Iranian society that tried to compete with the clergy for leadership of the Iranian masses against the Shah was the clerisy, the secularized intelligentsia, historically a small but influential group in Iranian society.

It is important to note the long tradition of nonreligious writing in Iran, which did not encompass many people but was nonetheless politically influential and culturally constitutive. As Bernard Lewis recently remarked:

> Medieval Islam, unlike medieval Christendom, had not one but two literate elites, each of which produced its own distinctive literature and even language. In Western Christian lands, for centuries the clergy were virtually the only literate class. In the Islamic lands in the same period there was a second literate elite, consisting in the main of what one might call the scribal class—those who in various ways served the central and regional bureaucracies. (1988, p. 27)

In premodern times a literati surrounded the Shahs. These *divani,* or premodern royal bureaucrats, wrote the pronouncements and protocols of the Shahs that were then carried across the Persian Empire. This role of writing the Shah's commands was an elevated and desirable social position that was maintained within select families for generations. This process of enscribing royal decrees also helped to develop a specifically literary linguistic style, *ketabi,* distinguishable from an oral colloquial style, *mohavereh' i.* This flows over into current linguistic usage which depends heavily on formal courtesy, *ta'arof,* which differentiates according to the perceived social status of the communicator vis-à-vis the communicatee (Hillmann, 1981).

Royal support also helped to maintain artistic traditions, such as the production of lavish handwritten and illuminated books—collected in extensive libraries in Parsagardae and Shiraz—and the emergence of palace miniaturists in the Ottoman, Moghul, and Persian empires. In the latter, the Shahs also enjoyed and employed poets laureate, the best known being Saadi and Hafez, who were literate, and Rumi, who brilliantly extemporized in verse that was written down by a scribe. Dictionaries were compiled more than 900 years ago, the oldest by Assadi Tusi known as "Persian Word."

In the nineteenth century, with the process of modernization and increased contact with the West, a new secular literate tradition emerged, independent and often critical of the centralized monarchy. The development of newspapers, the increase of intellectual debates about modernization, and demands for political reform, much of which was orchestrated from exile, culminated in the constitutional revolution of 1905-1911.

The role of this new clerisy was kept strictly in check by the royal dictatorships of both Pahlavi Shahs, but reemerged during periods of central state weakness such as 1945-1953 and 1977. The most important tools of the middle class were the *anjoman,* pressure groups, and the press (Cottam, 1964). Yet a combination of high rates of adult illiteracy (despite frequent royal proclamations about new literacy initiatives) coupled with strict censorship over newspapers and books created an environment hostile to both writer and reader.

Despite the considerable historic cultural involvement with the production, translation, criticism, and elucidation of texts, crucial elements of the cultural behaviors of even the clerisy remained oral and premodern. The main social arenas for middle-class intellectuals were the universities or schools, where oral performance was stressed above all else. Even in the 1970s, meetings in governmental bureaucracies or universities would typically begin without an agenda, have no secretary recording the proceedings, and set no predetermined end. Meetings could, and did, take all day (with sweet tea served intermittently for sustenance), and subsequent meetings would spend time in often acrimonious recapitulation (rather than on agreement over minutes) and renegotiation.

Secular social organization unsupervised by the state was disallowed, so independent political parties, trade unions, and pressure and interest groups could not exist, eliminating any social fora where secular intellectuals could interact with other sections of Iranian society and propound their secular ideologies. Publishing, both popular journalism and academic discourse, was severely controlled, thus forcing the clerisy into silence, exile, or writing in isolation without the possibility of readers.

Although Ong (1982b, pp. 78-79) and others argue that writing is the most decontextualized of communicative forms (the "text" presenting itself, not the author), in Iran the provenance of the author was and still is crucial in deciphering the text. Perhaps because of the severe circumscription of debate, a text received far less attention than the assessment of the background of the author, particularly in attempting to place him or her within the political spectrum and thus prejudging the text; and among secular political activists, far more energy was spent in character assassination than in critique of argument.

The clerisy was also deeply divided, many in the pay of the state in the educational system and cultural arenas despite their antipathy to the regime. A substantial number of the clerisy were involved in the development of state-run radio and television, which expanded enormously in the 1970s. Yet, as already mentioned, much television content was imported and, while programming was technically quite sophisticated, few original genres or individual programs were produced except for some socially conscious soap operas and some attempts at discussion programs as the political movement grew in the late 1970s.

The clerisy also lacked immediate arenas for public oral communication (except schools and universities, which were highly controlled); their access to print was also tightly censored; and they were unable to develop a culturally authentic voice in electronic media. In addition, the clerisy developed secular critiques of the regime couched in the languages of Marxism, using class terminologies and notions of imperialism and nationalism. These models were analytically more complex than those used by the religious leadership and employed terms not immediately familiar to most Iranians, apart from small cadres of politically-activist workers in some well-established industrial areas. Thus not only did the clerisy lack the channels through which to speak or write, but they were also out-languaged. The religious leadership offered a simpler binary model of oppressors (*mostakbarin*) and oppressed (*moztazzafin*), which the clergy proposed at national and international levels, and it called ι pon well-known identities, particularly religious ones. While the clerisy played key roles in opening up the mass mobilization of 1977, they were overtaken by the dynamism of the religiously oriented movement and later complained that Khomeini, whom they considered the bulldozer of the revolution, had usurped their rightful leadership role.

The Masses

The third group that needs to be inserted in our media map is the masses. We shall explore their involvement with media, their preferred forms of communication, and their attitudes toward authority.

Rural Iran is configured into more than 50,000 villages, many untouched by the rapid development of industrial and urban areas. From the 1960s on, extensive urban migration occurred, so that by the mid-1970s 29% of the population lived in towns of more than 100,000. Almost one-half of the entire population is less than 25 years old. Illiteracy ran at about 60% under the Shah, higher for women than men, despite literacy campaigns and UNESCO conferences. Under the Pahlavi far more emphasis and resources were placed on the development of radio-television than on literacy. In the postrevolutionary Islamic environment, a new thrust toward mass literacy has been introduced through the *Jihad Farhangi,* the Cultural Jihad.

In Iran, as elsewhere, nonliterates clearly coexist with literates in a typographically complex environment of street signs, advertisements, newspapers and magazines, bus tickets and political leaflets, letters, legal documents, and books. Illiterates know that they "lack something." The term for illiteracy in Persian is *bi-savad,* which literally means "without knowledge." The cultural implications are clear. Islam values *elm,* knowledge, which is essentially accessible through texts, and the cleric and the teacher traditionally have held the highest respect in the community.

Illiterates often possess texts they cannot "read," the major one being the Koran, in Arabic, a foreign language. Thus the main cultural appropriation of the Koran comes through memorization as with the five-times-daily recitative of *namaz* prayers, a clear example of noetic, formulaic ritual. Ong notes that "Koran" means "recitation" (1977a, p. 260). This is reinforced by regular oral performance at Friday prayers, now strictly enforced in public schools, offices, and other work environments of the Islamic Republic. Through repetition, one comes to know and "read" the Koran. Indeed, it is interesting to note that in Persian, the term for "reciting" prayers is *namaz khandan,* a verb which also means "to read." From earliest times, nonliterates have memorized the entire Koran, and annual international competitions now award prizes for the best complete recitation.

The importance of memorization extends to poetry, a vital and popular part of Iranian culture, and while Saadi and Hafez now exist as texts, many nonliterates can recite lengthy passages. Much school and university work depends heavily on rote memory, with city parks filled at exam time by students wandering up and down, reciting passages of text over and over.

A variety of oral performances is still very important in maintaining and reinforcing collective memory and religious identity. The *naqqal,* professional storyteller, can be found in the teahouse, where mainly men congregate, play backgammon, smoke water pipes, read news stories aloud, conduct business, and exchange gossip and rumors. The most common narrative is that of Ferdowsi's *Shah-nameh,* Book of Kings, which is retold a section at a time with the *naqqal* acting out the parts during the recitation. In the *zur-khaneh,* house of strength, attended by craftsmen and apprentices, the Islamic virtues of physical strength and moral steadfastness are encouraged, and traditional exercises are practiced to drum rhythms and the chants of the *murshed* who encourages with verses from the *Shah-nameh* (Beeman, 1982). During the month of Moharram in particular, gatherings for the preaching of homilies by a *rowzeh-khan* are popular, where with the help of a large curtain pictorially representing the story, the martyrdom of Hossein, a key Shiite figure, would be recounted. Two forms of traditional theater, *Ta'azie* and *rou-howzi,* also play on Shiite narratives and often take on a political resonance in the theme of just struggle against unjust tyrants. Of great emotive power, such performances were banned by the Shah, yet resurfaced in attempts by secular intellectuals to preserve traditional folkloric culture. With the Islamicization of Iran, they are spontaneously being practiced again. All of these traditional yet currently popular cultural events build on known and valued narratives and themes that are repeated over and over again.

Literacy might be expected in the public documentation and recording of private events. Under Reza Shah in the 1920s, birth, marriage, and death certificates were introduced in Iran. This was also the time of the adoption of surnames, which seem to have been chosen at will so that brothers in the same family have different surnames. In industrialized societies, most commercial transactions have become written transactions, whether by hand on a check or credit card transaction or in the electronic transfer of funds from one location to another. Iran, like much of the Third World, is still predominantly a cash economy, and most daily economic events, such as shopping, as well as major purchases are conducted in cash. The bazaar in particular works with cash, and young boys can be seen safely carrying huge trays of coin and notes for bank deposit.

To aid illiterates in their interactions with official bureaucracies, an interesting form of entrepreneurship exists. Outside many public offices, particularly the Ministry of Justice, modern-day scribes, equipped with manual typewriters perched on folding tables, sit ready to read letters or documents and type out replies. Both the cash economy and this letter-writing process speak powerfully to the level of social trust and safety that exists— one is tempted to say "still" as though it will inevitably disappear.

Daily life hardly demands literacy. Shopping is conducted in small specialist shops (the butcher, the baker, the candlestick maker) with personal interactions with known individuals. Under the Shah, from the mid-1970s Western-style supermarkets with mass-produced processed foods and printed labels spread in major urban centers for the educated middle class. Economic dislocation, shortages, and deliberate policy mean these are now poorly stocked with limited variety, another blow for literacy. Yes, the illiterate will miss out on street signs, shop names, and graffiti, yet even here, despite the importance of written slogans, posters and stencil images were widely used as public expressions during the popular anti-Shah movement. With the establishment of the Islamic Republic, the most common decoration of buildings, both inside and out, are huge wall murals or photographs of Khomeini and other religious leaders, visual icons of a charismatic political movement.

Iranians, literate and illiterate, took eagerly to television. In the mid-1970s the interior of a simple village house often would consist of whitewashed walls adorned with a few family snapshots, a Persian carpet, and no furniture other than a huge television console with wooden doors to protect the screen, which would be ceremoniously turned on when visitors came. In villages without electricity, television would be run from a portable generator. New patterns of time-use and sociability grew, as viewing patterns came rapidly to resemble those of the West. While we lack clear research results, it certainly appears from the immense popularity of television across the developing world that the grammar of television is a comparatively easy one to learn, certainly easier than the grammar of print. This does not imply that the meanings or satisfactions derived from television content will be the same, but merely that as a technical medium, it does appear readily accessible to illiterate populations.

Yet, despite state control, television did not serve to legitimize the Pahlavis, and all the pomp and imagery of development that was broadcast did not prevent the burgeoning of a retraditionalizing popular movement centered on religious figures. Able to decode and to be absorbed by television as a medium, the population clearly did not so readily appropriate its messages. The model of "communication and development" of Daniel Lerner (1958) and Wilbur Schramm (1964), which suggested electronic media might endow a regime with legitimacy and help to create a unified political order, and indeed Ong's own arguments that secondary orality reverberates with the original oral situation, both suggest that television would have a special kind of influence on illiterate populations. The Iranian experience suggests that active Third World audiences are well able to use electronic media for entertainment without accepting the political legitimacy that state-run media may try to project. Thus the medium alone cannot create legitimacy, but can be used effectively by those groups that already possess authority.

Ong and Iran: Theory and Actuality

Ong has argued that "media in their succession do not cancel one another but build on one another" (1967b, p. 89), and I have tried to extend the sociological analysis of the groups in Iran that have utilized specific forms of media the most. The political dimension of this process has been stressed, particularly the competition for social authority and political power that has accompanied the utilization of different forms of media. Several questions remain, however.

Lana F. Rakow (1988) has argued that men and women have differential access to the creation and development of technologies and different relationships of use; thus communications technologies play a part in the articulation of gender. As C. Jan Swearingen and Ruth El Saffar point out elsewhere in this volume, feminist scholars have begun to analyze the relationship of gender and communication in Western cultural history, a subject that Ong has repeatedly explored (1971, pp. 113-141; 1974a; 1981a). Given the very particular gender relations that Islam constructs, there is clearly much interesting work to be done in exploring the relationships of men and women to the various media examined here, and how and in what manner the patterns of media use, habits, and tastes reinforce—or perhaps bring into question—the differential power and authority of men and women in Iranian society (Abu-Lughod, 1989).

The argument that print supports the development of decontextualized, rational argumentation through its radical separation of author and reader and the anonymity of the text itself is tempered in the Iranian case by the prevailing political culture and level of repression, which blocked this kind of evolution. Similarly, to the claim that writing helps create new forms of authority, more objectivist than communal, the same factor of political repression can be invoked to explain what was essentially a lack of opportunity for the clerisy to develop either their critique of the Pahlavi dictatorship or their plans for a future Iran. Religious authority clearly resonates powerfully with oral communication, not only in Christianity as Ong has described in detail, but also in Islam. If oral culture is essentially "communal, nonindividualistic, and authoritarian" (Ong, 1967b, p. 283), religious affiliation and duty support those tendencies, while the formal features of broadcasting, the presence of voice and image, may reinvoke ethos and reinforce charismatic authority.

A key political question remains as to the relationship between print and democracy. While the availability of print channels alone does not guarantee democratic rights and participation, perhaps their absence or constraint renders such phenomena unattainable. Print allows for sustained, cool reflection unpressured by another's presence, direct or electronically mediated. And only print fosters individual assessment, observation, and objectivity that are the bases of political critique and rational action vis-à-vis the repressive powers of states, whether secular or theocratic.

Ong acknowledges that "orality is not an ideal and never was" and that literacy is one of the cornerstones of development, and democracy (1982b, p. 136). Electronic media appear to offer powerful tools for political systems and those with economic power, at least as currently organized and funded in much of the world, but generally appear to offer limited democratizing possibilities to their audiences. Paulo Freire argues that literacy empowers, since "acquiring literacy [involves] an act of creation and re-creation, a self-transformation producing a stance of intervention in one's context . . . a sense of empowerment" (1974, p. 48). Perhaps a more explicit valuation of literacy needs to be made as a necessary tool for democratization in the Third World as elsewhere.

10

Television, Rhetoric, and the Return of the Unconscious in Secondary Oral Culture

ROGER SILVERSTONE

Television has become the source, site, and symbol of most of what is particular to contemporary culture. Its importance is rarely denied; its influence, rarely questioned. As medium, as message, as the carrier of messages, as the articulator of custom and morality, and as intermediary between public and private, present and past, the familiar and the strange, it seems to dominate by its ubiquity, by its very presence. We watch it intensely, and there is little sign that with rapidly expanding communication technologies we are going to watch it any less. We believe television to be powerful: of itself, as technology and as culture, and by virtue of its embeddedness in the politics of the complex societies in which we live.

Walter Ong's work touches the medium of television at a number of points. Television is something which, together with other electronic means of communication, particularly the telephone and radio, has substantially undermined the dominance of literate and print-based culture. Television at the same time is an agent of return, creating through its forms and formulae a noetic world that recalls without entirely reviving the sonorous immediacy of preliterate societies. Ong's seminal notion of secondary orality captures precisely the essence of this technological and cultural dialectic: the identities and differences between the present and a world we thought we had lost.

Ong, however, is not in any sense preoccupied with television. His work, unlike that of Marshall McLuhan, with which it shares a general orientation, has its scholarly focus elsewhere. He is not so much concerned with the contemporary or with the specificities of technological or cultural difference. While the concept of secondary orality powerfully illuminates the character of our media-dominated world, it has not really radiated into the cracks and shadows of social and cultural processes.

In this essay I explore the place of television in contemporary culture and identify key elements in the processes of its integration into the practices of everyday life and into the fabric of social and cultural relations. The starting point is Ong's own discussions of these issues. But in pursuing these I want to explore an approach that extends Ong's perspective in two directions. The first is outward, toward a sociology of television. The second is inward, toward a psychoanalytic of television. An adequate account of this most complex of media requires this equally complex intellectual journey. I will attempt this in five stages, each corresponding to the following sections of the essay. The first will pursue the notion of secondary orality and engage in a sociological questioning of it. The second will explore the significance of television as a primary source of secondary orality in contemporary culture. The third will discuss the relationship among television, technology, text, and context. The fourth will discuss some of the implications of seeing television as a rhetorical medium for an understanding of the dynamics of contemporary culture. And I will end with a discussion of Ong's notion of interiorization and its relation to the unconscious.

Secondary Orality

The essence of Ong's position, as I understand it, is that substantive and substantial technological changes of the kind that mark the transitions from writing to printing to electronic communication affect the social, cultural, and psychological fabric of our lives in the profoundest possible ways by influencing the way in which we think and the way in which we organize ourselves. Instead of the linearity of print-based texts, infinitely recoverable and structurally complex, the new media provide us with increasingly formulaic and fragmentary texts, recognizable and understandable on a single hearing or viewing. Their appeal is to the group—or in the case of broadcast television the as-if group of the mass viewing audience—rather than to the individual. They offer a shared, not a private, experience. What distinguishes secondary orality from primary orality is its continuing dependence on the analytical and technical and narrative skills that in turn depend on print. Secondary orality is a displaced orality. This sense of displacement is indicated by a recasting of the formula by the slogan and by the planned spontaneity of group experiences. The new orality is action-oriented and thus is oriented to the future, not to the past (Ong, 1971, p. 299).

Ong defines secondary orality in the following terms:

This new orality has striking resemblances to the old in its participatory mystique, its fostering of a communal sense, its concentration on the present moment, and even in its use of formulas. But it is essentially a more deliberate and self-conscious orality, based permanently on the use of writing and print, which are essential for the manufacture and operation of the equipment and for its use as well. (1982b, p. 136)

And elsewhere Ong characterizes secondary orality in this way: "Secondary orality is founded on—though it departs from—the individualized introversion of the age of writing, print, and rationalization which intervened between it and primary orality and which remains a part of us" (1971, p. 285). Secondary orality is a hybrid. Technological change brings with it social, cultural, and psychological change, though neither simply nor in an unqualified way. The forms of expression and experience, which have dominated our lives since writing and print, have now been both compromised and supplemented by those associated with, and created by, the newly emerging oral-aural communication technologies. Television is a hybrid. Dependent technically on the competence that only literacy skills can provide and supported culturally by a secondary popular literature of written schedules and commentary, it is quite undemanding of those same literacy skills that have hitherto marked those who possess them as educated beings.

Television and Contemporary Culture

The most spectacular and intrusive of the recent technological transformations of the word, television, manifests perhaps most clearly, and certainly most massively and deeply, the breaking up of the closed systems associated with the verbal art forms generated by writing and print. Television blurs the fictional with the real on a scale previously inconceivable. It does so not through deliberate choices made by executives, directors, writers, technicians, performers, or viewers, but rather of its very nature. The "tube of plenty" has generated an other-than-real world which is not quite life but more than fiction. (Ong, 1977a, p. 315)

Ong's most sustained analysis of television as a medium goes some way to relating his phenomenology to the particular exigencies of United States culture, where, he notes, it operates relatively free from direct influence of government (1977a, pp. 315-323). It is television's peculiar capacity to present presence and to blur the live and the staged, the real and the imagined, the spontaneous and the rehearsed, that marks it as an open system (as opposed to the relatively closed system of writing and print). Television is narcissistic, but television is also participatory. While its audience is displaced and in a real sense a fiction, the identity of experience that a single shared viewing creates is a powerful force for community. The murder of Lee Harvey Oswald, the Churchill funeral, "Dallas," and a royal wedding all provide an occasion for that sense of participation. As such television is neither necessarily benevolent nor malevolent. The key, of course, to Ong's position is his view of television as a phenomenon *sui generis,* irreducible to society or culture (though its particular relationship to commerce in the United States is one that he finds somewhat perplexing). Television has a nature.

There is much here that is both attractive and plausible. But there are dangers and difficulties as well as encouragements in such a position. Let me offer a brief review. There is no doubting the pervasiveness of television as a technology. More than 95% of households in the industrialized societies such as Western Europe, North America, and Japan have one television set, and many have more than one. VCR, satellite, cable, and all the associated communication and information technologies and services have reinforced television as the primary information and entertainment medium of our time. We take it entirely for granted. We are lost without it.

There is equally no doubting the pervasiveness of television as a cultural force. American television programs, their forms and their formats, are being seen in almost every country in the world: a veritable "Dallas" syndrome. African countries receive reports about events in their own countries from First World news services (Golding & Elliott, 1979). Television advertising is ubiquitous. Television sells. Buy television.

There is finally no doubting that television requires little in the way of formal literacy from its viewers and that making sense of moving images and recorded sounds is a relatively easy skill to acquire, and, it would appear, almost instantly pleasurable. As writers from Aristotle to Ong have pointed out: Mimesis is a fundamental source of delight for human beings. So too are stories. Narrative is a universal phenomenon, and television provides, even in the fragmentation of its texts, much of our current mythology, our folklore (cf. Barthes, 1977, p. 79).

There is, it would seem, a *prima facie* case for seeing television as all of a piece and as a compelling technology that must have affected and must continue to affect cultural forms and content, what Ong would call cultural sensibility. Our behavior changes with television; we see the world through television; we are increasingly dependent on television. Ong's argument (albeit qualified) is that the quality of the technology defines the quality of the content, which in turn defines the quality and the intensity of response. The appearance of television, historically and physically, is sufficient cause (together with the appearance of other adjacent technologies) for major cultural, social, and personal change.

There are two ways in which this argument can be understood. The strong case brooks no exception; it is in effect an argument for technological determinism, which accords the appearance of a new communication technology, or set of technologies, irrespective of context, the power of major and unitary social and cultural influence. Ong does not hold this strong position, despite the occasional arguments that may seem to suggest otherwise (e.g., 1977a, p. 315, quoted above).

The weak case is, of course, more complex and less conclusive. Briefly, it could be summarized by saying that the appearance of a new communication technology that requires different skills of both sender and receiver, as well as a different relationship between message and referent than those required by previously dominant communication technologies, has the capacity to influence, often quite profoundly, the nature and quality of the lives of those who use it. This is an argument about potential as well as achievement. It is essentially and importantly a phenomenology. It leaves open the questions that relate to context, to cultural difference, to social and political contradiction, and indeed to the nature of the mechanisms that link technology, text, culture, and personality. It is still a strong argument.

And it can be pursued in relation to television in a number of ways. We can note, as Ong does and as I have already noted, a number of the qualities of television as a medium. We can examine the qualities of television's textuality, the particularities and consistencies of its narratives, its genres, its rhetorical claims (concerning the narrative of television, see Alvarado, Gutch, & Wollen, 1987; Ellis, 1982). And we can explore the implications of these characteristics for an understanding of social and cultural change. Television then becomes a source of contemporary myth or ritual, and as such it can be shown to preserve (or redefine) a dimension of cultural experience that was otherwise neither recognized nor acknowledged as being of significance in the modern world. And then television becomes the focus of a whole series of questions about cultural persistence or regression and about influences and effects. At this point questions of its global status arise, and we can, if we wish, start talking about secondary orality.

There are many advantages in so doing. Not only does the notion focus attention on the significance of media technology, but it does so, I am bound to say, dialectically. Television, paradigmatically, defines a set of cultural possibilities that involve a complex interplay of modes of communication;

secondary orality is a hybrid, and it is also a kind of synthesis: the present and two pasts. But there is a further dimension to the dialectic. It is one that has already been mentioned a number of times in this essay but that now requires attention, for it is relatively neglected in Ong's work. It is the dialectic of technology, text, and context, of message and response, and it goes to the heart of the matter as far as the significance of television in contemporary culture is concerned.

Television, Technology, Text, and Context

The study of the impact of the mass media in contemporary culture is currently much exercised by two problems: the first is cultural difference and the second is the active audience. The two are fundamentally related.

"Dallas," for example, is seen by Californians and New Yorkers, by Londoners and the citizens of Dhaka and Manila and Jerusalem. It is watched in high rises, on ranches, in grass huts, in suburbs, and in slums, by men and women and children, by peasants and industrial workers, by managers and academics. It is watched by varying ethnic groups. It is watched in pubs, communes, and prisons. It is watched with subtitles, and it is watched dubbed. How is it watched? And how differently? Is there one "Dallas" or many? How are we to understand its significance in this multitude of settings? There is evidence that "Dallas" is read and received differently by different groups and that it is watched actively, in the sense that different viewers will bring different expectations to what is being shown and be able to approach it with different degrees of critical distance. It can be argued at the same time that the particular morality, the particular display of American life represented in the series, leaves the viewer little room for maneuver. "Dallas" is America for the non-American (for scholarly literature on "Dallas," see Ang, 1985; Katz & Liebes, 1985).

"Dallas" spawned a number of national imitations. Europe was once awash with them. "Dallas" itself has its precursors. It is not unique, only perhaps uniquely successful. It is the tip of a cultural iceberg; an example of cultural imperialism; a successful international product—television's Coca-Cola—homogenized and homogenizing. It will be replaced by another.

The problem posed by "Dallas" is the problem of television, and the problem of secondary orality. It is at first blush a perfect illustration of the symbiosis of technology and text: a literary-oral product matching perfectly other products and expressing in form and content much that is recognizable in the oral narratives of preliterate or subliterate society: the predictability and redundancy of plot, the persistent stereotypicality of character, the narrative of fragment and pyramid in constant tension; an invitation to the receiver to identify with, to remember, to compare, to accept; a national and an international shared experience. And so it is.

Television is remarkably similar across the world, not just by virtue of the presence of identical products but through the influence of forms and genres. Television news, the soap opera, and the ads are bare respecters of cultural difference, generating a universal language, not for an educated elite this time, but for all of us. Television is becoming the source of a new global vernacular at odds with national cultures: an agent, perhaps, of a kind of regressive progress. But its relationships to those cultures, particularly those that have survived the traumas of literacy, can only be extremely complex. They have hardly begun to be studied. Once they are, of course, our sweeping generalizations about television's influence (or lack of it) will have to be modified and developed.

There is a sense of this, and of the complexity of the relationships involved, in a passage in *Rhetoric, Romance and Technology,* where Ong is talking about the indeterminacy of medium and message and about the inadequacy of our metaphors to deal with the nature of communication:

> The medium is not the message, for one medium will incarnate many messages. But medium and message interact. The medium is neither container nor vehicle (*pace* I. A. Richards) nor track. The message is neither content nor cargo nor projectile. Medium and message are interdependent in ways none of these carton and carrier metaphors can express—indeed, in ways no metaphor can express. In the last analysis, the medium is not even a medium, something in between. Words destroy in-betweenness, put me in your consciousness and you in mine. There is no adequate analogue for verbalization. Verbalization is ultimately unique. True information is not "conveyed." (Ong, 1971, p. 290)

Ong's difficulty is a real one and it involves not just the relationship between medium and message, technology and text. It cannot be resolved by appeals, however substantively grounded, to interiorization or noetic difference. It requires, as he acknowledges time and time again in relation to the work of Havelock, Parry, and Lord, and as he demonstrates in his own work on Ramus and Hopkins, a detailed understanding of the particularities of culture, text, and social context. And it requires, if his argument is to be pushed to the limit, an understanding of the mechanisms by which texts (as both medium and message) make their appeals to individuals, groups, and nations, and how such appeals are received. It is to some of the issues raised by these requirements in the context of the place of television in contemporary culture that I now turn.

Television and Rhetoric

Ong's writings on rhetoric are extensive, rich, and multifaceted. For the purposes of the following discussions, I want to choose one aspect for consideration in relation to television: rhetoric and textuality.

Television has its rhetorics. It has them by virtue of its technological shape and character and by virtue of its history and culture: the rhetoric of look (how the camera is positioned, angled, moved, with its figures and its tropes in the disposition of lighting, or in the patterns of editing); the rhetoric of image (how what the camera sees is shaped, framed, and arranged, with its figures and tropes in the metaphors, the stereotypes, the ironies, and the surprises of its composition); the rhetoric of the voice (how the written and spoken words are constructed with the figures and tropes of classical rhetoric—the ellipses, metonymies, apophases and the rest—which have marked persuasive language always, and do so now, even in the flattest of documentary realist accounts). It has them in its music.

Television also has its narratives; the strategies of chronology: the mythic and the mimetic, the arguments and the stories, the logic and the chronologic of the texts' temporality. Fragmented and coherent, infinite and unique, appealing to reason and to emotion—television's genres are many and various. But they are dominated by a few: the soap opera, the news show, the advertisement, the magazine program, the game show. In each the formula and the familiar, both in structure and content, define a certain indigenous quality, exclusively televisual, which is itself determined by the ephemerality of the communication: its predominantly oral character. Only the feature film (and to some extent also, the documentary), a throwback to the security of a literate world, it would appear, requires the solace of a clearly defined and maybe masculine narrative (Modleski, 1983, discusses narrative as gendered). Indeed, as Ong points out, our television narratives are marked still by their dependence on literacy.

But none of this occurs in a vacuum. If we are to be concerned with the mechanisms of television's textuality (indeed with the dynamics of secondary orality), then we must ask also about production and reception. For the present purposes I will restrict my discussion to the dynamics of reception (for a discussion of production, see Silverstone, 1985).

The television audience is a displaced audience. The rhetorical claims of television—for attention, assent, community—are made, of course, from a distance. Power is exercised across that distance, but how much and of what kind and in what way is very much a current issue. Technology, especially those secondary oral technologies that so concern us, must be user-friendly. Our rhetoric, of machine and message, is an irenic rather than an agonistic one. What freedoms do we have to dissent, aesthetically, morally, politically, from this combined agenda of seduction? (Colin Mercer, 1986, also asks this question; he too finds himself invoking the significance of rhetoric for an analysis of the power of television.) What tactics do we have at our command to transform and transcend, to privatize and personalize the public and the impersonal (Silverstone, 1990)? These are questions that go to the heart of the problem of secondary orality, but they are far from easy to answer.

The history of mass media research has been dominated by a concern with influence and effects, it must be said, not principally the influence of the technology as such, but, by virtue of the technology, of its content. The pendulum of research activity has swung from seeing the audience as entirely passive to seeing it as sophisticated, critical, and actively participating in the pleasures to be had from the flickering screen, and back again. We are able to say of the mass media that they are generally reinforcive, pacifying, consensual. And this is hardly a surprise. Anything else remains inconclusive. There is a very good reason why this is so.

Empirical research techniques construct an audience in a particular way, above all as conscious beings responding (or not) to distinct content in a broadly measurable way. This is not entirely surprising either, given the nature of contemporary scientific epistemologies. But behind this construction is an assumption, and of course, a denial. What is assumed is that cultural processes are discrete and that our relations to them are manifested exclusively in behavior or attitude. They can be assessed, measured, discussed, and if they cannot, then they are discounted. What is denied is the possibility that cultural processes in some way may be unconscious; that is, they are not amenable to ordinary forms of empirical analysis, because they are inaccessible, non-rational, or even uniquely individual. It is possible that the relative poverty of much empirical media research in this area can be explained by its failure to take into account unconscious processes, both individual and general. On the other hand, the assumption that the unconscious is the key to the unlocking of the problem of culture, and that the history of communication technology's influence on humankind can be explained exclusively by reference to it, is not by itself an answer either.

Television and the Return of the Unconscious

If writing and printing bring with them an increasing privileging of consciousness, drawing humankind away from its unreflexive, unconscious, primitive state, a state itself determined by orality, then the emergence of the new technologies of communication, in inaugurating a new age of secondary orality, in some sense must bring with it a return of the unconscious. The last element of the dialectic may also be the most important.

In this final section I want to shift attention to television as a cultural rather than a technological phenomenon. I am not suggesting that the two are separable. Indeed the previous discussion, as well as that of Ong's work as a whole, requires that technology and culture be treated as inseparable. I also want to draw in, albeit schematically, another body of theory—object relations theory—to complement and to expand what I have been attempting to argue in my dialogue with Ong up to this point.

The principal theorist whose work I regard as being of substantial relevance to the discussion of both culture and technology is D. W. Winnicott (esp. 1974 and 1975). And the point of entry is his discussion of what he calls transitional phenomena and transitional objects.

The point of doing so is this. Ong posits, particularly in his discussion of literacy, a process of interiorization that is perceived, relatively unproblematically, as the incorporation of the requirements of the new technologies into the minds of those who use them: "Technologies are not mere exterior aids but also interior transformations of consciousness, and never more than when they affect the word" (Ong, 1982b, p. 82). How these technologies enter the minds of humankind does not seem to be in question; nor indeed in question is what might be called the cultural inflection of such a process. There is, to put it baldly, a gap between technology and mind that must be filled despite the certain knowledge that filling it is likely to be both extremely difficult and uncertain.

Winnicott's work offers an opening, as I hope to be able to show, for it involves a theory of child development that indicates the primary importance of the symbolic to such a developmental process, and that in turn focuses on the central role of mediation and illusion to that process. It does so in a way that allows a parallel discussion of technology and culture to be undertaken. It also provides some basic clues as to the mechanisms of engagement between mind, culture, and technology and some hints as to a plausible explanation of our dependence on the new secondary oral media.

Object relations theory, to which Winnicott's work is a substantial contribution, looks for an understanding of psychodynamic process less in a study of the instinctual and the monadic individual, emphasizing more the subject's mode of relation to his or her world (Laplanche & Pontalis, 1973, p. 277). For Winnicott, a central element of this relationship as it emerges in normal child development is the transitional object. The transitional object—Linus's blanket in the Schulz cartoon is the perfect example—is an object that emerges in the early months of a child's life:

> a bundle of wool or the corner of a blanket or eiderdown . . . which becomes vitally important to the infant for use at the time of going to sleep, and is a defence against anxiety. . . . This object goes on being important. The parents get to know its value and carry it round when travelling. The mother lets it get dirty and even smelly, knowing that by washing it she introduces a break in continuity in the infant's experience, a break that may destroy the meaning and value of the object to the infant. (Winnicott, 1975, p. 232)

The transitional object is transitional in two senses. The first is because it mediates, that is it both separates and links the child with the mother. The second is because it occupies a similar mediatory position between the first stages of a child's complete identification with the mother, at a time when it is presumed that the child has no sense of itself as an independent being, and one at which, with maturity, there is just such a sense of self and an equivalent sense of the boundary between self and reality. The transitional object is the first "not-me" possession. It is something to which the child ascribes meaning and affect, and it is effective by virtue of the intensity and familiarity of feeling, in providing a "magical" defense against anxiety, a magical link with the most powerful and most basic feelings of attachment to the mother—a comfort.

The transitional object is the first symbol, the focus of the first cultural experience (the interaction of inner and outer worlds), the container of the first illusions. The transitional object mediates both chronologically and synchronously between self and other, between a sense of belonging and one of separation. It provides trust and security. It stimulates and contains fantasy. It is the seed of culture:

> This intermediate area of experience, unchallenged in respect of its belonging to inner or external (shared) reality, constitutes the greater part of the infant's experience and throughout life is retained in the intense experiencing that belongs to the arts and to religion and to imaginative living, and to creative scientific work. (Winnicott, 1975, p. 242)

That television can occupy the status of transitional object is illustrated by many familiar examples of the way in which it becomes part of a child's and indeed of an adult's life. Consider the child who comes home from school, runs into the house and immediately switches on the television, runs into the garden to play, yet returns to switch it back on immediately after the mother, noticing an empty room, turns it off. Consider the child who is comforted by a particular television title sequence and none other. Consider the adult who cannot bear a silent house or who cannot even go to sleep at night without the television being on in the room.

This is, of course, an extremely condensed account of a deceptively simple body of theory, but I hope some of the connections between Winnicott and Ong's discussion are beginning to emerge. There are a number of points I would like to make briefly.

The first is the link between phylogenesis and ontogenesis. The early experience of the child is an oral one; the early experience of humankind is also an oral one. Whether this provides a warrant for an argument of equivalence remains to be seen, but it does suggest the possibility of exploring some parallels. Specifically, it invites attention to the elemental and elementary aspects of culture and to the significance of illusion, play, myth, and fantasy, both for the child and for preliterate society. If psychoanalytic explanations have any credibility at all, then their analysis of basic processes of mediation in relation to the individual must still in some way be relevant to the group.

If this can be accepted, then what Winnicott has done is to identify the mechanisms of a primary psychodynamic process of individual and collective cultural experience: a mediatory and mediated space for the development of the symbolic and the technological that is both cognitive (we learn both about ourselves and reality) and affective (it provides us with comfort, security, a defense against anxiety, a sense of belonging). This space of mediation has been variously allocated to play, myth, rhetoric, technology, and television, by different theorists, Ong among them. What unites them is a perception of a stage of individual and collective cultural development that will be transformed by literacy: a participatory, inclusive, shared, mnemonic, formulaic, reassuring culture articulated orally and verbally without the benefits of advanced technology.

Secondary orality creates something of that world anew, and our mediatory technologies occupy that space: a space of creative dependence. Our relationship to television, then, is, in a nonpejorative sense of the word, regressive—both culturally and individually. The power of television lies in its capacity to offer texts that are regressive: They create (or recreate) narratives (and narrative fragments, and formulae) which encourage a sense of participation, not just with each other, but with our own pasts, comfortably. We are drawn into an experience that is both passive and active. We contribute to it—indeed, in a sense we do create it—though the object itself, the television text, is given, and the result is and must be illusion. This is not simply an argument about the role of technology, therefore, nor even one about communication technologies; it is an argument about technology and text, and about the overdetermination of the former by the latter. I want to suggest that it is not just television *qua* technology that can be seen as a transitional object, but that the key to the effectiveness of the medium as a transitional object is to be found and defined in a study of its narratives: their structure, rhetoric, genres, and context.

Conclusion

Walter Ong's discussion of secondary orality opens up a powerful field for investigation. I have tried to relate it to the specific quality of television, both as technology and medium, in contemporary culture. The argument has, as I initially suggested, moved in two directions. The first was toward a concern with the sociological: with issues of context, power, and the negotiation of meanings and realities that differently situated individuals and groups are able to generate in relation to the universalizing dominance of television culture. The second was toward a concern with the psychodynamic and with issues of what Anthony Giddens (1984) talks of as ontological security: that is, with the dynamics of individual and collective unconscious processes that engage with a medium like television in such a way as to create and sustain a firm, trusting, and secure basis for existence in a troubled world. Television has a crucial significance in creating and articulating the particular and various qualities of our secondary orality. There is a great deal still to do if we are to understand fully those particular and various qualities.

11

Postmedieval Information Processing and Contemporary Computer Science

PHILIP LEITH

Too frequently formalists' desires for purity of system lead to forgetting that many of the mistakes they might make have actually been made in the past. Either the belief in a new method, the belief in new ways of setting out knowledge, or the belief in new fundamental insights leads formalist computer scientists to look only to the present, ignoring lessons learned from the past that might be useful and insightful. This essay looks for such connections between the past and the present. Judged from an emphasis upon the sociohistorical, this essay will succeed if the reader understands that the past is important for understanding the present.

This essay looks to a postmedieval researcher, Peter Ramus, who has been described as the world's first programmer, and examines the relationship between method, logic, and information. Importantly, Ramus can be described as one of the early formalists, advocating that knowledge can be axiomatized by a simple methodological technique. Taken together with the description of him as "the first programmer," this makes him an interesting figure to study. The method that Ramus used in his logic to handle information was formalist for several reasons. First, he believed that knowledge could be fully axiomatized and set out in his logical system. Second, he held that the method was more important than the social/intellectual context in which it was used. And, third, his method was a form of the "soft technocratic" use of logic.

AUTHOR'S NOTE: This essay is a shortened version of Chapter 4 of Philip Leith, *Formalism in AI and Computer Science* (Chichester, England: Ellis Horwood, 1990), pp. 73-91. Additional lines of inquiry, examples, and illustrations can be found in the original.

Ramus lived in the postmedieval period during which the world was breaking free of the chrysalis of medieval handwritten manuscripts. Printing had become common and gave an intellectual spurt to the concept of just what "information" actually was. Pierre de la Ramée (Latinized to Ramus) was born in 1515, the son of a French charcoal burner (whose family had once been noble), and died in the St. Bartholomew's Day Massacre in 1572. At his death, he was one of the most influential thinkers of all the postmedieval world. Though obviously highly influential, Ramus was a controversial figure. In fact, he was a highly controversial logician who made many enemies.

Given the significance of Ramus's logic in the sixteenth and seventeenth centuries, it is striking how little information can be found about him in the current histories of the discipline. He has been wiped from the standard history books of mathematics as though he had never existed. That this dismissal of a logician should have occurred is an indication that we cannot believe everything that we read in current histories of a discipline: Each new generation massages and amends the history of its predecessors to provide a coherent and, indeed, formal picture of its own knowledge as a true and unfolding path. Ramus's work, unfortunately, does not fit in with this formal historical picture.

Perhaps the classic work on Ramus is Walter Ong's *Ramus, Method, and the Decay of Dialogue,* which was published in 1958. Since its publication, it has been used as a source in disparate fields, since, as I shall argue here, Ramism strikes many chords in our current world. Ong himself, when the text was republished in 1983, wrote of its starting point:

> The book grew from a hunch . . . that the intellectual "reforms" so passionately advocated by . . . Pierre da la Ramée and by his thousands of followers across central and northwest Europe, somehow registered a major shift in consciousness marking the transit from the ancient and medieval world into the modern. Ramus' streamlined reorganization of the age-old Western tradition of logic and rhetoric seemed to signal a reorganization of the whole of knowledge and indeed of the whole human lifeworld. (Ong, 1958a, p. vii)

Ong's text has been used in many areas: philosophy, literature, linguistics, in the history of memory systems and the history of medicine, in anthropology, sociology, psychology, theology, education, and intellectual and cultural studies generally. However, there has been no work done in its relationship to computer science, though Ong himself wrote in the 1983 edition:

> Were I to do this work again . . . I know there are many things that would need reconsideration and revised assessment. One connection that would have to be brought out would be the resemblance of Ramus' binary dichotomized charts . . . to digital computer programs. Like computer programs, the Ramist dichotomies were designed to be heuristic. . . . The quantifying drives inherited from medieval logic were producing computer programs in Ramus' active mind some four hundred years before the computer itself came into being. (Ong, 1958a, p. viii)

I had not read Ong's note on this connection when I began my work on the relationship between computer programming (particularly that of logic programming) and Ramism, but I too saw that this was the case. Logic programming is an attempt to program computers solely by the use of logic. Its proponents, but not its critics, argue that logic is the most effective way to process and handle information, and thus should be the most effective way to get all users to program or interact with computers. Logic programming is one of the largest research areas in computer science, and consumes large quantities of research funding. Ramus was, indeed, an early programmer. His whole attitude towards algorithmic method, knowledge, and handling information is strikingly modern. (In fact, it could be said that he invented the term method as we now know it; see also Gilbert, 1960.) He would have found little difficulty in settling into the logic programming section at Imperial College, London, or the artificial intelligence (AI) laboratories at Stanford University.

Ramus, then, gives us early insights into our own discipline. He leads us to begin thinking about how a particular method affects our consciousness; printing, I shall argue, altered that of Ramus, while digital programming alters ours. This, of course, is a resetting of the social element of computer knowledge within a slightly different framework. It begins to lead to questions about how the "computer culture" is changing how computer scientists see what is possible: If we believe that we have methods to handle information, for example, we will not look too closely at "information" since it will seem unproblematical to us. Indeed, we do see information as unproblematical, and my thesis is that this is due, in large part, to the way that computers have changed our perspectives.

Looking back to Ramus, we can see why he can shed highlights on computer science. His was a period when the world was becoming only slightly used to the notion of printing technologies. The view had been, in the early stages, that printing was just another form of writing. Ramus changed that, for since the concept of space on the printed page was different from that of the written page, his logic utilized new means of textual layout; these were impossible in manuscript format because of the different processes involved in manuscript production and printing. Space, as a form of closure or fixing of the written word, was highly significant in the setting up of his own logical system. Whether he saw how much he owed to printing is not important: What is material is the fact that his method was really only possible because of the technology of printing.

There are a number of strands in Ramus's work that I am only beginning to untangle—another is related to the rhetoric of computing. One that I have so far untangled is his relationship to logic programming; in order to deal with this I shall provide some background about his influence and his method. Ramus is, of course, being set out here as an example of formalism in action; he was both technicalist and axiomatist. These faults are still being carried through in the current fashion for logic programming.

Ramist Influence

It is useful to look to just how influential Ramism actually was. His ideas had been taken by the Pilgrim Fathers to the new colonies, where they provided the intellectual foundation for Harvard University as a Ramist citadel. Miller has written that "while Augustine and Calvin have been widely recognized as the sources of Puritanism, upon New England Puritanism the logic of Petrus Ramus exerted fully as great an influence as did either of the theologians" (Miller, 1939, p. 116). John Milton, author of *Paradise Lost,* was a Ramist of sorts; he also wrote a *Logic* (1672/1982)—a textbook on the subject—which expounded and extended Ramist principles. Sir Philip Sidney, whom Buxton (1987) tells us was influential in initiating the English Renaissance, had a biography of Ramus dedicated to him; Sidney also paid for the education of Abraham Fraunce, who advocated Ramist logic in law (Fraunce, 1588/1969). More generally, Ramus gave the world concepts such as method, logical analysis, and system, which were so influential on philosophers such as Liebniz, Descartes, and, we might argue, today's computer scientists.

With the rise of artificial intelligence in the 1980s, there has been a related rise in interest in those philosophers who, prior to the AI movement, had looked to the rationalization of thought (see for example, Davis & Hersh, 1986). Two of these were, of course, Descartes and Liebniz. Descartes published his *Discourse on Method*, and Liebniz searched for his *charateristica universalis,* that is, the universal method. On more than terminological terms, we can argue for a direct descent from Ramus to artificial intelligence.

This picture takes full account of the importance of Ramism to the sixteenth and seventeenth centuries; in many ways, Ramus was sixteenth-century man, but long after his death his influence continued to be felt. There was no single point when Ramism, as an intellectual pursuit, died. Rather, it seems to have been watered down and slowly forgotten: The interesting aspects such as method and logical analysis were taken up by others, and Ramism was diffused into our intellectual culture and heritage like a salt dissolving into solution.

Ramist Method

It would not do my own argument about the social complexity of knowledge and technology much justice if I were simply to suggest that Ramism could be expounded in a short section of an essay. Ramism is a complex phenomenon that touches upon many aspects of pre-Ramist thought and that, even during Ramus's lifetime as well as after his death, went through a continual process of change as it was criticized, improved, and moved over as a means of analysis into ever new areas. Thus the exposition I can give here will provide only an overview of the method and its origins. However, as Ong himself has said, the comparison between computer programming and Ramist logic is compelling; it is this central facet of Ramist thought with which I shall deal, and not any of the other expressions of his thought style.

What is this Ramist logic that is so closely intertwined with current computing? *It is a two-part process or method that claims the ability to analyze information and, from that analysis, allow it to be reformulated through synthesis as new knowledge.* It is thus an example of postmedieval information processing.

Any subject or discipline, Ramus claimed, could be processed by means of the method, whether art, physics, medicine, law, or (dangerously, given the times) theology. The first act was analysis, by which the field can be "sown asunder" (that is, divided) by logic into its two component parts. The method thus began by dividing a subject into parts through a process of binary division. And thus begun, it continued, with successive divisions by this means of bifurcation until the subject was split into its component parts. In today's terminology, this was a *knowledge-handling formalism.*

The method was diagrammatical and was set out with the discipline at the left-hand side of the page, and the elemental parts of that discipline at the right. When one page was insufficient to cope with all the information, as in Abraham Fraunce's *The Lawyer's Logicke* (1969), it was continued on other pages in a manner similar to the way that computer programmers break up their program into subroutines or modules or segments. As an example of the method in practice we can see how Ramus' own dialectic (as he called his logic) could be expressed (see Figure 11.1, *Tabula Generalis*).

Ramist logic is divided into two parts: invention (discovering and classifying the art or science) and judgment (referred to as IVDICIVM in the diagram), which was a synthesis from the constituent parts on the left-hand side of the diagram. Judgment was, as a method, a process of gluing together those parts that logic (dialectic) had divided. Ramus asserted that things are "glued" in nature and that the mind also glues things together in thought in the same manner. The two kinds of glue are connected either by simple axioms or by discursive reasonings. Miller gives an example:

> We have two axioms, each composed of arguments, "fire makes heat" and "heat warms the body." We put them together, exactly as we put arguments together to frame the axioms, and so achieve the discourse, "When the body is cold it is wise to light a fire." . . . We may be compelled to plead, "fire makes heat, heat makes warmth, ergo, fire makes warmth," or we may, on so obvious a matter, fashion our oration by simply listing the axioms in intelligent sequence. (Miller, 1939, pp. 131-132)

The process was always, Ramus claimed, the same. First we produce individual arguments (rightmost on the page), then we can combine individual arguments together to form a conclusion. If in doubt we join the arguments together with a syllogism. Our axioms or conclusions from our syllogisms then need only to be set out in an organized fashion to produce a discourse, a sermon, or any representation of "knowledge" that we wish.

I want to emphasize the common methodology between today's logic programmers and those of the Ramist persuasion. Logic programmers in the computer era claim that we simply need to set out our knowledge as a series of axioms (rules), which we can then encapsulate within our logic program. These axioms can then be combined together by deduction (i.e., by means of the syllogism, as Ramus might have put it), in order to produce conclusions or new knowledge. *It is striking that the method of logic programmers is identical to that of Ramus.* Although Ramus used, as I explain below, the new technology of printing, logic programmers use the new technology of computing; apart from that, there is little difference between their methods, for both make use of the concepts "logical analysis" and "logical conclusion."

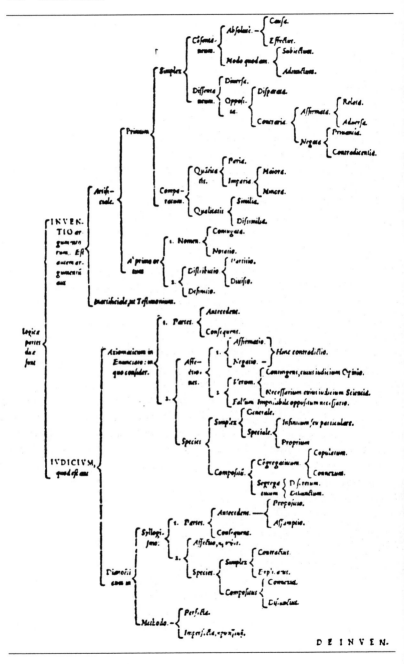

Figure 11.1. *Tabula Generalis*

Ramus has been accused of having the most reckless means of logical quantification that the intellectual world has ever seen. It was so reckless that, even when he was setting out the axioms of his own system, the elements varied on every occasion that he did so. The randomness of the analytical process meant that there could be no exposition of a subject that was similar to any other exposition of that same subject: The epistemological foundations were entirely ad hoc. But this is just the problem with logic programming: It embodies one of the most reckless means of quantification that the twentieth-century intellectual world has seen. For example, we can look to the way that John R. Ennals suggests that logic programming is usable in historical research (Ennals, 1985). Ennals may well cite Collingwood, Wittgenstein, and Elias in his discussion of just how complex is the nature of knowledge and rules, but—constrained by his method—he can offer us only a knowledge representation formalism without any indication of just how we apply the closure from real world knowledge to logic: We are left with entirely ad hoc means of quantification. Not only that, but it is not the method that is to be blamed (that is, logic programming and the computer) if anything goes wrong but it is us:

> The program is only as good as its weakest link—and that could be the original description of the archaeological or historical knowledge. . . . The computer will not make logical errors; but we may inadvertently give it information that is ambiguous, inconsistent, or downright incorrect. The blame rests with the human author. (Ennals, 1985, p. 93)

For all of Ennals's attempts to provide a philosophical context to his method, he is stumped by this notion of information as logic—it is our fault, not the method's, that we cannot give it information that is not ambiguous, inconsistent, or downright incorrect. But real historical knowledge is rarely consistent, unambiguous, or correct. For example, take the simple sentence, "Elizabeth was crowned Queen Elizabeth II in 1953," a sentence that we might believe to be factual. But, of course, it is only factual from one particular perspective: There are many who point out that she is not Queen Elizabeth II, but Queen Elizabeth I, since Scotland was not part of the United Kingdom in the reign of the first Elizabeth. Living in a part of the world with two opposing cultures (which necessitates two separate histories), it is clear to me that historical fact is not so unproblematic as Ennals suggests.

The problem, of course, is that Ennals' method and knowledge representation affect the way that he sets out his description of the world. That is just what happened with Ramus and his colleagues through their graphical technique. In the next section, I will look to the way that printing affected Ramus's method; this, too, closely relates to the way that computing has affected the method of logic programmers.

The Word in Space

It is a common assumption, and an errant one, to believe that the manuscript was just an earlier version of the printed text. The same errant viewpoint seems to suggest that the only difference between electronic publishing and printing is that electronic publishing allows quicker access. In fact, the information handling mechanism is highly important in deciding just what kind of information can actually be held.

The matter is seen most clearly with the indexing and diagrams found in manuscripts and books. In books, the fixing of the contents of a page (each page is identical because each page comes from the same printing plate) means that it is possible, and indeed highly efficient, to index the various elements of the book. While it takes some time to construct the index, typeset, and print it, this saves a considerable amount of time for future readers who wish to consult that indexed book. Similarly, with diagrams and pictures, it becomes an efficient strategy to take the time to make high-quality block prints that can produce the same diagram over and over again. Many early diagrams in books indeed show that substantial effort was put into effecting these.

Only when the word became *fixed in space* on the printed page—that is, when printing allowed each word to be given a set location on a set page—did indexing become a widespread practice. At this point, the title pages of books began to advertise the fact that the book contained an index, so important an advance was this considered.

Much the same problem about fixing in space can be found with diagrams, pictures, and such in manuscripts. In printing, only one person needs to know what the diagrammatic representation arises from: For example, if I were printing a text on tulips in the seventeenth century, it would be possible to get an artist to prepare the block prints that would clearly show the differences between the various tulip stems, bulbs, heads, and so forth. These would then be fixed and could be reproduced any number of times, and each reader would see exactly the same differentiations that were highlighted by the artist. With manuscript format, though, on each occasion that the tulips were being reproduced, they would be done so by people who had not actually seen the original flowers, but who had only seen a copy of a copy of a copy of the originals. Rather like the children's game of whispering a word from ear to ear around a circle, the final version of a tulip would be as different as the final word was from the children's first whisper.

Printing, thus, allowed the diagram to be as fixed in space as it allowed the word to be. Each diagram was an exact replica of the initial one and would appear in the exact place in each copy of the text, and it too could be indexed just like the words and concepts. It was little wonder that pictorial representation was taken up by Ramus, since it was a technique that became available as a thinking or communicating tool just as effectively as Latin was a thinking or communicating tool to intellectuals of that time.

Since my argument is ultimately about computer science, it might be useful to have a small example of the way that electronic media are changing the nature of "print" space and, thus, our notion of what "information" is. No longer, in electronic media, do we have the concept of the fixed location of a word (that is, fixed for all time). Rather we have the idea of digital space as being a temporary, changeable location: We index in information retrieval systems by location on a disk, which represents nothing we can see; the indexes do not lead to a page, but rather to a block of digital information that we can display on a screen. And, due to the easy way we can update our information retrieval systems, we can easily run an indexing package upon them so that new temporary (and, to the eventual user, unknown) locations are given as our storage system is expanded with more and more information.

Further, given the easy way we can copy and edit information held on magnetic media, we are moving—in some ways—back to the manuscript format: Our data can be re-edited in ways that we might not wish, or we can actively aid this. I can give one small example. I was responsible for the design of a computer-assisted learning (CAL) authoring package, called LEXICAL (Leith, 1988), which allows lawyers to produce tutorials in law. It seemed to me that one advantage of the CAL tutorial was that it actually allows others to re-edit and change the tutorial so that it suits their own teaching practices. I realize that not all authors would be keen to have their knowledge so manipulated and, perhaps to their view, bastardized, but it seems to me that we should not necessarily stay with the traditional fixing of knowledge and word as we have come to expect in the age of printing. Just as manuscripts were the work of a collection of authors (because of the changing contents of the manuscript), it might well be that computer-produced teaching media will become the work of a collection of twentieth-century teachers.

Returning to Ramus, we can now see the importance of his diagrammatic technique. It was a technique that came about only because of the nature of the new communicating technology. Ramus was one of the most effective users of this new craft. Without printing, Ramus's logical diagrams could not have been reproduced properly. But also, as Ong is at pains to emphasize, the change in consciousness that printing brought about gave a push to the perceived usefulness of graphical techniques anyway; as in our day, when we want to try some new intellectual activity, we most often wonder whether it can encapsulate computers (computers and law, computers and history, computers and grammatical syntax, etc.). In Ramus's time we might have wondered how graphics could have been used.

There is a further layer of complexity here that relates to the nature of medieval memory as a series of places or loci (see for example, Frances Yates' *The Art of Memory,* 1966). Undoubtedly, this too was a strong force in the uptake of diagrammatical techniques in print. I mention this factor because I wish to emphasize that social forces are rarely simple and one-dimensional. It would be a useful study to see how our electronic storage media now relate to this idea of storing knowledge in electronic loci—memory locations and sectors on hard disks. There is also, on the surface at least, a similarity between many of the diagrams used to represent the medieval mind as a series of places connected with diagrams (see, for example, Figure 11.2) and the use of diagrammatic techniques in both computer science and cognitive science. I bring this to the fore because it seems to me that we use diagrams in computer science almost because we are expected to, and that there must be some social factor acting upon us here, perhaps in the same way that it acted upon Ramus, if not so forcefully as upon him.

I cannot claim to have any full understanding of the role of diagrams in computer science, either as a clarifier or as a confuser, but can point to the interesting comments of Ludwik Fleck on medical diagrams, where he notes that diagrams are never fully representative of the subject they are supposed to present, and that they always contain a highly theoretical element within them (Fleck, 1979, p. 33). Fleck calls these ideograms since they carry a message in their symbolism. In software engineering the notion of a "software life cycle" is usually represented diagrammatically in the *vade mecums* of software engineering. Much of the power of the concept of the software life cycle, it seems to me, has come from the fact that it is so easily representable by a diagram (although every diagram representing it is different in some way or another). It has been an ideogram for a way of thinking (or not thinking, more accurately—see the comments in Hekmatpour & Ince, 1988) about whether there is such a thing as a simple life cycle for software. The ideogram has acted as a means of mental control. It has been more

Figure 11.2. The Geometry of the Mind

difficult to escape from the simplistic view due to the very power of the ideogram of the software life cycle.

It is interesting, then, to see how a sociohistorical study of Ramism begins to highlight other aspects of our discipline that might have laid buried under the idealism of the formalist program, which suggests that we should not look back from our "radical novelty."

The Social Context of Ramism

Formalism as a tendency is always awaiting an opportunity to strike like some intellectual man-eating tiger, but some social situations bring it to the fore more readily than others. In Ramus's case, the social situation that brought it to the fore was the battlefield of the medieval university, and in this section I look to what was happening in that situation that caused Ramism to flower. My argument should be seen as mirroring an argument that formalism in computer science is as much the product of current university computer science education as was Ramism the product of medieval logic teaching.

Ramism found itself at the center of a battle among three intellectual forces. These were theological scholasticism (best represented perhaps by Thomas Aquinas), arts scholasticism (represented by the lesser abilities of those teaching in the typical medieval university—sometimes termed the Schoolmen), and humanism, the movement to which Ramus was bound. In logical terms the division between these three forces (and, once again, I emphasize that in a short space I can give only the flavor of the argument) was relatively clear. The theological scholastics had a logical system that was complex, highly specific, and little understood by the general population much, we might say, like mathematical logic of today.

Arts scholastic logic was nowhere near as complex. It represented the attempts to take Aristotelian logic and teach it as a practical subject to the adolescents in the care of the Schoolmen. It had been much bashed about by various simplifications brought to bear to make it easier to understand and so forth. Ong has pointed out that although it claimed that Aristotle was its source, much of the *Organon* was left out, and other sections added to the logic textbooks of the time—for example, Peter of Spain's *Summulae logicales* (Hispanus, 1947).

Between these two forces there was obviously tension. One was much more elitist and much more related to theological research. The other was far from elitist and was related to pedagogical needs.

Peter of Spain's text seems to have been the linking between the two forces. In its original form it was a complex body of logical and rhetorical knowledge, and yet it was much simplified as it was transferred over to the arts scholastics. Although the *Summulae logicales* was strikingly modern in much of its outlook, it was produced in a time that was ideologically divergent from our contemporary scientific/technological one: Peter of Spain, Ong tells us, after acting as Pope Gregory X's physician, became Pope himself, and "merely dabbled in theology. Great as it was, his posthumous reputation as a logician was second to his reputation as a physician—a practitioner both of medicine and of all sorts of physical experimentation, including black magic" (1958a, p. 55). Isaac Newton, too, although a father of modern physics, had similar sorts of interests; and we should be careful to remember that, although in some terms we can look back in history easily, our scientific ideology is not a necessary part of human nature that we can automatically take back in time with us.

Humanism, the third of the intellectual forces, can best be seen as a response to Peter of Spain. It was also an attempt to move the focus of attention from the teaching system to practical usefulness: No longer was logic to be simply the rote learning that it had become under arts scholastics. Now, it was to be put to practical use. As Ramus himself expressed it:

> After my regular three and a half years of scholastic philosophy, mostly the *Organon* of Aristotle's logical works, terminating with the conferring of my master's degree, I began to consider how I should put the logical arts to use. But they had left me no better off in history, antiquity, rhetoric, or poetry. Thus I went back to my study of rhetoric, ended when I began my philosophy course four years before. My aim was to put the logical books of the *Organon* to the service of erudition. (Ong, 1958a, p. 41)

Ramus's basic charge against the arts scholastics was that "ordinary people don't talk like that." There were problems in logic that were imposing other strains upon the teaching methods at that time, as well as those of the lack of usefulness of the taught systems. This was caused by the lack of an adequate symbolism that would have allowed the mechanics of these systems to be discussed and expounded. Given the age of the students expected to understand this logic (less than 15 years), it was little wonder that cracks were showing in the logistic plans of the arts scholastics. The problem was not really to be solved until the nineteenth century, when the study of logic got a new impetus from symbolic techniques. However, it should be noted that scholastic logic's interests are highly agreeable to those of philosophical logicians today: They were interested in language, ontology, and epistemology. In fact, Desmond P. Henry, in his *Medieval Logic and Metaphysics,* informs us that "an intelligible conversation between medieval logicians and modern philosophers could be quite profitable" (1972, p. 1). My point is that we should not take the view that all our current knowledge is more sophisticated than that of our intellectual predecessors.

Ramus's method was conceived as a way to overcome the failure of the arts scholastic process. It utilized the existence of a new technology (the printing press), which gave the technological/intellectual means to take the arts scholastic on in the battle of logic. In many ways, then, Ramism was a socially produced phenomenon owing its life force to university culture and printing culture, which too can be viewed as a social or sociohistorical fact. Ramism was not a way of viewing the world that sprang independently to life, nor did it grow as a necessary outcome of the intellectual system that it attempted to replace.

And since it was, I suggest, the first attempt at what we now call "computer programming"—the method as a set of simple steps of analyzing a problem or a body of information and setting it out in an early sort of flow diagram, showing the connections and the divisions that could be made—we should take heed that this first example of programming was so socially produced. Ramus was not aware of the social construction of his formalist grand plan—to him his method was just as unproblematical as those methods that computer science produces. Similarly, most computer scientists are not aware of the social construction of their own discipline: where their research agenda comes from, what makes a proper subject for study in the terms of computer science, and so on. But that does not mean that today's computer science is not as bound by social facts as was Ramism.

Conclusion: Imperialism and the Quantification of Success

One of the most striking aspects of Ramism, as a technicalist enterprise, was its incessant imperialism and hubris. It believed no area would not succumb to the method and was prepared to go out and prove it. Ramus himself had a tremendous—almost charismatic—enthusiasm for logic as a practical tool. His public lectures attracted large crowds, who would be entertained by his melodramatics and his attacks upon his logical opponents.

As pronounced as the enthusiasm for his method was Ramus's enthusiasm for all it could do; that is, he had no qualms at all about its being a highly successful methodology. No area of intellectual life, he thought, was not amenable to his axiomatization: Any subject—theology, mathematics, poetry, and so on—could be logically analyzed and broken down through the binary method to the particulars of the discipline, and then—once again through the method—recombined into new knowledge. We are told that before Ramus started work on axiomatizing the Bible, he possessed only a New Testament. So too, mathematics was not, it seems, his strong point, for he would make frequent errors while on the lecture dais, calculating with his abacus.

The same kind of imperialism seen in Ramus has been observed by several commentators in the research process of artificial intelligence. For example, Sherry Turkle, in her sociopsychological analysis of the AI community, notes:

> Being in a colonizing discipline first demands and then encourages an attitude that might be called intellectual hubris. You need intellectual principles that are universal enough to give you the feeling that you have something to say about everything. The AI community had this in their idea of program. Furthermore, since you cannot master all the disciplines that you have designs on, you need confidence that your knowledge makes the "traditional wisdom" of these fields unworthy of serious consideration. Here too, the AI scientist feels that seeing things through a computational prism so fundamentally changes the rules of the game in the social and behavioral sciences that everything that came before is relegated to a period of intellectual immaturity. And finally you have to feel that nothing is beyond your intellectual reach if you are smart enough. (1984, p. 260)

Technicalism is, of course, always an imperialist program since there is the belief that some technique or knowledge can give insights or solve problems that are not amenable to other means. The very act of discarding the social and problematical elements of a discipline and concentrating upon the formal nonsocial elements is imperialist, because those formalists are acting in a way where their imperialism brings a blindness to the already known knowledge of the occupied discipline.

For all technicalists, the belief in the technique seemed to be unaffected by any lack of success: The imperialism of the method left a tunnel vision that immobilized any fuller understanding of aspects of the discipline that could not be handled by that method. Of course, Ramist technique was not static: It developed through Ramus's own lifetime and after his death. It must have been much like current logicians always being aware that there were problems with their logistic enterprise, but believing that by some logical fix or extension, these problems would melt away.

Ultimately, we know the final result of Ramism as a technique: It is now seen as an errant period in the history of logical thought. And we can also look back with some detachment at the manner in which Ramism was carried out as an evolving political and social force that existed in a given sociohistorical context. Hindsight gives us these detached insights into the errors of Ramism, yet in Ramus's own time there was no clear agreement on the success or failure of Ramism. No doubt, opponents saw it as a false and simplistic pursuit; and no doubt, proponents saw it as a new "Kuhnian revolution" or paradigm, as we might call it today.

PART IV

Studies of Consciousness

Introduction

BRUCE E. GRONBECK

As the opening essay in this anthology suggests, perhaps Walter Ong's greatest contribution to American cultural studies is his work on consciousness. Given the domination of American cultural studies by sociological, political, and social thinking, concerns for the sensate self often have been left behind. Even American psychological theorists have spent much time on mind and its cognitive contents (beliefs, attitudes, opinions, values), devoting but little time to the *cogito* that convinced Descartes to assert his selfhood *sum*. Ong is one of the few native American intellectuals of this century to address the problem of consciousness-in-society again and again.

More specifically, not only does he discuss consciousness, one's sense of I-ness as distinct from everything else, but also gets caught up in the study of psychic development in order to complete his system of thought about psychocultural life. That is, Ong works from a great dictum of the twentieth century, "Ontogeny recapitulates phylogeny," but modifies it so that he traces parallels between individual growth and cultural (rather than racial) development. His key to understanding both lies in communication processes. The defining aspects of any given medium, together with its habitual usages by social actors, allows us to see traces or echoes of both consciousness and culture in the everyday intercourse of people.

So far, so good. Yet, Ong has refused to leave his discussion at this level of generality. Consciousness is a bedeviling concept—too often merely an unknown constant worked into the equations of life when investigators run into epistemological or ontological trouble. Ong wants more than a way out of trouble. He seeks in consciousness to understand how the self—"the 'I' [that] identifies itself by its self-awareness and by this alone" (1981a, p. 194)—can move back and forth between the interior and exterior worlds. Via consciousness, internal understandings are matched or tested against

179

external perceptions and admonitions; consciousness negotiates relationships between the individual and others. How does all of this occur and with what force?

These are difficult questions to answer, for various perspectives can be assumed in pursuit of responses. Ong himself has moved from one perspective to another over the 50 or so years he has pursued the "I" of life, working in tandem with sociobiologists, historians of consciousness, Freudian and Jungian psychoanalysts, epistemologists, rhetoricians, theologians. In the past decade, he even has gone to a neologism, *noobiology,* to capture his ideal—"the study of the biological setting of mental activity (Greek *nous, noos,* mind)" (1981a, p. 11).

Others have followed Ong down multiple paths in the search for cogent and useful understandings of the relationship between consciousness and life. Part IV is devoted to studies of those relationships. We open with the work of Ruth El Saffar, set out in Freudian terms, to understand the consequences of separating body from mind. She sees in the rise of modern science the propensity to split consciousness, to disembody the self, tracing through the language of Francis Bacon the murdering of the mother in nature and in the human psyche. Freud then is depicted as the instrument for restoring the mother, for making pleasure rather than knowledge the goal of science, though he himself is seen as repressive—still resisting the mother-principle in his articulation of consciousness. To El Saffar, only post-Freudians (including Ong) are able to overcome mind-body and gendered oppositions to construct unified theories of consciousness.

Laboring in some of the same territory is Thomas Farrell. He seeks to understand today's "secondary oral culture" in terms of Neumann's stages of the evolution of consciousness, that is, to essentialize cultural evolution in terms of dominant forms of consciousness. Farrell characterizes Neumann's stage seven as a period of androgyny, with masculine and feminine impulses working out their relationships, and stage eight as the time of self-actualization and transcendent integration—Jung's holy wedding. The coming of secondary oral culture thus is seen as a force in evolving consciousness to states of wholeness and health.

Jan Swearingen approaches the gender gap even more directly than does Farrell. Ong's *Fighting for Life: Contest, Sexuality, and Consciousness* (1981a) is certainly a controversial work (a) in grounding gender (social) distinctions in sexual (biological) terms, and (b) in its seeming rationalization—and hence perpetuation—of hierarchic, gendered social practices. Swearingen first reviews the feminist debate over gendered social practices, then outlines Ong's positions in *Fighting for Life* on sexual and gender differences between males and females, focusing particularly on gendered argumentative discourse. She next presents Gilligan's analysis of logics of justice/ethics of care so as to parallel Gilligan's and Ong's thoughts on the complementarity of masculine and feminine language and voice.

David Payne concludes the section with a study of social character drawn from very different angles. He explores the relationships between media structures and the shaping of individual and social character. Working from the perspective of what he calls characterological rhetoric, he is in search of the "rhetorical technology" by which we manifest in symbols, narratives, and dramatic action our personal identities. This move ties Ong's work, not to psychoanalysis, but rather to sociological study of character in the tradition of David Riesman, Christopher Lasch, Richard Sennett, and Robert Bellah. Riesman provides Payne a framework for exploring relationships between tradition-directed and primary oral culture, inner-directed and literate culture, and other-directed and secondary oral culture. That framework allows Payne to take on television, more particularly the characterological struggle among orientations toward shame, guilt, and anxiety in the multiplicity of situations, ethics, and instructions presented to us in various programs.

12

The Body's Place:
Language, Identity, Consciousness

RUTH EL SAFFAR

The scientists and philosophers who laid the groundwork for the modern industrial and technological world built their theories and experiments out of a dualistic worldview that came to rely on the eye and the "I" as the basic instruments of observation. In "I See What You Say," Walter J. Ong catalogs the sensory metaphors by which we represent understanding, showing how the preference for the visual privileges knowing based on separation (1977a, pp. 121-144). The hypervaluation of the visual as a cultural dominant in Western consciousness coincides roughly with the Copernican revolution. Like the sun, the eye fosters clarity and distance, and associates knowing with information gathered about "others"—about things outside of and apart from the body and the self who observes. Knowledge that might be gained through tactile, olfactory, or aural means, though more intimately grounded in the body's sensual apparatus, tends to be held suspect when compared with visually apprehended information (Gallop, 1982, p. 27).

The technology for disseminating the written word that developed in the Renaissance further enhanced the mind-body split so characteristic of Western epistemology in the modern period. Dualism is a byproduct of script culture and certainly antedates Gutenberg, as Eric A. Havelock (1963) has shown. It was not until the seventeenth century, however, when the effects of easily reproduced written material had impacted the culture through expanded and radically altered schooling practices, that dualistic thinking became a veritable cultural dominant.

The cultural and political consequences of the effort in Western Europe to distinguish the thinking from the embodied self, and culture from nature, continue to manifest themselves in our collective experience. In what follows

I want to trace some responses to the split in Western consciousness. In keeping with Walter Ong's developmental perspective, I have divided the work into three sections designed to trace the movement toward, into, and back away from the dualism that is still powerful as a Western construct.

The first section of this paper will deal with the rise of modern science, and how the drive for consciousness is represented as the achievement of clarity, dominance, and power. In the next section I will discuss, through the pivotal figure of Freud, the ways in which the need for distancing and separation begins to break down. Finally, I will offer in the last section a sampling of post-Freudian thinkers whose work begins to seek recovery of the imbalances inherent in a consciousness oriented toward separation and mastery.

Dualism and the Classical Scientific Paradigm

The move in Western science from an earth-centered to a sun-centered cosmology is dramatized in the sixteenth-century struggle between alchemy and animism on the one hand, and mechanistic philosophy on the other (Yates, 1964, 1979). The victory of the mechanistic over the animistic attitude is one that has been studied by such historians of culture and science as Brian Easlea (1980), Carolyn Merchant (1980), Allen Debus (1978), Sandra Harding (1986), Evelyn Fox Keller (1985), and P. M. Rattansi (1963). Striking in all of these writers' accounts of sixteenth- and seventeenth-century philosophical change is the role that body and woman play in the verbalizations surrounding the relationship between the knower and the known. In "The Masculine Birth of Time" (1604), for example, Francis Bacon refers to the scientist's aim to bind "Nature with all her children" to his service and "make of her [his] slave" (quoted in Leiss, 1972, p. 197).

More overtly aggressive and militaristic aspects of Bacon's approach to knowledge can be seen in his call for men to make peace among themselves so they can turn "with united forces against the Nature of Things, to storm and occupy her castles and strongholds, and extend the bounds of human empire" (quoted in Easlea, 1980, p. 7). The political ramifications of equating knowledge with power were being enacted in the contemporaneous coloniz-ing of the non-European world. Since the task of the rational man is to dominate nature, the scientific and the imperialist enterprises would be supported by an identical ethos.

The "Masculine Birth of Time" heralded in Bacon's essay attests to a shift in consciousness that both Ong and Erich Neumann (1966) have discussed in connection with the ego's need to separate from the mother. Of the range of bodily senses presently recognized, Ong associates vision, paramount after the seventeenth century, with the "male sky god," and touch with "mother and earth." Ong says:

> Mother (earth) and father (sky) are related to one another as tactile to visual. Mother and earth are close to us, ground our sense of touch (which develops in contact with mother), and deeply involved in subjectivity; father and sky are more remote, more object-like, apprehended more by sight than by touch. (1977a, p. 143)

Neumann, who, like Ong, records a shift between the fifteenth and the seventeenth centuries in the collective relation to maternal and paternal archetypes, links the differentiation of consciousness that begins to take place in the Renaissance with the psychological imperative to "murder the mother" (1966, p. 104). Merchant (1980) further elaborates on the dissociation of the earth/Great Mother that takes place in the sixteenth century. Her analysis of the move from an organic to a mechanistic worldview shows how technological development, first seen as assaultive to the body of Mother Earth, eventually produced in mechanism a view of the earth less likely to induce guilt. Easlea (1980) has shown, finally, how an end to the persecution of witches intertwined with the birth of modern science. The great advantage of the mechanistic over the animistic worldview, according to Easlea, was that mechanism sapped the lifeworld of its vitality and therefore undermined the idea that witchcraft could affect anything.

The growth of consciousness and ultimately of science is clearly linked in the analyses of Ong, Neumann, Merchant, and Easlea with the effort to contain the irrational qualities associated with women, nature, non-European "natives," and the body. As early as 1486, in the *Malleus Maleficarum,* the earth cults' powers were linked with the devil. By the time of the Spanish playwright Calderón in the seventeenth century, nature was clearly associated with danger (El Saffar, 1989, 1990). Nature confuses and distracts, pulling the subject into realms where passion and the imagination work to destabilize the self and the social order. So heavily is sixteenth- and seventeenth-century thinking invested in projecting danger and corruption onto the feminine that Saint Teresa's canonization caused major consternation. Efforts during her lifetime to denounce her visions and revelations later reverted to praise at the Saint's escape from her female body (Weber, 1990).

The use of Latin in the schools and for philosophical and scientific discourse further accelerated the process by which thinking was separated from the body and the oral culture. Ong writes of the Latin taught in school that it "had certain advantages in keeping the human lifeworld at a distance. As a male-polarized language . . . Learned Latin provided a special instance of the sometimes devious role of writing in the emergence of the modern consciousness" (1977a, p. 35).

The development of the expectation that science would allow "man" to be the master of life may have been, as Ong has suggested, an inevitability in humankind's drive toward full consciousness. The break with the organic worldview and the oral culture that consciousness seems to have required produced, however, a dangerous imbalance. It was Freud, toward the end of the nineteenth century, who began to excavate in the regions of the repressed. His early work with hysterics reintroduced the figure of the woman that has lost all connection to reason—the woman Freud himself explicitly related to the witch (Freud, 1892-1899/1966, p. 242). It is to Freud's complex position in the relation of the body to consciousness that we must now turn.

Freud: Discovering/Resisting the Mother

Freud's work sustains the separations of knower from known and mind from body basic to Western science, but inverts the hierarchy on which the terms are ordered. Unlike earlier theorists of modern science, Freud proposes that pleasure, not knowledge, is the goal of the human organism. *Civilization and Its Discontents* (1930/1961) clearly places Freud between classical science and the newly emerging paradigm of a more participatory, body-centered relation to the lifeworld. In that work, Freud writes:

In the last generations man has made extraordinary strides in knowledge of the natural sciences and technical application of them, and has established his dominion over nature in a way never before imagined. . . . But men are beginning to perceive that all this newly won power over space and time, this conquest of the forces of nature, this fulfillment of age-old longings, has not increased the amount of pleasure they can obtain in life, has not made them feel any happier. (p. 46)

Freud's search for a scientific understanding of the human psyche, essayed as early as 1895 in his *Project for a Scientific Psychology* (1895/1966), was an attempt to return consciousness to the body from which with Descartes's *Discourse on Method* (1632) it had decisively been separated. The institution of the "talking cure," and the clinical focus on hysteria, draws Freud's work, at its inception, into the ambit of the spoken word and the female body. The rediscovery of the child's longings, and the body's search for pleasure, though developed in the work of some of Freud's followers, does not grow in Freud's work in the direction of gratification. In Freud the repressed returns, but it returns through a structure designed to contain and divert the pressures rising up and seeking release.

The need to suppress desire for the mother built into Freud's theory establishes him as a participant, albeit reluctant, in the dualist paradigm. Freud's early fascination with the accounts of female hysterics gave way after his crisis of 1897 to a practice largely centered on the problem of neurosis. His last major effort to write out a female case was that of Dora, which he himself described as a continuation of his own self-analysis (Bernheimer, 1985, p. 17). In an interesting commentary on Freud's failure with Dora, Collins, Green, Lydon, Sachner, and Skoller (1985) observe:

> Throughout the analysis Freud acts as if the mother were of no consequence in Dora's psychic life. . . . Did he not find intolerable the very notion of aggressive wishes directed toward the mother? If he did, this could elucidate Freud's complicity with Dora in the repression of her mother. . . . Might not Freud's parallel occulting of the mother in the Oedipus complex conceal a similar involvement on his part? This hidden preoccupation with the mother could be viewed as an individual phenomenon. But is it not more useful to see this blindness in so astute an analyst as the manifestation in him of a perversion—the repression of the mother—which lies at the root of Western civilization itself? (250-251)

A great deal of the work of psychoanalytic theorists in the generation after Freud has been devoted to reinstituting the importance of the mother as a figure through whom early development is shaped. The object relations school of psychoanalysis, best represented in the work of Melanie Klein (1975) and Margaret Mahler (1980), brought the mother and the whole pre-Oedipal experience into analytic discourse. The mother in object relations theory, however, is seen primarily through the lens of the child's envy, greed, rage, and desire, and thus she becomes, once again, that from which the child must escape. The goal of individual development remains separation, and the obstacle continues to be the mother, and by extension, the bodily and unconscious pleasure (and pain) she represents.

Significant at this point is the recognition that discontinuity and dualism remain unruffled by psychoanalysis. Although Freud's idea of the sexual etiology of hysteria was a first step in his often-repeated desire to heal the split between body and mind by showing the bodily basis of mental images, the images were seen as disguises through which the body's unacceptable drives reach expression. The analyst's task was to reveal the desires embedded in the images, and thereby to free the subject of the power of those desires over him. Like the body from which it emerges, therefore, the image becomes an essentially resistant object destined to be subdued by the analyst's powers of intellect.

The two contradictory pulls that appear to govern the psyche as Freud envisions it can be considered in terms of the struggle in his work between two theories of seduction. Freud's best-known seduction theory is based on the model of father incest, formulated early in his career out of the narratives of his female hysterics. His abandonment of the theory later in 1897 marked a significant turning point in his thinking. Freud's alliance with the figure of the father after 1897 may not be insignificantly related to the death of Jacob Freud and his subsequent assumption of a paternal role with respect to the whole movement of psychoanalysis.

Freud's exculpation of the father goes deeper still, as Harold Isaacs (1978) has discovered in Freud's partial reading of the Oedipus trilogy. Freud's assignment of guilt to Oedipus is more severe than Sophocles's. Freud's interpretation is also strangely protective of Oedipus's father Laius, who in fact initiated Oedipus's problems by trying to kill him peremptorily. But in Freud's reading it is the Oedipal figure who is ultimately responsible for his own fate. Freud's Oedipus and castration complexes, his envisioning of the psyche as tiered in the triad of id, ego, and superego, and even his theory of competing and irreconcilable instincts, are rooted in the parental battle being fought in the psyche of the child.

The id, associated with the antisocial desires and impulses that civilization has been created to hold in check, is the place in the psyche of desire. That desire, though apparently originating in the infant, as the abandonment of the paternal seduction theory would suggest, in fact has its genesis in the seductive activities of the mother, who, as Freud explains in "Femininity" (1933/1964, pp. 112-135), satisfies her desire for a penis by possessing in the figure of her male infant the masculinity that fate has denied her. The castrating effect of the possessive mother on her child is something developed in greater detail in the work of Klein (1975).

One of the principal effects of Freud's abandonment of the paternal seduction theory is that it turns the object of disturbance away from the external world and focuses it within the subject. By locating conflict in the innate drives of the infant, Freud breaks not only the relation of desire and the primary processes with outside events, but also of desire with the secondary processes by which they are contained.

The split between mind and body, which Freud sought to resolve by recognizing the embodied nature of consciousness, is also a factor in Freud's severance of id impulses from the super-ego. The image of a divided self, one part of which is designed to impose control over the other, emerges after Freud's renunciation of the seduction theory of hysteria. Discarding that theory, however, meant denying not so much the fact of seduction, as its attribution to the father. As Jean Laplanche has put it in *Life and Death in Psychoanalysis*:

> Despite the incessant oscillation between such terms as reality, pure imagination, retrospective reconstruction, etc., Freud will affirm with increasing insistence the fact of seduction, going so far as to present it, at the conclusion of his work (in the *New Introductory Lectures,* 1932/1964)[*sic*] as a quasi-universal datum, for there is indeed a form of seduction which practically no human being escapes, the seduction of maternal care. (1976, p. 33)

Freud's whole theory of the unconscious, as it develops after *Three Essays* (1905/1953), rests on a longing to recover that oneness with the body of the mother that acculturation and the acquisition of language force the child to relinquish as the price of entry into the social order. Forever barred from the real object of desire, the human subject can never, in action or in language, make anything other than an approximation of that Other, which is also Nature, Reality, the Body, the Woman.

This view of the split between systems of symbolization and the realities they seek to define, explicate, or re-create, makes of language an instrument by its very nature alien to that which it evokes. In the evolution of Freud's work, and in its elaboration through the French neo-Freudian Jacques Lacan, language comes to be associated with the intervention of the father. The Oedipal drama, for Lacan as well as for Freud, is one that results, if successfully enacted, in the child's rescue from what is seen as the regressive pull of the mother.

The identification of language with a mastery that overcomes the pain of maternal loss inevitably separates language from the body. Language, and what Lacan calls the "Symbolic Order," are understood as a substitute for the gratification and sense of wholeness that was once the child's experience with the mother. Like culture, they sublimate the child's unrealizable wish for symbiotic union. The implication for language is that it has separation built into it. It does not affiliate, as in Ong, with mother and body, but rather, with father and culture.

What Freud initiates for twentieth-century thought is the process by which the dualisms of self and other, knower and known, inside and outside, on the basis of which mechanistic philosophers paved the way for the growth of modern technology, are broken down. Freud's discovery of the Other within, of the unconscious that, glimpsed in dreams, jokes, and slips of the tongue, in fact drives not only consciousness but civilization, marks the beginning of a turn in the Western psyche back toward an awareness of unity, however much it seems to emphasize division and inner conflict.

Twentieth-Century Efforts Toward a Recovery of Holism

Freud's opening to the importance, however occluded, of the mother provided the means through which his early disciple and later rival Carl Jung would seek to undo the Western attachment to rationalism. Jung's excavations, precisely in that "pre-Minoan" territory of the mother that Freud despaired of approaching, led Jung eventually back to the sixteenth century and the pre-mechanistic philosophers who sought a unified worldview based on the interconnections between spirit and matter, male and female. Jung's work with the alchemical tradition and his highlighting of the feminine represent one effort to bring the opposites into better harmony and interrelation.

Jung's move, first developed in *Symbols of Transformation* (1956), offered a revisionary view of the incest taboo. By establishing a level of the psyche beyond the personal repressed, Jung was able to reclaim, at the level of what he called the collective unconscious, the place of the mother-son dyad that the rationalist-materialist orientation would have had to repudiate. Jung's engagement with universal myths, fairy tales, and cross-cultural dreams led him back to the Paracelsians and alchemists whose animistic vision of the universe had been suppressed in the scientific revolution. It also allowed him to develop, through work with what he called "active imagination," a practice of consciousness no longer exclusively reliant on objective, intellective processes, and no longer dependent on hypervisualism.

Jung is hardly alone among twentieth-century thinkers in reclaiming a place of importance in consciousness for the image. The image in its affiliation with affect and lived experiences has an immediacy and a power that shamans and healers have long used. Like the spiritual exercises of Loyola that Ong describes at length in his book on Gerard Manley Hopkins

(1986a), the contemplative use of the imagination brings the practitioner to levels of consciousness in which the self comes into contact with the essence of its being. Heiddegger, Merleau-Ponty, and the whole school of phenomenology have also sought a way out of dualism through a more bodily sense of presence to the world.

The recovery of the *vis imaginativa* and of an animistic world view is associated in Jung's work with the unconscious, and with the recognition of the desire for the body of the mother. In the past several decades the importance of the body as the locus of another kind of wisdom has spawned many studies, not only on the alchemical and occult traditions in early modern Europe (Couliano, 1987; Debus, 1978; Yates, 1964, 1979), but on the pre-Socratic and earth deity cults that went underground under the pressure of patriarchally centered religions (DuBois, 1988; Gimbutas, 1982; Keuls, 1985; Spretnak, 1978). Jung's effort to open up a territory of the psyche beyond the individual's repressed desire for the body of the mother led him not only to a different image of the psyche, but also away from a view that saw the alienated, divided self as the ultimate expression of developed personhood. In its fullest evolution, the Jungian psyche is capable of bringing the opposites into fruitful interaction and, in some Jungian revisionist thought (Hillman, 1975), of also abandoning the need for the unitary world view implicit in the Apollonian attitude.

Abandonment of the demand for a single paradigm within which all experience can be explained has also taken place in the natural sciences. Starting with Göedel's mathematical proof that no theorem can be both consistent and all-inclusive, science in the twentieth century has progressively let go the absolutist, objectivist stance characteristic of classical science. Relativity and speculations arising from quantum mechanics have led scientists such as Heisenberg and Pauli, and more recently, David Bohm (1980), David Peat (1987), Fritjof Capra (1983), and Ilya Prigogine and Isabelle Stengers (1984), to imagine a universe not simply made up of separate entities, but interconnected in a way that makes each element a part of the whole, itself understood as a living organism. This "implicate order," as Bohm has called it, or the "pleroma," as Jung and Wolfgang Pauli have named it, returns science to the *unus mundus* perspective of the Renaissance magi and alchemists. It provides a way out of the deterministic, linear, dualistic, and causal habits of thought, offering instead a universe involved in dense and intricate interrelations among its parts and formed in the interest of both individual and collective growth.

The emphasis on relationship and spatial, as opposed to temporal, ordering brings the emerging scientific paradigms into the ambit of what had been relegated in dualistic thinking to the realm of the feminine. Jung's synchronicity and Rupert Sheldrake's notion of formative causation, for example, call attention to relationships among events based not on sequencing, but rather on simultaneity. The assumption underlying synchronicity and formative causation is that at any given moment all things exist in relationship to one another, and that they emerge out of the pleroma, or creative matrix, because of that relationship.

The concepts of interrelationship and a unifying matrix developed in field theory and quantum mechanics also have correlate expressions in Piaget's structuralist model. That model has an interactive, creative, non-deterministic basis that emphasizes organicity over mechanism, and inner dynamism rather than objective passivity. The work of psychologist Jessica Benjamin (1988) also presents human beingness as interaction among selves rather than as an ongoing struggle for dominance among separate entities. Challenging the object relations model that traces the infant's movement from an idealized symbiosis with the mother to an equally idealized autonomy, Benjamin proposes a mother-infant dyad built from the beginning on the "simultaneous presence of two living subjects" (p. 16). Her work, like that of Carol Gilligan (1982), is based on the idea that development entails not growing out of relationships, but rather "becoming more active and sovereign *within* them" (p. 18), a point also basic to the notion of differentiation as outlined in the recent work of Michael Kerr and Murray Bowen (1988).

Although most French feminist and poststructuralist theorists do not make overt alliance with a relationship-based understanding of the lifeworld, such writers as Helene Cixous (1981) and Luce Irigaray (1985a; 1985b) seek recovery of a territory outside of patriarchy for theories of language and human relations. They employ metaphors of space and body in ways that enhance presence and body rather than deny them. As Jane Gallop (1985) has pointed out, the separation of subject and object and of male and female into hierarchized positions of dominance and submission puts woman in the place of subversion. As women begin to enter a cultural system in which they had functioned as Other, they tend to undermine the clarity and separateness so prized in hypervisualist economies. Gallop says: "Woman's ambiguous cultural place may be precisely the standpoint from which it is possible to muddle the subject/object distinction, that distinction necessary for a certain epistemological relation to the world" (p. 15).

Conclusion

The figure that the whole composite of Freud's writings describes, the figure embattled, forever caught between the regressive pull of the mother and the need to establish an identity separate from her is one that Ong clearly distinguishes as male. Ong's writing on what he calls noobiology, as well as his extended study of sexuality and academia in *Fighting for Life,* seek, as did Freud, to establish the biological setting of mental activity. From the womb in which the fetus is embedded to the realms of family and of culture, environment is feminine. Presenting male efforts to conquer and subdue as defensive maneuvers within a universe favoring female survival, Ong gives a masculine valance to the drive for autonomy that was for Freud the essence of adult human development. By showing how the thought processes typically associated with rationalism and mechanism developed in academic settings that were nearly exclusively male until very recently, he also gives a historical coloration to the success men have had in separating.

Ong's analysis of cultural history links Renaissance schooling practices with the development of modern scientific thought. The fact that Latin was associated exclusively with the "letter" and used principally by males becomes, for Ong, highly significant. Divorced from the oral culture, separated from the realms of the mother, the voice, the mouth, and the ear, Latin became in Ong's words "eminently useful for thought struggling to be abstract and especially for budding scientific thought endeavoring to maintain a contact with the physical world that worked from immediate, continuous, but unemotional involvement with objects toward full abstraction" (1981a, p. 114).

Having associated spoken language with the mother, the body, orality, and the unconscious, and Learned Latin with the separation from those elements, Ong sees the scientific revolution of the early seventeenth century not as the victory of reason over unreason, or culture over nature, but as part of the evolution of consciousness at whose heart is a "dialectic of masculine and feminine" (1981a, p. 116). He further sees how the distancing involved in the development of abstract thought is associated with a mentality of domination (1981a, p. 121). With Ong, then, we can begin to historicize not only the "absolute and universal truths" of the scientific revolution, but also the efforts of present-day scientists, philosophers, and psychologists to recover relationship and the interaction of living subjects as vital aspects of an evolving lifeworld.

Ong suggests that consciousness is moving beyond the need for opposition, which grows inevitably out of the metaphysical binarism that has dominated Western thinking since Plato, toward an awareness of an interdependence that recognizes both individual differences and the need for mutual support. The shifts that Ong intuits in the patterns of thought and relationships in late twentieth-century culture are related, as always in his analyses, to changes in information storage and retrieval. The renewed importance of aural receptivity that the growth of electronic media has fostered has worked to attenuate hypervisualism. Ong's valuing of hearing is part of his recovery of oral culture, not as a primitive and outmoded predecessor to script culture, but as a mode of orientation to the world rooted in identity and valued on its own terms.

The secondary orality of which Ong writes represents a collective tendency, made possible because of the overdevelopment of the intellect in the past 400 years, to restore balance to a consciousness excessively dependent on visualism. The hearing sense that is reactivated due to recent developments in the technologies of communication brings back into the noobiological system a connection to the lifeworld that breaks down distance and alienation. That Ong specifically presents the senses and the whole development of modern science as gendered places him firmly within the tradition flagged by Evelyn Fox Keller that invokes "gender and the use of sexual imagery . . . in the description of nature" (1985, p. 35). What is striking, however, about Ong's gender-based metaphors is the consistency with which he projects a model of harmonious interrelationships in the place where earlier writers proposed conquest or separation.

Ong's early fascination with the oral (Hopkins's "sprung rhythm," 1949); his efforts to see in orality not primitivity but an integral and highly sophisticated means of communication (e.g., "African Talking Drums," 1977a, pp. 92-120); his view of Western scientific thought as the product of cultural and historical conditioning (1971); and his contextualization of the phenomena of consciousness not only historically and culturally but also biologically (1981a) have provided invaluable guideposts for those looking for ways to repair the fabric of the human lifeworld. Ong's efforts to recover balance—between the masculine and the feminine, between culture and the environment, between consciousness and the body, between orality and literacy—are part of a general cultural shift that he both reflects upon and exemplifies.

13

Secondary Orality and Consciousness Today

THOMAS J. FARRELL

Hope characterizes Walter J. Ong's treatment of our secondary oral culture (1967b). Ong uses the term "secondary oral culture" to distinguish contemporary Western culture from the primary oral culture out of which Western culture emerged after the development of vowelized literacy. While many intellectuals today lament the waning of the inner-directedness associated with manuscript and print culture in the West, Ong radiates hope because of what he senses as the potential of secondary oral culture. He does not believe that we are headed for a perfect state of existence, and he is critical of certain aspects of secondary oral culture (1971, pp. 284-303; 1977a, pp. 305-341; 1978a, pp. 100-121). But he does regard secondary oral culture positively, not as the disaster some do. The purpose of this essay is to use some hints from Ong's works to suggest a possible basis for such hope; I propose to discuss Ong's work on primary oral, literate, and secondary oral culture in terms of Erich Neumann's (1954) Jungian stages of consciousness, Jean Houston's (1980) psychohistorical stages of development, and related works.

Ong and Neumann on Psychic Development

In *The Presence of the Word* (1967b), *Rhetoric, Romance, and Technology* (1971), and *Interfaces of the Word* (1977a), Ong formulated and developed the thesis that "major developments . . . in culture and consciousness are related . . . to the evolution of the word from primary orality to its present state" (1977a, pp. 9-10). Moreover, he claims that this thesis is not reductionist, because his "works do not maintain that the evolution from primary orality through writing and print to electronic culture, which produces secondary orality, causes or explains everything in human culture and consciousness. Rather, the thesis is relationist" (p. 9). A relationist approach to analyzing cultural data emphasizes relationships among phenomena, because "cause and effect [are] often difficult to distinguish" (p. 10). As I hope to show, a relationist analysis of Ong's work on communication and culture with reference to works by Neumann, Houston, and others suggests that secondary orality is related to the integrative stages of consciousness. Thus a relationist analysis suggests a basis for the hope Ong sees for contemporary culture.

Ong calls attention to Neumann's description of the stages of consciousness to help us identify aspects of consciousness associated with secondary orality. In *Rhetoric, Romance, and Technology* (1971, pp. 10-11) and in *Fighting for Life: Contest, Sexuality, and Consciousness* (1981a, pp. 18-19), Ong identifies twentieth-century personalism with stage eight of the eight stages of consciousness Neumann describes (1954). Ong makes this identification in the context of summarizing Neumann's largely Jungian account of the stages of consciousness:

> The stages of psychic movement as treated by Neumann are successively (1) the infantile undifferentiated self-contained whole symbolized by the uroboros (tail-eater), the serpent with its tail in its mouth, as well as by other circular or global mythological figures, (2) the Great Mother (the impersonal womb from which each human infant, male or female, comes, the impersonal femininity which may swallow him up again), (3) the separation of the world parents (the principle of opposites, differentiation, possibility of change), (4) the birth of the hero (rise of masculinity and of the personalized ego) with its sequels in (5) the slaying of the mother (fight with the dragon: victory over primal creative but consuming femininity, chthonic forces), (6) the slaying of the father (symbol of thwarting obstruction of individual achievement, to what is new), (7) the freeing of the captive (liberation of the ego from endogamous kinship libido and emergence of higher femininity, with woman now as person, anima-sister, related positively to ego consciousness), and finally (8) the transformation (new unity in self-conscious individualization, higher masculinity, expressed primordially in the Osiris myth but today entering into new phases with heightened individualism—or, more properly, personalism—of modern man). (1971, pp. 10-11)

Although Ong here refers to a primordial myth involving a masculine character, he could just as aptly have referred to the story of Psyche to illustrate the emergence of a feminine mythic character into stage eight (Johnson, 1986). Robert Bly (1990) has published a significant study of male growth that correlates with Neumann's account of human development. The red warrior, the white warrior, and the black warrior as described by Bly correspond to stages four, five, and six, respectively, in Neumann. In Bly's account, the marriage of the boy, who is the son of a king and queen, and the girl, who is the daughter of a king and queen, represents the wedding of the masculine and the feminine dimensions of the psyche in stage seven, and the emergence then of the previously shadowy figure of Iron John as a king exemplifies the emergence of stage eight in the male.

While Ong identifies personalism with stage eight, he does not discuss Neumann's account of the integrative stages of consciousness (stages seven and eight) in much greater detail. However, he does make it clear in other places that he considers personalist philosophy to be one of the unique and great developments of twentieth-century thought. To him, personalism is subject-oriented without being subjective. Under this expansive concept he would include the work of Martin Buber, Pierre Teilhard de Chardin, Gabriel Marcel, Karl Jaspers, Gaston Fessard, Bernard Lonergan, Karl Rahner, and others. In an important work Robert M. Doran (1990) integrates the key insights of Lonergan's work with Jungian psychology. The freeing of en-dogamous kinship libido, referred to by Ong above, is styled affective conversion by Doran. Doran refers to the growth process involved in stage eight as psychic conversion (cf. esp. pp. 3-352, 630-680).

In the course of this essay, I identify the concepts of various other writers with stages seven and eight as described by Neumann. For example, with stage seven I identify androgyny (Woolf, Heilbrun, Singer), generativity (Erikson), self-actualization (Maslow), and meeting the challenge (Houston); with stage eight, ego-integrity (Erikson), transcendence (Maslow), and self-realization (Assogioli). Both stages involve what Jungian analysts call the integration/individuation process. Those integrative stages of consciousness follow the formative stages four through six in Neumann's account. (While I have not studied Eric Voegelin's work, I am well aware from reading Doran's book that Voegelin has already essentially worked out in greater detail than I do here some of the major correspondences I note in this essay, especially with respect to stage eight.)

When Ong in *Fighting for Life* (1981a, esp. pp. 183ff.) points out that a new relationship with the feminine is being worked out in popular culture today, he in effect is saying that more individuals in contemporary oral culture are moving into stage seven. Many men and women today talk about working out a new relationship to one another, just as many also report working out a new relationship within their own personal psyches between masculine and feminine tendencies. Consequently, we learn about the androgynous person.

We may surmise from such talk that the speakers are giving voice to movements within their own psyches. If we make this inference, then we can say that the speakers are moving into or are in stage seven, the stage of growth in which a new relationship with the feminine is gradually worked out. I presume that Ong refers to such reports when he writes in *Fighting for Life* (1981a) that a new relationship with the feminine is being worked out in popular culture. In other words, Ong's relationist approach to cultural phenomena links the development of secondary orality, which he considers to be literate orality (unlike primary orality), with the development and spread of both stage seven (in popular culture, especially in the women's movement) and stage eight (in the development of twentieth-century personalist philosophy). Paradoxical or not, these developments fully accord with Ong's basic claims about the impact of the interiorization of vowelized literacy and the interaction of orality and literacy on human consciousness. Thus from a relationist standpoint, secondary orality is related to the widespread popularization of the integrative stages of consciousness.

Neumann refers to the entire process of development of consciousness as a masculinizing process (1954, pp. 63, 94, and elsewhere). By "masculinizing" he means individuating, and so he sees the development of consciousness in women and men alike as masculinizing. Similarly, Ong says, "Consciousness arises out of the unconscious by differentiation and thus has a masculine quality" (1981a, p. 115). In the formative stages of ego-consciousness (stages four through six), the developing person is strongly antifeminine, which is to say that the person develops through resisting those psychic attributes considered by Jungian analysts to be feminine (e.g., interdependence). Both males and females are antifeminine in those stages of growth, although antifeminism is typically more pronounced in males than in females.

Feminine and masculine orientations belong to the fullness of every human person, male and female. In this essay, the feminine orientation is linked with a set of characteristics that Ong discusses in his extensive treatment of cultural history, while the masculine orientation is associated with others. Specifically, primary orality (and by extension the mother tongue), openness, participation, embodiedness, concreteness, and practicality are considered in this essay to be expressions of the feminine dimension of personhood. The disembodiedness of language in writing and later in print, closure and individuation, distanciation, and abstractness are here associated with the expression of the masculine side of the human psyche. Since technology involves material embodiment, technology is linked here with the feminine side of life, as is the natural physical environment.

Doran points out that the masculine and feminine dimensions of the psyche constitute a dialectic of contraries (1990, p. 349). However, social conditioning in Western culture has often led people to consider them as contradictories and therefore to shape their lives too exclusively around one dimension or the other. In a dialectic of contraries, Doran notes, "both poles are to be affirmed, each in its appropriate relation to the other" (p. 503). To establish an appropriate relationship between the masculine and the feminine in the psyche, people need to avoid overdoing either dimension to the near exclusion of the other. To check themselves from overdoing one or the other, people need to develop in their psyches both a healthy antimasculism and a healthy antifeminism, bearing in mind that neither misandry nor misogyny is healthy. To check themselves from underdeveloping one dimension or the other, people need to remember that the fullness of life emerges from maintaining the proper tension, balance, and interaction between these two poles of the human psyche.

Stage Seven: Psychic Integration Begins

The psychic movement into stage seven is characterized by a new relationship with the feminine, and this is the stage Jungian June Singer writes about in *Androgyny* (1976; discussed below). The corresponding stage seven in Erik H. Erikson's (1963) account of human growth is characterized by generativity. "By generativity," Houston says, "Erikson means the responsible guiding of the growth of others and the caring and concern for social organizations and other activities" (1980, p. 24). However, Carol Gilligan shows that women in the formative stages of consciousness value the relationship between self and other more than men do. In the integrative stages of growth, according to Jungian analysis, women may very well continue to value "the ongoing process of attachment that creates and sustains the human community" more than men in these stages do (p. 156).

The beginning of the end of the multistaged formative period of ego-consciousness (the masculinizing/differentiating process both sexes grow through) is marked by a sharp turning in consciousness—what Aristotle in discussing tragedy in his *Poetics* calls a *krisis* (turning) and what Neumann styles a Copernican revolution in the psyche. This turning is a potential breakthrough, an opening up, that might seem like a breakdown, as it does in *Oedipus Rex*. But such an opening up to the feminine forces in the human psyche does not necessarily lead to positive results, as it does not for Oedipus in *Oedipus at Colonus*. Thus the full odyssey of Oedipus provides a striking contrast with that of Odysseus, who eventually discovers the life-giving powers of the feminine dimension of life.

What follows the initial turning toward or opening up to the feminine forces in the psyche is a kind of agonistic reconciliation with the less dominant polarities in the psyche—in a kind of Hegelian synthesis. Since the development of consciousness in both males and females is a masculinizing process, the initial reconciliation process that one turns to in stage seven is a reconciliation largely with the life-giving and life-threatening forces of the feminine orientation of the human psyche. The feminine contains both. Consequently, this initial stage of the integrative process involves real struggle. In concrete and imagistic language, the struggles of Odysseus after the shipwreck on his voyage home and the struggles of Oedipus on his pilgrimage in *Oedipus at Colonus* are representations of the struggles of ego-consciousness in stage seven.

Stage seven is the psychic voyage begun by some persons in consciousness-raising groups, by others in psychotherapy, and by yet others in less programmatic life experiences that lead to deep reflection about their lives. A kind of reconciliation of seeming opposites takes place; it is simultaneously agonistic and assimilative. Boundaries and psychic bonds dissolve as the psyche is gradually liberated from endogamous kinship libido. That is, energies that are wed within the psyche to primordial familial images are liberated from those images. In short, one comes to an objective awareness of familial relationships, oneself, and consequently others. More specifically, one frees judgment of self and others of infantile affectivity. The chthonic darkness of infantile affectivity dissipates and one is able to judge reality soundly.

This recognition/reversal process resembles that which Aristotle detected in tragedy as it had developed in ancient Greece. That is, one recognizes that one's relationships/actions in the present and past are in truth sort of a reverse of what one had imagined them to be, but this recognition only follows upon a turning in one's psyche or consciousness. This reversal/recognition process is symbolically manifested in Romanticism, as Raymond Benoit's *Single Nature's Double Name* (1973) and M. H. Abrams' *Natural Supernaturalism* (1971) suggest. Dorothy Sayers (1949, pp. 25-50) in effect describes how Dante moved into this stage of consciousness as his treatment of Beatrice progressively deepened in his works, and Ruth El Saffar (1984) shows how something similar happened in Cervantes's writing about women. I have suggested that this stage of consciousness is manifested in the rhetoric of certain contemporary women authors: Virginia Woolf, Vivian Gornick, and Sally Quinn (Farrell, 1978-1979).

But while this protracted process of reconciliation with the feminine is potentially liberating, it is also potentially destructive, if one succumbs to the lure of the Great Mother archetype in its life-threatening dimension. The difference between the life-giving and life-threatening dimensions of the feminine can be expressed in imagistic symbols as the difference between Athena and Circe in the *Odyssey;* in Erikson (1963) it is the difference between generativity and stagnation. If the life-giving forces of the feminine gain ascendancy in the psyche, this stage in the struggle for integration can result in great productivity or generativity. However, it need not, as it did not for Oedipus, who succumbed to the life-threatening forces of the feminine and stagnated.

Heilbrun and Singer on Androgyny

Thus, stage seven is androgynous, for in it the masculine ego-consciousness works out a new relationship with the feminine. Literary critic Carolyn Heilbrun's *Toward a Recognition of Androgyny* (1973) and Jungian analyst June Singer's *Androgyny* (1976) are both uneven but still useful studies of a subject that is difficult to discuss sensibly. They are of particular interest here because they presume that a positive relationship with the life-giving dimension of the feminine can be worked out in stage seven, and both authors urge people in contemporary culture to strive to do so.

Heilbrun urges her readers to recognize the heritage of androgyny in Western culture. She turns to Jesus Christ as a model of an androgynous person and looks primarily to his active ministry to make her point. In addition, she identifies certain signs of androgyny in selected women writers and even some men writers from around the end of the eighteenth century onward, although she fails to note the parallel psychologically androgynous movements in the Romantic writers of the same period. The traditional (male) invocation of the Muses in antiquity is a manifestation of psychic androgyny because the female Muses are ostensibly projections from the (male) psyche. The artists who invoked the Muses seem to have been conscious of the fact that creativity is the offspring of the harmonious and androgynous interplay of masculine and feminine in psychic union.[1]

Because Heilbrun focuses on the presence of female protagonists as the sign of androgyny in narratives, she overlooks more complex manifestations of the working out of androgyny in other narratives. In Thomas Hardy's *Far from the Madding Crowd,* for example, not only is Bathsheba somewhat masculine, but Gabriel Oak, who almost rivals Penelope in patient faithfulness, is somewhat feminine. D. H. Lawrence's *Women in Love* is another example of a novel where the development of androgyny is central to the development of both the female and the male characters. In other words, if one takes to heart Heilbrun's exhortation to recognize androgyny in our cultural heritage, one can begin to recognize examples beyond the ones she provides.

Like Herbert Marder (1968) and Nancy Topin Bazin (1973), Heilbrun regards Virginia Woolf and her major works as androgynous, a point Heilbrun treats at length. Woolf formulated explicit ideas about the significance of psychological androgyny in intellectual activity. In *A Room of One's Own,* she cites Shakespeare as an example of an androgynous mind: "The androgynous mind is resonant and porous . . . it transmits emotion without impediment . . . it is naturally creative, incandescent and undivided" (1929, p. 102). Woolf formulated her ideas about psychological androgyny in direct response to Coleridge's observation, "The truth is, a great mind must be androgynous" (1835, p. 153).

Jungians consider feminine and masculine to be fundamental, given orientations in the human psyche, and Singer in *Androgyny* (1976) offers a number of perceptive comments that can amplify the observations Heilbrun, Woolf, and Coleridge offer:

> The key to an understanding of androgyny is the recognition that androgyny is a way of life into which energy can be effectively directed. Androgyny is the act of becoming more conscious and therefore more whole—because only by discovering and rediscovering ourselves in all of our many aspects, do we increase the range and quality of our consciousness (pp. 134-135). . . . [Androgyny is] the rhythmic interplay of Masculine and Feminine within the psyche of one individual (p. 226). . . . In the differentiation of [opposites—initially in Neumann's stage three], the way is opened for the recognition and ultimately for the marriage of the pairs of opposites [in the working out of stage seven] (p. 100). . . . We need to think of ourselves . . . as whole beings in whom the opposite qualities [of Feminine and Masculine] are present (p. 275). . . . [Androgyny involves] working with oneself toward levels of consciousness in which the opposites within one's own being become apparent (p. 323). . . . Androgyny is not trying to manage the relationship between opposites; it is simply flowing between them. (p. 333)

Singer sums up her thoughts about androgyny thus: "Androgyny is the outcome of a dynamism based on the application of energy in an organic system that is open-ended and that interfaces with an open-ended universe" (1976, p. 276).

Androgyny has sometimes been popularly associated with actual bisexuality and/or homosexuality, but the psychologically androgynous person is not necessarily associated with any genital acts. The androgynous person is psychologically bisexual. As Singer suggests, androgyny is primarily an interior process. Furthermore, androgyny characterizes the self-actualization of stage seven. The various adventures of Odysseus after the shipwreck symbolically represent the working out of this stage, which is aptly described by Houston as "meeting the challenge" (1980, p. 29).

Consciousness and Western History

From Antiquity to Romanticism

As noted, Ong (1971, pp. 255-283) attributes the rise of Romanticism and the Industrial Revolution to the deeper interiorization of literacy and literate modes of thought; but he does not indicate explicitly how he would relate Romanticism and the Industrial Revolution to the stages in Neumann's (1954) account of consciousness. However, the studies of Romanticism by Benoit (1973) and Abrams (1971) in effect suggest that the rise of Romanticism marks the movement of Western culture into stage seven of the eight stages of consciousness in Neumann's account—a new relationship with the feminine. Romanticism expressed in words and images a new attitude toward nature, while the Industrial Revolution expressed in action a new relationship with matter. I interpret these new cultural movements as a sign of a new relationship in the human psyche with the feminine.

According to Ong (1977a, pp. 18, 129), Western consciousness moved from the empathetic identification of the knower and the known of primary orality to the distanced and reflective stance of the formal study of rhetoric and logic with the aid of alphabetic literacy. As literacy and literate modes of thought gradually became interiorized, consciousness evolved.

Ong's account of rhetorical/logical culture of the West from ancient Greece through the middle of the eighteenth century corresponds with stages four through six in Neumann's account of consciousness, the formative stages of masculinizing tendencies in the human psyche (which Gilligan, 1982, refers to as separation). In the introduction to Milton's Ramist *Logic,* Ong (1982a, pp. 144-205) points out that formal rhetorical culture in the West began with Aristotle's invention of logic, the handmaid of formal rhetoric. Ong distinguishes between the primal practice of rhetoric in a primary oral culture and the formal art of rhetoric, which was made possible by the development of vowelized literacy and literate modes of thought, even though it involved the residual use of oral modes of thought. Moreover, Ong identifies the formal art of rhetoric with its handmaid logic as stage four in the stages of consciousness described by Neumann, the rise of masculinizing tendencies in consciousness. Ong (1981a) repeatedly notes that masculinizing tendencies are associated with differentiation.

His identification of masculinizing tendencies with differentiation clearly aligns his analysis of literacy as involving diaeresis (1977a, pp. 20-21) as contributing to masculinization, whereas his analysis of primary orality as process-oriented (1967b, pp. 111-138) aligns orality with feminizing tendencies. In effect that which fosters what Gilligan calls separation and independence is masculinizing. That which fosters what she calls attachment and interdependence is feminine in Ong's usage. Orality, the mother tongue, represents nurture, and literacy represents culture of a certain kind. Of course, Ong sees literacy and literate thought as gradually interiorized over the centuries. While Ong refers to manuscript, print, and secondary oral cultures as large "stages" in this interiorization process, he clearly notes (1971, pp. 255-283) that the accrued noetic control associated with the interiorization of literacy reached a new level by the latter part of the eighteenth century. If one allows that Ong's long stage of print culture could be subdivided about that time into two stages and that his long stage of manuscript culture could be subdivided into the classical and the medieval periods, then one would see that the psychohistorical stages identified by Houston (1980) broadly correspond with the psychocultural developments Ong notes. (Houston cites neither Ong's nor Neumann's work.)

Houston implies that she is describing worldwide historical stages of psychic growth, not just stages specific to Western culture. However applicable her stages may be to other world cultures, certain periods of Western culture do broadly fit within her schema: Ancient Hebrew and preclassical Greek culture fit her preindividual stage; classical Greek, ancient Roman, and early Christian cultures, her protoindividual stage (stage four in Neumann); the culture of medieval Europe from about the fall of the Roman empire to about the rise of the Renaissance, her midindividual stage (stage five in Neumann); Western culture from the rise of the Renaissance through the rise of the Enlightenment, her individual stage (stage six in Neumann); and the rise of Romanticism in all its guises down to the present in Western culture, her postindividual stage (stage seven in Neumann).

Historically not that many persons have yet grown into stage eight. Consequently, Houston's psychohistorical schema does not include anything comparable to what Neumann describes as stage eight. The psychohistorical crisis Houston (1980, p. 29) identifies with each stage can be conveniently listed with the numbering system Neumann uses for the stages of consciousness: (stages one through three) birth trauma, leaving the tribe; (four) separation drive of protest, rage; (five) withdrawal and self-mortification; (six) dualism and divisiveness, breakdown of meaning; and (seven) meeting the challenge.

The Nineteenth Century

While there are many dimensions to androgyny in Virginia Woolf's life and work, her explicit comments in *A Room of One's Own* (1929) reveal an awareness of this psychic movement, and she may have sensed the psychohistorical movement towards androgyny (stage seven). Sex-change in Woolf's novel *Orlando* can be seen as a symbolic representation of Western culture's movement from a muscular masculinity coming out of the Renaissance, as Orlando does, and extending through the Enlightenment (stage six) to working out a new relationship with the feminine (stage seven) with the rise of Romanticism around the latter part of the eighteenth century, which is about the time of Orlando's sex-change. As the essays in this collection by David Heckel and Ruth El Saffar suggest, Francis Bacon can be seen as an emblematic figure of the muscular masculinity coming out of the Renaissance. In effect Orlando is a personification of the spirit of Western culture from the Renaissance to the 1920s, when Virginia Woolf wrote *Orlando*.

In this period, classic American philosophy developed. Mary B. Mahowald argues that "crucial insights of American philosophers are the very themes often invoked to describe the special traits of women, as different from men" (1986-1987, p. 410). The special traits frequently attributed to women are "an emphasis on feeling or emotion, devotion to detail and to practical, immediate needs, and orientation toward affiliative ties or relationships" (p. 411). These traits she describes as feminine elements. The contrasting traits frequently attributed to men are "an emphasis on rationality, long-range and abstract concerns, assertiveness and drive for individual success" (p. 411). These traits she describes as masculine. While a Jungian would posit that these feminine and masculine traits can be developed in all persons as they grow toward maturity, Mahowald makes no such assumptions, and so she is surprised to find feminine elements valorized among American philosophers such as James, Peirce, Royce, and Dewey. If "women are more devoted than men to detail, to the concrete than to the abstract," Mahowald reasons, then American philosophy's critique of Cartesian rationalism and emphasis on practicality manifest a feminine orientation:

James describes [his] pragmatic theory of truth [as] consisting of ideas proceeding from experience, dipping forward again into experience as the cycle
continues. Peirce defines belief as the resolution of felt doubt in a decision for
action. Royce distinguishes between internal and external meaning of ideas but
ultimately integrates these through practical purposiveness. And Dewey views
truths and ideas as instrumental, i.e., serving the practical ends of individuals.
(p. 413)

Mahowald is providing data for viewing American pragmatism as an
expression of stage seven of the development of consciousness. The personalism
associated with stage eight carries the concern with particular experience
forward to accentuate the particular person and his or her ability to make
meaningful decisions and to transcend absurdity. Seen from Mahowald's
perspective, American pragmatism seems to foreshadow some of the concerns valorized in twentieth-century personalism. Moreover, her
arguments about considering practicality as a feminine orientation provide an additional way of viewing the practicality of the Industrial Revolution as feminine in orientation, and thus related to the development of
stage seven. Mahowald also calls attention to the influence of American
feminism and of individual women on the formulation of American
pragmatism (pp. 414-416).

To turn to another sign of the shift of consciousness in the nineteenth
century, Ong's observation (1982b, pp. 159-160) about the rise of women
writers after the attenuation of the old rhetorical/logical cultural tradition
calls attention to the growing influence of women in cultural developments
in what he styles the Age of Austen. In another way, what Ann Douglas (1977)
describes as the feminization of nineteenth-century American culture also
calls attention to the influence of women. Consequently, the various signs of
a contemporary working out of a new relationship with the feminine can be
seen as the culmination and popularization of the evolution in Western
consciousness that started two centuries ago. Moreover, this very popularization may presage further development toward the fully individuated personalism of stage eight. Neumann does imply that the movement from the
formative stages of consciousness (four through six) to the integrative stages
(seven and eight) is more difficult than the movement from stage seven to
stage eight. Even so, reaching stage eight is not easy. If this relationist
analysis is correct, however, these developments suggest why Ong views
the emergence of secondary orality today with hope.

Stage Eight: Ego-Integrity

If the psychic movement into stage seven is like a Copernican revolution in the psyche, then the subsequent turn into the transcendence of stage eight is like the discovery that there are galaxies other than the one in which the earth, sun, and moon are located. The rise of what Ong calls personalism in real (as distinct from symbolic representations of) life involves wedding one's energies to God or some transcendent being or principle such as love or truth. Jung refers to this as *hieros gamos,* a holy wedding, and it is something quite other than a wish-fulfillment. Nor is it uroboric or self-indulgent. This holy wedding serves to direct one's energies more fully toward a higher goal in life than one's own solipsistic gratification. It is subject-oriented without being subjectivistic.

Whereas working out a new relationship in the psyche with the life-giving feminine can result in the type of generativity that Abraham Maslow (1971, pp. 41-52) terms self-actualization, the fuller integrative working out of the individuation process in stage eight involves what Maslow calls transcendence and what Roberto Assogioli (1965) refers to as self-realization. Self-realization or transcendence requires the consciously willed wedding of self to the transcendent, and for this marriage to endure and grow one must continually exercise will to keep it intact. In short, while symbolic representations of the achievement of personalism might be presented as a single dramatic act or struggle, repeated acts of will are necessary to sustain the integrity of self in stage eight in actual life. Despite the necessity of consciously enacting acts of the will, however, willfulness is not characteristic of personalism. Willfulness, such as Oedipus' murderous insistence on his having the right of way on the road, is probably the sort of assertiveness that Mary Lynn Broe (1980, p. 21) and other feminists find ludicrous.

The movement through stage seven eventually culminates in a crucible, a deathly struggle, which marks the psyche's movement into stage eight. Houston, in her review of literature, notes that stage eight as Erikson describes it is the arena for a crisis between wise integrity and bitter despair: "If integral mastery is gained, then the person is truly in a golden age, one in which all the previous stages are consummated in his being, and he knows himself one with self, his environment, and his life" (1980, p. 24). Augustine's *Confessions* is the record of one man's struggle for integral mastery; the famous scene with his mother in the garden presumably marks the culmination of stage seven in his life, and his writing of his *Confessions* presumably marks his successful negotiation of the crucible of dying to the old man and putting on the new to enter stage eight. Erikson would say that women and men need to experience such a stage of growth, as the stories of Pysche and Osiris suggest.

In Erikson's abstract language this later struggle in the integration process is between integrity and despair (disintegration). Personalism or full individuation arises with the rise of integrity. But this involves dying to one's old self and rising to new life. This deathly crucible is symbolically represented in the story of Psyche, as Johnson suggests (1986), although he does not develop the point. In Psyche's fourth task, she undertakes the risky journey into the underworld, returns, and then awakens to new life. Her awakening represents the freeing of the captive (her sleeping self) and the liberation of Psyche into new life. In concrete and symbolic language this movement is also enacted when Odysseus the king-come-back-as-a-beggar returns to his true identity (comparable to Psyche's awakening after her return) by taking up the bow and the position that are rightly his. When Odysseus overcomes the forces within the kingdom that are devouring it (which I take to symbolize the need all of us have of right-ordering the appetites, disordered affections, and potencies within ourselves by cultivating the quaternity of cardinal virtues of temperance, fortitude, prudence, and justice), he carries out his rightful responsibility and achieves integrity of self. Significantly, the stories of both Psyche and Odysseus show the awakening of new life as following a visit to the underworld, which probably symbolizes a deep reflection on one's own life such as Augustine manifests in his *Confessions*.

Conclusion

Secondary orality appears to foster psychic androgyny. While Woolf (1929) and Coleridge (1835) agree that a great mind must be androgynous and that Shakespeare is an example, becoming androgynous is no guarantee of becoming a great mind. Nevertheless, the apparent interrelationship of greatness and androgyny calls attention to the promise of our contemporary secondary oral culture. According to Maurice B. McNamee (1960), the quest for greatness or magnanimity has been a perennial concern of Western culture. Secondary oral culture seems to have brought with it the psychological conditions for the rise of magnanimity or greatness on a scale unprecedented in Western culture. While we may not be heading for a perfect state of existence, the potential for human flourishing is greater than ever before.

Elsewhere in this collection Noël M. Valis notes that Romanticism is associated with pure interiority. Indeed, the freeing of endogamous kinship libido, in stage seven, is a purely interior process. The categories developed by Thomas Patrick Malone and Patrick Thomas Malone for describing the human person might further elucidate the difference between stages seven and eight. They distinguish the *I*, the *me,* and the *self* as constitutive aspects of each person, which they claim are different from Freud's id, ego, and superego (1987, pp. 30-46, esp. p. 32). To use terminology employed by David Payne elsewhere in this collection, the *I* is outer-directed; the *me,* inner-directed; and the *self,* other-directed. As noted, Ong associates the development of inner-directedness in Western culture with the interiorization of literacy and literate modes of thought. This development proceeds through stages four to six of consciousness, culminating in the pure interiority of stage seven. The movement into stage seven involves fully discovering *me.* Being conditioned by the regression to the unconscious, as Roger Silverstone suggests television conditions people, would enable individuals to move into stage seven when they are psychologically ready to do so.

The movement into stage eight involves discovering the *self,* which entails overcoming alienation from one*self* and others and thereby developing human authenticity. The joyousness that Valis notes in the dying words of Fortunata and in Ong's writing from *The Presence of the Word* (1967b) onward is the expression of the deep self-acceptance experienced in stage eight. Psychic conversion develops in its fullness in stage eight. Lonergan (1972, 1991) has formulated the self-affirming precepts that people need to follow to move into and live in the transcendence of stage eight: Be Attentive, not inattentive, to the data of empirical consciousness, including not only sensory data but also the data of imagination and feelings; Be Intelligent, not stupid, in considering alternative interpretations and explanations of the data of empirical consciousness; Be Reasonable, not silly, in affirming our judgments about what is; Be Responsible, not irresponsible, in the actions that arise from our empirical, intelligent, and rational levels of consciousness; and Be in Love, not the opposites, when we use our empirical, intelligent, rational, and existential levels of consciousness.

The self-affirming precept to Be in Love has priority over the other four precepts in moving us toward transcendence, because if we are not in love, why would we bother to be responsible, reasonable, intelligent, or attentive? When we avoid the contrary of love (indifference) and the contradictory (hate), then following the precept to Be in Love will lead us to want to Be Responsible, Be Reasonable, Be Intelligent, and Be Attentive, because they are the ways to actuate love in our lives. Thus, the reason for following the other four precepts is not simply to avoid being irresponsible, foolish, stupid, or inattentive but to find love as fully as possible in every act.

Similarly, there is a hierarchy of priority among the other four precepts. If we are not trying to Be Responsible, why would we bother to be reasonable, intelligent, or attentive? If we are not trying to Be Reasonable, why would we bother to be intelligent or attentive? If we are not trying to Be Intelligent, why would we bother to be attentive? In other words, we try to Be Attentive so that we can be intelligent. We try to Be Intelligent so that we can be reasonable. We try to Be Reasonable so that we can be responsible. We try to Be Responsible so that we can be in love. And we try to Be in Love so that we can experience the joy of living that accompanies the experience of self-transcendence.

Although Ong does not explicitly refer to the emergence of cosmopolis envisioned by Doran in his synthesis of Lonergan's work with the work of Jung and Voegelin (1990, pp. 355-386), the hope Ong sees for contemporary culture implicitly anticipates the emergence of cosmopolis. As Doran explains, people need to develop world-cultural consciousness for cosmopolis to emerge fully in the world (pp. 527-558). People in stages seven and eight are more likely to lead the full development of world-cultural consciousness than are people in stages four through six. That is certainly a good reason to see hope in the rise of secondary oral culture, as Ong does.

Note

1. In *Fighting for Life,* Ong cites Sandra Gilbert's work and observes that "feminine creativity would seem to be more unisex than masculine creativity is, to seek its inspiration not in the opposite sex but in women's world" (1981a, p. 115). Even so, feminine creativity probably proceeds from psychic androgyny.

14

Discourse, Difference, and Gender: Walter J. Ong's Contributions to Feminist Language Studies

C. JAN SWEARINGEN

A woman must not practice argument: this is dreadful. To be ruled by a woman is the ultimate outrage for a man.

—*Democritus of Abdera, 420 BCE*

Recent feminist scholarship on gender and language has generated a debate about the merits of studying gender differences in language. To study differences, some propose, is to perpetuate them; we cannot study the differences of the present without examining them through the distorting lenses of centuries-old, biased definitions of masculine and feminine (Epstein, 1988). To avoid the study of difference entirely, however, seems an act of willful ignorance, even if the avoidance is justified as an interregnum between the categories of the past and the yet-to-be-defined categories of the future. Walter J. Ong's contributions to the study of gender and language both complement and supplement the work of feminist scholars who are forging a middle ground in this debate. His rhetorical, psychosocial, and literary analyses of the links among ceremonial contest, argument, rhetoric, logic, and linear, argumentative text conventions illuminate the tenacity with which men have defended their control over these central and privileged Western discourse paradigms. In the history of women's exclusion from academic training in Latin, argument, and logic, Ong identifies paradoxes that deserve further study, such as the prominence of women as vernacular literary authors in the rise of the modern novel (1982b, pp. 159-160). His social history of classical discourse patterns as male-controlled, and his psychological profile of the importance of these patterns to masculine identity define numerous directions for further analyses of the evolving and recursive relationships among the identities, roles, and language of men and women.

The Debate Within Feminist Language Studies

Among feminist scholars a widening gap separates those who support the ongoing study of gender differences in language and those who propose a moratorium on such studies until the terms of the comparison can be thoroughly overhauled (Elshtain, 1986; Hill, 1986, esp. chap. 1; Illich, 1982, pp. 132-139; Poynton, 1989; Rosenthal, 1983). The debate now extends to cover not only the study of language differences but also comparative studies of reasoning ability, moral decision-making, and "logical aptitude" (Gilligan, 1982; Miller, 1986). Like those sociolinguists concerned with cultural bias in IQ tests, feminists want to reshape the measures and methods used in comparative gender studies before any more misleading comparisons are conducted (Belenky, Clinchy, Goldberger, & Tarule, 1986; Epstein, 1988; Gilligan, 1982; Kittay & Meyers, 1986). Critics of comparative studies such as Robin Lakoff's *Language and Woman's Place* (1975) that are said to be polarizing and methodologically unsound warn that to isolate, describe, and define differences between male and female discourse patterns only perpetuates the perception and stigmatization of those female patterns of speech and thought as "outside" the mainstream of privileged and traditionally valued forms. Woman always ends up being the exception to an implicitly and often explicitly male norm, the other, the aberrant, the unknown "dark continent" of Freud's metaphor. Jean Bethke Elshtain criticizes the language of feminist theory itself. She proposes that feminist "narratives" of gender differences can create "lock-step sexual scripts" in which women are depicted as "prisoners of gender, caught in the snare of a systemic *sex-gender system*" (Elshtain, 1986, pp. 5-7). Gender lurks just beneath the surface, and sometimes on the surface, of much language. What is lacking is an acceptable methodology for defining the issues that should direct the ongoing appraisal of gender difference. Ostensibly "neutral" forms are imposed on—or are available to—all of us. Yet even in these forms, "consistently, male speech dominates" (Illich, 1982, p. 136). Thus, in the ostensibly neutral language of the academy, women continue to be studied as outsiders, to be viewed by women and men alike as "objects." They seldom speak as subjects *in* an authentic voice, and of a differently constituted object. Difference compounds and cements difference, creating a new gender prison house of language.

An alternative position is taken by feminists who promote complementary, revisionist studies of male and female discourse and reasoning patterns (see Illich, 1982, pp. 61-62). Carol Gilligan's *In a Different Voice* both defends and exemplifies such an approach and has been widely received as a groundbreaking prolegomenon for redefining and studying male and female patterns of identity formation, reasoning, and articulation. Single norm developmental approaches might have been simpler, but Gilligan adroitly explains how they insidiously yield polarized results. Instead, Gilligan defines multivariable, revisionist categories for appraising the stages in identity formation and male and female patterns of moral reasoning that are the vehicle for these stages and for evaluating them alongside one another.

Unlike Lakoff, who examines why women's language is deemed inferior by male standards, Gilligan reassesses the language and thought of each gender as having distinctive limits and merits. The feminine "ethic of care," she proposes, should be reconciled with the masculine "logic of justice" so that men and women alike can move toward "a greater understanding of both points of view and thus to a greater convergence in judgment" (1982, p. 167). *In a Different Voice* provides an extended review of traditional appraisals of gender differences in the language and reasoning of moral decision-making, but also reevaluates the traditional findings that "women perceive and construe social reality differently from men" and that "these differences center around experiences of attachment and separation" (1982, p. 171). Because women's sense of their own reality has not had a voice, Gilligan proposes to hear the different voice, the values of care and attachment it defends, and the logic of interdependence rather than autonomy that it defines. Instead of positing two different and mutually exclusive modes, Gilligan goes on to define "a more complex rendition of human experience which sees the truth of separation and attachment in the lives of women and men and recognizes how these truths are carried by different modes of thought and language" (p. 174). Along with other revisionist feminist scholars, Gilligan is building a new set of terms and methodologies that facilitate the observation of integrity and validity of women's thought and language in its own terms instead of viewing them as deviant or deficient when measured by male norms. "The parameters of the female's development are not the same as the male's [separation, dominance, and subordination], and the same terms do not apply" (Miller, 1986, p. 86).

Like recent feminist scholars whose revisionist methods emphasize complementarity rather than polarized comparative rankings, Ong's work has for decades focused on interrelations among gender, language, consciousness, and culture. Though sometimes interpreted as a lament for the passing of an all-male, Latin-based, agonistic academic environment (George, 1979, pp. 864-865), Ong's work provides extensive descriptions of that world from which women were so long excluded. Of most value, perhaps, are Ong's many hypotheses concerning the effects of this exclusion on women, on men, and on the evolution of consciousness. As a historian of consciousness, Ong identifies as one of his primary subjects the ongoing "male-female dialectic," the evolving "syntheses of masculine and feminine" (1981a, p. 208). Unlike many male scholars, Ong repeatedly and pointedly addresses gender issues tied to the history of Western education and logic, the development of literature, and the psychology of identity formation. The male need for separation and differentiation from the feminine world of the mother and the mother tongue, he proposes, explains the prominence of argument and disputation as distinctly male forms of ceremonial combat, which, he proposes, functioned as puberty rites and bonding rituals in the old masculine academic world.

By identifying traditional modes of rhetoric, argument, and logic as historically male puberty rites, as agonistic, and as instruments of masculine separation from the maternal and from the feminine world, Ong helps explain the stubbornness with which men have excluded women from academia. With the entrance of women into academia, "something had happened to the previously ascendant masculinity of academia—and of course to femininity as well" (1974a, pp. 10-11). More recently, Ong proposes, the women's liberation movement marks the "emergence of a female identity crisis," but along with it has come "an even more intense male identity crisis" (1974a, p. 11; 1981a, pp. 147-148). By examining the gender ties of older discourse modes and uses Ong uncovers the pointedly male, and defensive, psychology that for centuries led men not only to exclude women from training in argumentation, from academia, and from Latin study but also to maintain that women were incapable of these modes of thought and language.

Lalling and Logic, Mother Tongue and Latin Text

Ong's account of the ties among the vernacular, the oral noetic, and the mother tongue focuses on the exclusion of women from training in rhetoric, logic, and Latin. The social history of these correspondences he supplements with appraisals of the psychic importance of the mother as the child's first interlocutor. "It is the mother or surrogate mother who by continual contact during the lalling stage converts the infant into a user of words" (1977a, p. 25). It is the mother's language that first gives the child its own tongue and then provides the paradigm against which children come to define their separate linguistic identities. Ong proposes that this alternating participation and differentiation is an ongoing process not only in the development of the individual but also in the ongoing development of consciousness as well. "A longstanding tradition treats the 'eating' of the written word, a metaphor for understanding, assimilating, taking into oneself. This rather than visual imaging represents the process by which the written word becomes truly oral again, thereby alive and real, entering into human consciousness and living there" (1977a, p. 24). Ong links the literary and linguistic practices of women to social roles and to psychic structures that at least appear to have been shaped by those social roles. Any methodology that gives social roles deterministic control over psychic structure and identity is highly problematic (Ortner, 1974, pp. 67-71). But it is equally foolhardy to contend that there is no relation between the two.

Ong's analysis creates much-needed methodological diversity and heuristic room for expansion in this polarized field of inquiry. The appraisal of the mother tongue as both a psychic structure and a social fact draws on psychology, sociobiology, and literary history (1981a, pp. 36-37; 1977a, pp. 22-34; 1974a, pp. 5-7). Likewise, it establishes numerous connections among the "natural" spoken word, the fact that the mother's is the first word; the associations among mother nature, nurture, and mothers; and the forces that alienate the psyche from its "linguistic motherland" (1981a, p. 38). A literal interpretation of Ong's experiential, symbolic, and metaphoric associations has drawn feminist objections on a number of points. In a cross-cultural anthropological study, Sherry B. Ortner documents the near-universal association of women with nature. Like Lakoff and Gilligan, Ortner finds this association problematic because it implies the belief that women do what they do by "instinct," that is, by "nature." Consequently, she proposes, what women do is seen as reflexive rather than intentional and is therefore held in lower regard. "Herein lies a paradox, for the very traits that traditionally have defined the 'goodness' of women, their care for and sensitivity to the needs of others, are those that mark them as deficient" (Gilligan, 1982, p. 18). Lakoff (1975), Ortner (1974), Gilligan (1982), and Miller (1986) show how politeness, care, and patience place women in the double bind of being punished for their definitive, "unique" virtues, partly because they are believed to be instinctual—mindless "nature" rather than choices born of careful thought and disciplined will.

The association among woman, mother, and nature is problematic for all the reasons feminists cite and tenacious for reasons that Ong, alongside many feminists, analyzes in depth. His account has been faulted for focusing on traditional gender roles and for seeming to lament their passing (George, 1979; Gilbert & Gubar, 1987). "Women" and "mother," in Ong's discourse, are too quickly and too often read literally as carrying Ong's ideological imprimatur instead of as readings of psychological categories and culture-wide symbols that have been important to the perpetuation of cultural dominance by males. Indeed, Ong's analysis illuminates the extent to which agonistic and argumentative categories of thought and language may be culturally and psychosocially restricted to males more singularly than has been acknowledged prior to his forays into gender-symbol-language inter-sections.

With considerable detail and cross-referencing to Freud and Erikson, Ong links the mother's symbolic function in early identity formation to questions of language (1967b, pp. 92-110; 1981a, pp. 188-209). "The language in which we grow up comes primarily from our mother but also belongs to some degree intrinsically to our mother's feminine world" (1977a, p. 23). Insofar as this is an important context of early identity formation and language use, Ong proposes that when we begin to "manipulate" language on our own, a certain alienation begins to occur, an alienation that is both good and bad, essential to identity formation yet also a separation from the comfort and security of nurture and continuity (1977a, pp. 22-34; 1981a, pp. 150-158). Beyond a certain point, autonomy, separation, and self have divergent importance for the psyche and consciousness of both men and women (1967b, pp. 92-110; 1974a, pp. 7-11; 1981a, pp. 188-209). Ong joins feminists in calling for further study of the points of intersection and diverg-ence in these developmental models and in promoting—as does Gilligan—research based on complementarity, an ever-changing "dialectic of mascu-line and feminine" (1974a, p. 8). Psychoanalytic concepts of development need revision to accommodate such study: "What we need is a phenomeno-logy of psychoanalytic concepts and then a phenomenology of phenomenological concepts" (1967b, p. 110).

If aligned with feminist studies of differences between masculine and feminine concepts of identity and self, Ong's work provides additional evidence of the male bias in most models of psychic and cognitive develop-ment, a bias that has stimulated the development of alternative models such as Gilligan's and Miller's. Ong proposes that from classical times, "the agonistic academic tradition has been structured by masculine needs" (1974a, p. 6). The Western academic tradition evolved out of classical rhetoric, a system of ritual ceremonial argumentation that early on was restricted to males. Oral rhetorical debate was supplanted gradually by logic and textuality; the "decay" of the *viva voce* "dialogue" that occurs when two persons argue was superseded by two views juxtaposed in a *disputatio,* which, though delivered orally in its original setting, controlled, contained, and internalized—within both psyche and text—the older agon (1958a, pp. 9-11, 195). Finally, Ong proposes, the interiorization of that textualized logic led to the "demise of the Muses, the projections of the male psyche concerned with generating its 'brain children' " (1967b, p. 252), and to the "atrophy of Latin as a sex-linked language" (1982b, p. 112). These changes set the stage for the Romantic conception of literary composition as creative and self-expressive rather than mimetic of both martial and verbal wrangling, and as an organic construction. Ong proposes that these changes marked, and were perhaps shaped by, "women's presence on the scene" (1967b, p. 253).

Fighting for Life and Fighting to Kill: Gender and Argument

Beginning with his study of Ramus (1958a), Ong has repeatedly drawn attention to the agonistic structures that have shaped academic discourse and traced their parallels to male verbal contests, ceremonial displays, bonding rituals, and puberty rites. His explicit and persistent attention to the ties between formal academic discourse and gender concomitantly revises cognate histories of argument and logic. Ong's analysis reveals the extent to which ostensibly neutral academic-discourse paradigms have been shaped by longstanding ties among gender, argument, and a male-dominated academia. Paradoxically, it is the history of the evolution of argument and logic that tends to provoke the most unease among feminists because it has seemed to suggest—much like cognate appraisals of Black English speakers—that women are either incapable of or uninterested in argument and logic, the undeniable mainstays of Western academic discourse. "But as folklore has it, 'women fight to kill'" (Ong, 1974a, p. 9). "Fighting by females is more straightforward, less spectacular, less 'abstract' and, when full blown, likely to be more lethal" (1974a, p. 10). Traditional male oral combat—argument, rhetorical display, the *miles gloriosus* tradition—is ceremonial. "Words can't really kill; so long as people keep talking they are still in contact" (1974a, p. 9). "So strong is the male bonding motive" that mortal enemies can become close friends after engaging in such ceremonial moots, carefully defined by rules much like those that only allow tackling within the boundaries of the playing field (1974a, p. 9). But "the *femme fatale* is lethal" (1974a, p. 10).

Many women, and academic feminists in particular, have understandable reservations about these definitions of argument as an exclusive male pre-serve. Masculinizing argument, and invoking folklore to do so, seems a double insult. It is one thing for Robin Lakoff to cite such stereotypes in a criticism of prejudices against women. It is quite another for a male to invoke them in an ambivalently neutral account of the history of argumentation. Yet feminist scholars can profitably acknowledge and then examine the origins— the partial if distorted "truth"—of Ong's portraits of women in verbal and symbolic combat. The notion that words cannot "kill," for example, may be both literally and metaphorically true. But without a heritage of using words with the assumption that they can't kill, women, and extra-academic men as well, have on occasion used words, like looks, to kill. It is not entirely false to say that "when women fight, they fight to kill," and that they resort to such fighting only under duress. Janet Lever's (1976, 1978) and Shirley Brice Heath's (1983) studies of cross-cultural gender differences in childhood games document conflict avoidance and consensus seeking among girls, and "play" fights among boys. Ceremonial fighting, verbal or otherwise, strikes many women as silly. Consensus seeking and compromise are often regarded by men as weak.

In *The Portrait of the Artist as a Young Man,* James Joyce depicts the artist as one who must survive through "silence, exile, and cunning." These traits of retreat, hiding, guile, and discreet silence have been developed by women as linguistic strategies. Joyce's association of silence, exile, and cunning with the "outsider" artist has been viewed as a mark of his androgyny (Heilbrun, 1973) insofar as silence, exile, and cunning have also been associated with the linguistic and social behavior of women as depicted in literary and cultural representations (Ellman, 1982).

Ong contends that between men, between women, and perhaps most notably between a woman and a man, it is silence, however hostile, rather than argument, that is the final "word" or the unceremonial end: "So long as people keep talking they are still in contact" (1974a, p. 9). And, "ceremonial combat among all species is male" (1974a, p. 9). Lakoff and Gilligan note the demeaning responses women receive for their "politeness" and for their silence, a silence that is as often offered in a spirit of receptivity and conciliation as in hostility. Receptivity and the silence of hostility get confused; the silence of deference, likewise, is seen as weakness of thought or character even when it is intended as a gesture of willingness to agree, find common ground, reconcile. Paradoxically, when a woman does argue, she is often seen as hostile, strident, or irrational; providing further evidence that women never were and still are not "in the game." Ong's forthright acknowledgment of these ties between gender and argumentation is far from a claim that women cannot or do not argue. Rather, it furthers the analysis of formal, academically structured argumentation as a decidedly gender-linked practice. One question that remains is what men and women have done with argumentation, for better or worse.

In seventeenth-century colonial Mexico, Sor Juana Ines de la Cruz (1651-1695), a self-educated nun, wrote literary and theological works prodigiously until she was warned by her bishop that her works were causing her danger. Her response, *La Respuesta* (1982), is a noteworthy example of carefully crafted argument and literary irony. (As Ruth El Saffar notes elsewhere in this collection, Alison Weber, 1990, examines in detail how Teresa of Avila employed her rhetorical skills differently in dealing with members of her own order and ecclesiastical and civil authorities.) Similarly, Sojourner Truth's "And Ain't I a Woman?" manifests superb logical and rhetorical craft, even though she learned no Latin and even less Greek. Moreover, Heath's examination of differences between the socialization of male and female black children provides a long-needed supplement to the study of black male contest rituals such as fliting and playing the dozens. Heath notes that, before the age of two, girls are not reinforced for conversational interaction. Unlike boys, they are not tolerated when they interrupt the conversational interactions of adults or when they imitate adult (male) ritual "challenge" patterns (1983, p. 96). When they do try to participate they "are either ignored or told 'Go 'way, gal, what you think you doin'?' " (p. 96). Heath notes, however, that girls develop contentious verbal behavior in a different and exclusively female register, "fussing" (pp. 95- 103). "Young girls have to learn to be 'fussers,' because if they do not, they cannot be expected to be good 'mammas,' able to protect their rights in the neighborhood" (p. 96).

Ong's forthright tracing of the links between gender and verbal contest patterns facilitates a synthesis between studies of many forms of verbal contest that evolve without formal school instruction, and the schooled and unschooled practices of contest and argument that reveal notable gender differences. Women fight but restrict their fighting to "serious" rather than "abstract" or "ritual" situations. Their avoidance of, or perhaps their succumbing to social constraints on them to avoid, "display" verbal fighting remains pervasive enough to explain the persisting stereotype of women who use words and not just looks to kill. That stereotype is defensibly the product of a male point of view, for reasons that Ong deftly surveys. "Antifeminism is most virulent among males. It is intimately associated with verbal performance, oral and literary, and with intellectual and academic activity, and is tied into male insecurity" (1981a, p. 70). Men, he proposes, must manufacture strife to establish their identity, an identity defined in significant part by differentiation from the feminine, hence the "irrational" resistance to women's entrance into the socio-academic realms of argument and debate.

Women are (at least in some men's perceptions) self-contained, complete in a way men are not or do not feel themselves to be, due to their inability to give birth or perhaps due to their need to separate. "Woman is interiority, self possession" (1981a, p. 90). Finally, Ong asserts, men seek an all-male refuge because:

> women know too much about secrets already. [They] must be kept away from the strictly masculine affairs so that the confected male secrets can be protected from disclosure and ridicule. For, deep down, the men know that they have no real secrets at all and, to make it worse, suspect that the women know it too. (p. 91)

Ong notes that discourse patterns of argumentation ebb and flow. Once available, they are never completely gone; furthermore, they are always changing. The rhetorics of women's liberation and black rights from the late 1960s to the mid-1970s, he notes, were adversarial, and contentious, concerned with the same "esteem building that was at work in the old agon; the functions of rhetorical contest are central to contemporary consciousness" (1981a, pp. 204-205). The spontaneous, natural, and untutored argument of women and men alike proliferates, suggesting the need for ever more precise studies of how much argument is a result of training and how much its effect, likewise, requires special orientation or formal instruction on the part of the hearer or reader. It is probable, for example, that Sor Juana's bishop would have appreciated both the rhetorical and the literary art of her *Respuesta*. It is much less likely that Sojourner Truth's audience, if they even thought of themselves as an audience, would have been counting tropes and good examples. Survival takes a different kind of attention; Sojourner Truth was fighting to kill, in order to stay alive.

Ong emphasizes that the paradigms of autonomy, control, agonistic logic and argumentation, and alienation accorded positive or inevitable value are Western school traditions and represent, in part, formalizations of masculine identity; at the same time they have shaped masculine concepts of identity because for so long they were paradigmatic in all-male settings. This second proviso helps in the construction of a way out of the impasse that is created when it is claimed that all argument, logic, or rationality is "male," an impasse that has created several unfortunate lines of polarized argument in current debates about gender. Defenses of these modes as male, or Western, and right nonetheless have resulted in *loci communes* whose import is that you will learn to do it our way or not at all; or, in a more patronizing version, "here, we will help you do it our way." Alternately, feminist resistance to "male" modes of thought and discourse have resulted in equally reductive and dangerous abandonments of any and all rationality simply because it is "male." Contemporary East German novelist Christa Wolf expresses "a genuine horror at that critique of rationalism which itself ends in reckless irrationalism" (1983/1984, p. 260). She readily concurs that it was "dreadful, shameful, and scandalous" that for centuries women were not allowed to contribute to culture, and proposes that this fact "is, strictly speaking, the weak point of culture, which leads to its becoming self-destructive—namely, its inability to grow up" (p. 260). Yet, she warns,

> it does not make it any easier to achieve maturity if a masculinity mania is replaced by a femininity mania, and if women throw over the achievements of rational thought simply because men produced them, in order to substitute an idealization of prerational stages in human history. The tribe, the clan, blood-and-soil—these are not values to which men and women of today can adhere. We Germans, of all people, should know that these catchwords can supply pretexts for hideous regressions. (p. 260)

Wolf's rebuke is a fittingly austere reminder of the dangers run by reductive polarizations, and employs the language of psychological development in a manner that, like Ong's uses of the same paradigm, proposes parallels between the evolution of cultures and of individuals. Though this parallel cannot be taken too literally, it is a way of seeing paradigms of thought, language, self, and identity alongside one another in heuristic analogies. Just as "male" should not be reductively linked to all rational thought as a grounds for its abandonment, obsessive male control over rational and cultural discourse should not be sustained, for this constitutes a masculinity mania, a fear of the Other, unease with proximity to the other, the mother, the feminine.

The Literate Self and Its Voice

Much like Ong, Gilligan has often been taken as a literalist and reductive dichotomizer, but her work promotes complementary modes of thought and language, a broadening of available resources for men and women alike that can be brought about when both women and men accept several alternate paths for reasoning, speaking, writing, and forming identity. If read carefully, her work provides needed appraisals of the logic behind what she terms the feminine "ethic of care." Through citations of her subjects' discourse she demonstrates that the moral reasoning of women is at times more complex, because multivariable, than some applications of the single-rule "logic of justice"—the more typical male mode. Similarly, the mature women interviewed in her study, though they did not satisfy the requirements of complete autonomy and independent postconventional thought central to conventional measures of emotional and psychological maturity, were articulate in self-reflexivity and self-reflectiveness. They go back and scan the stages in the formation of their mature whole current identity, the stages in life's way, to adopt Kierkegaard's phrase. They reflect with great care and detail on their choices, and the peace made with their most difficult decisions, including the decision to be a certain kind of self, to form a certain kind of identity. The elements in their thinking that did not measure up to the conventional psychological standards of total autonomy, separation, and independent postconventional thinking are expressed most amply in the self-descriptions of professional women in their 40s who, even though highly successful and satisfied in their professional work, defined the quality and sustainment of their relationships with friends and family as singularly definitive of their sense of identity. Their sense of self was based in ongoing relationships, in participatory and mutually sustaining identity rather than in autonomy and independence. Gilligan emphasizes the continuity of this value in girls and women in her study in order to correct the bias toward autonomy that she finds problematic in conventional measures of psychic health and maturity.

The parallel to discourse modes is most readily observable in the comparable emphasis given independent and original thought and in constructing an argument that "stands on its own" in most school writing. It is particularly difficult for many women to argue against the view of another for pedagogical purposes, not only because it seems an empty exercise but because it violates the "ethic of care" that forbids doing or saying something that will harm another. There are ways of presenting the value of logic and argumentation that do not require arguing against, particularly when arguing against is a classroom exercise. At the same time, the importance of boys' tendencies to play games of differentiation entailing lengthy disputes about rules cannot be ignored. Gilligan proposes that both gender paradigms are needed and worthwhile, and that overly rigid gender identity patterns can be diversified to encourage boys' sustaining of an ethic of care that teaches them to think in terms of the other's point of view, and to encourage girls to learn paradigms of abstract rules and logic as valuable in some circumstances.

Ong stands beside and not against feminist scholars who are working out revisionist approaches to Western cultural history (cf. Gilbert & Gubar, 1987, pp. 227-271). The ways in which Latin or academic discourses supplant and deliberately distance speakers and writers from their vernacular and mother tongues have been given painstaking attention, particularly within Ong's ongoing defenses of literacy and its modes of alienation as psychically valuable, not because inevitable, as some contemporary theory would have it, but because they provide the basis for evolving living discourses and for change and growth in models of identity. Ong has constructed "a model of orality that can stand alongside the Derridean constellation of qualities and attitudes associated with writing in its explicitness and comprehensiveness" (Sussman, 1989, p. 215). His sustained exposition of the value of orality, the vernacular, and the mother tongue not only stands alongside deconstruction's powerful dismantlings of textuality. The appraisal of orality and literacy as a complementarity proposes that we can only say "language speaks us" in the ongoing and self-perpetuating activity "we speak language."

The examination of any deep psychic structure such as gender makes it likely that "you will get your knuckles rapped no matter how you handle the subject" (Ong, 1979a, p. 872). Knuckles have been rapped and will no doubt be rapped again. After the ritual denunciations are done, feminists can continue to find in Ong's work a male scholar's insightful and suggestive historical and hypothetical forays into the domain of the masculine and feminine in language. Virginia Woolf's *A Room of One's Own* documents the social and educational settings that until recently restricted feminists to overhearing, guessing at, or, at worst, projecting what a masculine voice says or might say about feminine and masculine "voice." Ong's work boldly discloses a male voice speaking of masculine and feminine in issues of language and gender. Though the author's gender may always be a fiction, Ong has been unafraid to speak as a male, of masculine patterns, to the greater good of all of us.

15

Characterology, Media, and Rhetoric

DAVID PAYNE

Media structures and characteristics shape the most fundamental elements of our social and individual identities. Any medium creates technical possibilities for and favors certain techniques for knowing, internalizing, and expressing human character. Media technology, in a general sense as a technology of language and symbols, gives rise to modes of being and doing that are codified in the rhetoric of character operating at given points in a culture's evolution.

Contemporary rhetoric reflects a preoccupation with character in both theory and practice. We contend issues of moral, social, ethnic, national, corporate, and, especially, individual character. Whether interest is expressed in changing ethical practices of public discourse or in devising techniques of effective image maintenance, such concerns involve questions about the formation, propriety, functions, and execution of character in ethical choices and communicative acts. At the same time, significant strains of social philosophy, theory, and criticism have turned to analysis of public discourse and its role in socialization and preservation of human values (e.g., Bellah, Madsen, Sullivan, Swidler, & Tipton, 1985; MacIntyre, 1984). The widespread concern for symbolism of character and the role of public discourse informs our efforts at moral understanding, social engineering and reform, political and commercial advertisement, socialization and education, and the therapeutic practices of institutions and individuals.

The preoccupation with the rhetoric of character embodies a call for theoretical and technical knowledge about the psychosocial and interactive processes that undergird identity formation and maintenance (Baumeister, 1986). Attention to the symbolism and communication of identity suggests the presence of an active rhetorical technology, one that attempts to achieve the diverse ends of social persuasion while preserving the aims of individual autonomy and self-determinism of private character (Payne, 1989).

In speaking to the characterological concerns of individuals through the language of self-stylized identity, contemporary social practice rests its hopes of moral, political, and even economic sustenance on the prevailing drama- tism of individual character. The rhetorical technology whereby we attend to individual character is manifest in symbolization, narrative contextualiza- tion, and dramatic display of personal identity. These rhetorical features constitute important components of a characterology that has its roots in the dominant communication media of society. Walter J. Ong has offered a perspective on the evolution of culture and individual consciousness through communication media that enables us to understand the historical dimension of this characterological rhetoric. His contribution to understanding the relationships among media, character, and social structure is the subject of this essay.

The Characterological Concern

David Riesman's (1950) groundbreaking description of the relationship between character and social processes provides an excellent analysis toward which one may point the relevance of media and their role in developing individual consciousness. Riesman identified historical shifts between cultures of tradition-directed, inner-directed, and other-directed character, setting in motion a sociological critique of character that now has spanned 40 years.

Riesman attempted to downplay the apocalyptic vision his findings in- spired in others: that the breakdown of traditional moral codes and self-inter- nalized moral standards has led to a morally paralyzed culture and to individuals impoverished of social responsibility and ethical substance. But this apocalyptic conclusion was not eschewed by sociologists following the lead of his theory. In popular scholarship, Richard Sennett decried the *Fall of Public Man* (1979), and Christopher Lasch diagnosed America as *The Culture of Narcissism* (1979). More recently, sociologists attempting to discern the "habits" of the American "heart" conclude that many individuals are today "trapped in the language of the isolated self," which is a "therapeutic rhetoric" that, "through the medium of television and other mass communications, increasingly all Americans, cannot avoid" (Bellah et al., 1985, pp. 83-84).

The current apocalyptics of mass media, which are by no means limited to these examples, represent little more than a displaced critique of modern society and a lament for the loss of some idealized past (Jensen, 1990). Although these critics attempt to discern the American character from the artifacts of media and popular culture, they are sadly wanting for either a historical or functional perspective on communication and media. This makes Riesman's analysis, completed prior to the popular dispersion of television, a most inviting point of departure. Riesman's historical analysis of changing practices of socialization displays great insight and depth in how it conceives the rhetorical function of symbols of character.

Riesman views social character as the sum total of training and conditioning that makes conformity possible, which at base is necessary for a society to function as such (1950, pp. 5-6). Character, in this view, is a kind of least common denominator of all the socializing forces in a culture, one which seeks to instill a basis for conformity in individuals. By implication, the symbolism of character is crucial to the socialization process, and the rhetorical-motivational formation of character is transformed in different cultural epochs.

Western culture, at least, has evolved from a "tradition-directed" culture of *shame,* wherein myth, lore, ritual, and religion inform individuals of the codes of honor and dishonor in social conduct. In a culture of shame, people's behavior and standards for ethical evaluation are directed toward and through this tradition; tradition supplies unified images of character that a person emulates and against which one compares himself or herself in conducting life and action. The symbology of shame, one may posit, contains the rhetorical-motivational operations of tradition-directedness, insofar as invocations of and means for repair of shame enforce and perpetuate conformity.

In Riesman's analysis, the culture that has evolved from tradition-directed times to the mid-twentieth century culminates in inner-directedness. Inner-directedness emphasizes the individual's autonomous but subservient relationship to society. The individual is directed to internalize the standards of right conduct and social responsibility in personal and psychological make-up. Riesman likens this to an individual having a gyroscope in his or her character that provides the moral guidance to conformity or responsibility. The comparable rhetorical-motivational symbology to shame in this case is *guilt,* wherewith an individual is socialized to experience a psychological, inner sense of deviation and loss with behavior or thoughts that do not conform to the social code.

Of the contemporary age, Riesman's analysis is more provocative and less replete in description. Riesman discerns in the developing mass society of America that the guilt-based, inner-directed culture is eroding and is being replaced with a culture of "other-directedness," where other people and diverse social situations dictate the standards of conformity and appropriate social behavior. In other-directed culture, Riesman speculates, people develop a kind of "social antenna" that allows them to read others and social situations and to perform accordingly. There is a heightened sensitivity to others that is laudable, as well as an increased commitment to social harmony. One can extrapolate that there is also an intricate system of situational ethics at work, and a corresponding social relativity characteristic of recent society.

This thesis, of course, provokes the kind of apocalyptic "Whither morality?" interpretations of American society that have prevailed, and leads to the concern for the breakdown of social character and the social order it preserves. That individuals no longer have an honor- or code-based morality as a substantial part of their personal character and make-up is to be lamented and feared. Our traditional ideals of individual honor and morality are embarrassed by the suggestion that contemporary individuals are malleable and conform to the pressures of diverse social situations. In this other-directed culture, the need for or even possibility for achieving integrity in one's personal character is seemingly absent. An individual may be incapable of achieving an identity that integrates cross-situational performances and provides transcendent standards of self-evaluation.

The rhetorical-motivational structure that fuels the culture of other-directedness, comparable to shame and guilt, is *anxiety*. Anxiety about social performance at once erects people's social antennae to potential sanctions of others, gives them greater sensitivity to the needs and judgments of others, and, like shame and guilt, puts individuals in the deficit where they must compensate or in some way make things right through conformist behavior. Riesman's analysis was avant-garde, especially for his time, and we may wish to delay judgment as to whether "anxiety" is the right term. But for the moment we should trust his insight that situational conformity, spawned by the perception of some kind of personal shortcoming or embarrassment, might be comparable to shame and guilt as a culture-wide, socializing mechanism. The kind of social anxiety and need for approval that individuals currently experience suggest that he was fundamentally correct in his predictions for this culture.

Riesman's treatment of psychological conditions such as shame, guilt, and anxiety as social and cultural products makes a great contribution to understanding their symbolic, rhetorical, and mediated functions. His definition of social character, however, is too sociological in focus to explain the relationships among media, consciousness, and individualism that it implies. Riesman does not recognize explicitly the interaction among communication, character, and media whereby social character (and personal character) are created, sustained, and changed. This recognition directs attention to the role of dominant media in social evolution and the possibilities for individual consciousness—a central theme in the work of Walter J. Ong.

Individualism and the Evolution of Media

The stages of cultural transformation observed in Ong's history of media parallel the cultural shifts theorized by Riesman. Ong ties these changes to the changing communication technologies of primary oral, literate, and secondary oral or electronic cultures. The historical epochs operating within these dominant media are identical to the cultures of shame, guilt, and anxiety Riesman theorizes (Riesman anticipated the culture of anxiety at the same time television became popularized). Beyond the coincidence of their theories, however, there is a logical reason for these connections to be found in the characteristics of these dominant media.

The connections between a tradition-directed culture and a primary oral culture should require little explanation. Within an oral culture, tradition is maintained as the only objective, stable, and effective rhetoric whereby to insure community and continuity in a society. People are directed by oral history toward and by the symbols of character embodied in tradition. One is socialized to feel shame when one deviates from coded standards of character and motivation.

The parallels between an inner-directed culture, where people are socialized to have an inner, psychological experience of guilt, and the phenomenon of literacy are more interesting. Unlike the ephemeral, outer-directed events of oral exchange, the events of literacy are necessarily individual, psychological, and interior. The permanence of the written word and piety toward "The Word" could facilitate development of a kind of "gyroscope" in one's inner, privately experienced character. In Western culture, literacy culminates in the individual's ability to experience the word of God directly, rather than through an outer institution or the oral translations of a priest. Literacy leads to individual access to science and discovery, and it fosters the kind of independent moral substance presumed in modern notions of democracy. The experience of knowing through literacy is private, personal, and involves the internalization of knowledge within the individual consciousness. Literate consciousness is one in which individual responsibility (through guilt) could insure the common mores and participation of diverse people disconnected in time and space.

The connections between the developing electronic culture and the other-directed culture of anxiety Riesman describes are necessarily more speculative. Ong styles contemporary electronic culture as "secondary orality," indicating his view that the electronic age revives many features of a primary oral culture. This is logical, since radio, film, and television revive the dominant role of oral expression, aural reception, and active, physical events. The return to orality also has parallels in Riesman's characterological analysis. In the culture of anxiety, as in primary oral culture, people are turned toward an "outer" standard of judgment—not the shared and stable standard of oral tradition but the outer, variable standards of other people and their judgments. Either way, there is greater dependence upon public mores and their symbolic display, and less subscription to internal, individual, and private relationships to the objective, literate codes of guilt.

The connections between electronic media and a culture of anxiety are more suggestive than either Riesman or Ong is in a position to appreciate. In 1950 Riesman could not foresee that the culture of television populates—in fact saturates—our perceptual worlds with images of others, with their actions, reactions, and psychological anxieties and judgments featured in intimate proximity. Television is an intense and close-up language of interaction, such that we are trained in every nuance of anxiety, performance, and evaluation. No other medium could so effectively reinforce and perpetuate standards for social performance based upon experience and repair of anxiety.

Ong's analyses of secondary oral culture have not focused on television, and he too has missed this important point about the psychosocial dimension of electronic media. However, Ong has made very important contributions to understanding the role of media development in contemporary individualism and its culture. Ong believes that individualism has been in steady evolution in and through media development, and has traced individualist trends in the literature of the past few centuries (1962a; 1986a). Ong believes that the psychological and intimate character of modern media culminates in "personalism," a spiritual achievement of contemporary culture. While the "personalist drift" (1962a) of modern consciousness may be manifest in certain individualist indulgences, the general thrust has brought us greater spiritual actualization and higher maturity in individual consciousness. This enhanced personalism is found in examples such as the personalized cosmos of Pierre Teilhard de Chardin or the dialogic intimacy of Martin Buber. Ong's analysis of personalism in secondary oral culture and Riesman's "culture of anxiety" provide an interesting contrast. While they imply different evaluations of the current age, they both bespeak the other-directedness, sensitivity, and intimacy that is part and product of contemporary media technology.

Ong's analysis of the parallel developments of individual consciousness and media technologies provides a historical and functional context with which to consider the culture of anxiety. Ong's theory of media evolution posits an interaction between personality and culture. Evidence of this interaction is found in the strong parallels between phylogenetic evolution of culture and ontogenetic development of individual personality. The transformations involved in cultural evolution move from the oral stage, where our mythic grounds mark an "infantile undifferentiated self-contained whole," to a middle stage marked by the emergence of personalized ego and individual heroism, to a higher transformation, a "new unity in self-conscious individualization . . . today entering into new phases with the heightened individualism—or personalism—of modern man" (1971, p. 11). As Ong suggests, these transformations are similar to the development of personality in the individual:

> Ontogenetically, consciousness grows in individual human beings in the sense that for a normal adult more of life is under conscious reflective control than for a child. . . . The consciousness of the individual can be said to grow out of the unconscious and gradually to supersede the unconscious as a base of response to existence in more and more areas, without ever, of course, eliminating the unconscious (1971, pp. 42-43).

The theory of ontogenetic and phylogenetic developments of personality and culture have been previewed adequately by other essays in this volume. It is sufficient here to draw into focus the implications of this view for the development of individualism and corresponding possibilities for social character.

Rhetoric was developed in primary oral culture as the central medium of public communication. The epistemology, social organization, and modes of individual expression—what Ong calls the noetic economy—of oral culture were dependent largely upon the structures rhetorical practice assumed. One might simply note that the structures of epideictic rhetoric, in acts of praise and blame, were socializing forces and ways of reinforcing characterological virtues. The Western culture that specialized in rhetoric was transformed, but not eliminated, by the subsequent advent of literacy and print. With these newer technologies of public communication, the noetic order of rhetorical culture was summarized and proliferated in the rhetorical theories and guides of the Renaissance, but dislocated from its central role in the organization of modern consciousness.

The development of rhetoric until the age of Romanticism marks a kind of middle stage in cultural evolution, a middle stage that is paralleled by the adolescent stage of maturation and development in an individual. Rhetoric, in Ong's view, is an intermediate stage between the unconscious mythic past and the conscious control of maturity reflected in contemporary personalism. As a media technology, displaced by newer dominant media, rhetoric came to specialize in the "birth of the hero," denoting the "rise of masculinity and of the personalized ego" (Ong, 1971, pp. 10-12). The Renaissance, according to Ong, "in many ways represents the phylogenetic high point of rhetoric development," reflected in the "ego dominance fostered by rhetoric" that was characteristic of the age (1971, p. 15).

The connection between adolescence and the heroic quest of rhetoric is more than a simile, as psychoanalysts consistently note the heroic quest as a marked symbolic stage of adolescent development (Bettelheim, 1977, pp. 225-226; Ong, 1971, p. 11). Further, Ong contends that "rhetoric at its most impressive peak was heroic and masculinizing through its association with puberty rites" (1971, p. 14). As a middle stage of development, akin to male adolescence, rhetoric continues to have an affinity with both the mythic stages preceding ego development and heroism, as well as the continued development of personalism that succeeded the rhetorical culture. One should expect this specialized characterological function of rhetoric to continue to be manifested in diverse forms and formats of electronic culture as it serves the ontogenetic developments of the individuals in this culture. Ong attempts to demonstrate this in various analyses of artifacts in popular culture (1971).

This view suggests a significant historical relationship between rhetoric and the development of individualism and a structural relationship between rhetorical technology and the development of social character at any given point in the evolution of culture. The functions of rhetoric as they specialized in the noetic economy of oral culture and then literate culture have not disappeared, but rather have been "disrupted, displaced, and rearranged" within the noetic economy of electronic culture, such that the "history of rhetoric simply mirrors the evolution of society" (Ong, 1971, pp. 8-9).

An important contribution of this thinking to the discussion of character is that the changes and modes of character are part of a *transformation* and *evolution* of historical shame and guilt, at least within the parameters of Western society, not a loss of these structures and their replacement with nonmoral or immoral substitutes. This view gives greater insight into the passage of our culture from one of shame, then guilt, and now, possibly, anxiety. The tradition-directed culture of shame, through the noetic structures of an oral world, operated with external direction and reinforcement, while instilling a mythic, subconscious, inner character that aligned the individual with tradition. Guilt and literacy helped to bring this structure to consciousness, fix an individual's relationship to others and the world, and impart to the individual significance, identity, and direction toward both self and society. Rhetoric, in this noetic economy, specializes in the imaging and enactment of autonomy and control, necessary to adolescent passage into the world of adults. Without both the outer-directed and inner-directed structures evolved through such processes, neither heightened sensitivity to others nor effective responsibility and responsiveness of self to situation could be codified and elicited through manifest "anxiety" and its repairs.

The Characterological Struggle

The central issue advanced here concerns the description and treatment of contemporary characterology as represented in media and what consequences these phenomena and our criticism of them hold for understanding the contemporary rhetorical climate.

One obvious criticism of any attempt to characterize an age or epoch in such generalities as a "narcissistic age," an age of "individualism," or even those operationalized here, cultures of "shame," "guilt," "anxiety," "personalism," and so on, is that upon closer inspection more than one trend or pattern occurs in any given time. Further, every "new" pattern, upon final analysis, seems to bear close similarities to historical patterns or preceding conditions. This is because, as Ong says, cultural history is deposited in each new age in the form of personality structures (1967b, p. 178). Ong's complex and interactive reading of cultural evolution characterizes more diversity and movement, and simply accounts for more of the data than Riesman's sociological theory (originally based on fluctuating population trends). In addition, Ong's treatment of the developing psychodynamics of an individual's relationship to a prevailing medium and culture grants a far richer perspective on social character and an individual's internalization of social practice than does Riesman's taken-for-granted assumptions about the process of socialization.

Riesman's theory offers one further idea that helps to advance our understanding of contemporary character. He observes in the general population the likelihood of different groups who are acculturated to one or another of the three primary modes of character—shame, guilt, or anxiety. That is, in Riesman's terms, there may exist a "characterological struggle" between subcultures of shame and guilt and the emerging culture of anxiety, leading to interesting dislocations and conflicts across the cultural spectrum (1950, pp. 31-35). To the extent that his analysis of the primary bases of character is accurate, this seems likely.

Perhaps because Riesman's early focus was completely sociological, or perhaps because the intervening 40 years have created profound changes and reactions to certain conditions, this description of the characterological struggle overlooks a central possibility I will take here as a point of departure. *The characterological struggle among orientations toward shame, guilt, and anxiety as social structures of character and evaluation occurs within each individual who is socialized into this culture.* In other words, the dramatism of character in which this media culture is saturated preserves, enacts, and applies each of these structures in its discussion and treatment of individual character and social situations. It may be, and I think this is the case, that a certain degree of specialization has taken place with the kind and degree of situation toward which shame, guilt, or anxiety is applied in our current characterology. Nonetheless, it also seems likely that the rules and meanings of these different structures are unclear and open to change and interpretation—creating widespread ethical confusion among individuals and fomenting an ethical vulnerability that indeed can become morally paralyzing for individuals who are attempting to deal with issues of character.

Although different subcultures or age groups may be socialized primarily to the terms of shame, guilt, or anxiety, one likely effect of mass media and multiple literatures is that these structures have been widely dispersed as frameworks of interpretation and response, and specialized in their applications to public and private situations. This specialization surely has transformed them. Institutions claim to and are expected to hold to a higher code of honor and are subject to public shame when they fail. This is not generally true of individuals or of personal situations. Public individuals seem to deal most frequently with structures of guilt, with some confusion between legal and moral guilt often at issue. Public figures accused of moral guilt have a deft defense in saying that they are not legally guilty. It is common, in fact prevalent, for public individuals to effectively restore much of their socially held character by enacting guilt and penitence. For most individuals in most interpersonal situations, shame and guilt are not salient criteria for evaluating personal failure. Instead, individuals today experience widespread anxiety about peer evaluation and social performance, in personal as well as public roles.

Whether this description represents a complex contemporary characterology or pervasive ethical confusion—I think it is both—it remains to be asked how all of this relates to media, its functions, and developing individual character. Again, Ong's understanding of media evolution helps to formulate a more complex analysis of the psychological dimension in media ecology.

Ong's notion of the sensorium provides an excellent backdrop for understanding the multiplicity of media structures in contemporary consciousness. By the sensorium Ong means "the entire sensory apparatus as an operational complex" (1967b, p. 6). He writes that "[human] sensory perceptions are abundant and overwhelming. [We] cannot attend to them all at once. In a great part a given culture teaches [us] one or another way of productive specialization" (1967b, p. 6). What Ong in various places calls "personality structures" are the products of different media epochs. They are ways that the media ecology teaches an individual how to attend to experience. These personality structures are directly related to the organization of the sensorium, where there are shifts and balances of emphases according to the dominant media and their epistemological specialties.

The idea of the sensorium, together with Ong's description of media evolution, support the idea that in a given noetic economy there are multiple phenomena that lead to multiple structures of perception, personality, consciousness, and, by inference, character. New media and their epistemological bases do not, in Ong's view, erase historical and preceding structures, but rather dislocate them. There may be dominance and subordination of these structures, conflict and cooperation among them, and one or another may come to prevail and characterize the habits of a cultural age. Yet at any given time the sensorium of the individual contains traces and elements of past structures upon which new structures are continually being erected. "Maturity does not escape the past," Ong writes, "but structures it" (1967b, p. 104). This description suggests a process whereby shame and guilt become transformed within a new noetic economy and a new set of pressures upon the organization of the sensorium, leading to multiple characterological structures at play.

From this vantage, it is possible to see that the characterological struggle is basic to the multiplicity of situations, ethics, and instructions given to an individual of our culture and with which he or she must forge effective psychosocial character. Literacy did not erase classical shame, but rather transformed it into guilt, a more interior, personal, and portable socializing mechanism designed for the needs of expanding society and expanding individual consciousness. With that transformation came other incidental and consequential cultural transformations—individual heroism and personalized ego as developed by a transformed and specialized rhetorical technology. Likewise, electronic media have not erased guilt and its attendant characterology. The literature of romantic individualism contains the experiences, occasions, and consequences of guilt, and this literature is one of the primary subjects that music, television, and film translate and transform into a contemporary dramatism of character. Especially, and pervasively, this is the case with adolescent materials that saturate these media.

Evidence of the characterological struggle, that is, the conflagration of shame, guilt, and anxiety, is strongly present in media drama that addresses issues of identity. Benjamin Braddock in *The Graduate* must deal with parental and family shame, personal guilt over sexual indiscretion and loss of inner direction, and his own numbing anxiety toward his life, role, future, and the terms of shame and guilt with which he is confronted socially. These same themes occupy the popular *The Dead Poets Society* nearly 30 years later, although with different results. The adolescents are beset with issues of social and family shame, are confused and confounded about finding their inner direction, must deal with institutional and family guilt for deviance from standards of success, and are consumed with anxiety about performance before peers and authorities. The characters of the television show "Thirty-Something" exhibit perpetual anxiety and personal doubt, much of which focuses on whether they should feel shame or guilt in relation to their peers, spouses, and roles. The same absorption in anxiety is the character of the mature voice-over that speaks the psyche of the preteen hero in "The Wonder Years," another popular adolescent drama.

These casual examples are but mere indicators of the language and drama of characterological treatment that flourish in the electronic media.

These media are technologically adroit in inspecting intimate and psychological dimensions of interpersonal relations. Noteworthy in these examples is that shame, guilt, and anxiety are all presented as social structures with which persons are confronted, with which they must deal, and through which they must sort for guides to personal identity and social performance. The multidimensional characterology is scarcely limited to narrative drama. The public enacts shame as structure in which Exxon must operate to restore its image after a costly oil spill; the public responds to Richard Nixon with expectations that he should confess to guilt for his actions in Watergate; Jim Bakker, Jimmy Swaggart, and Gary Hart are profoundly embarrassed by publication of their sexual indiscretions, the inadequacy of any suitable response leading to prevalent anxiety over media exposure. In the latter cases, different elements of the public expect that the individual should enact the results of shame, by shrinking in disgrace, or guilt, where confession and conversion make repairs, or simply be embarrassed, where the individuals should show greater discretion and caution in their public lives (manifest anxiety).

The public struggles of these individuals to deal with the multiple codes and expectations of the public is merely indicative of the ethical confusion to which each individual may be subject when dealing with issues of personal character. The polythematic narratives of our media complicate our readings of characterological expectations and procedures. The struggle with personal integrity and social performance dominates key forms of advertising and consumerism, situation comedies, professional dramas, romance, psychodrama, political dialogue, and to some extent virtually every other dramatic form in our media.

The heroic quest and romantic individualism are prevalent themes in the socialization of adolescents in this culture, and nonconformity to traditional expectations of character and maturity is chief among those themes. Anxiety is the condition of the adolescent, where characterological expectations are apparent, yet one does not have yet within oneself the guides, experience, and confidence that one is meeting the requirements of a particular situation. Social performance and evaluation are very much on the minds of adolescents and maturing adults in this culture, yet there is little affirmation that one or another character will yield success. The motives and strategies of the inner-driven person do not very well answer to the real demands of social performance, and when put into practice in our organizational lives, inner-direction often represents a form of antisocial, self-denying individualism of antiquated origins. In short, the characterological struggle may be between the desire for autonomous heroism, adolescent rebellion, and ego-integrity toward which we are socialized, and the tremendous demand for situational conformity placed upon the individuals of this culture for social and economic success.

The rhetoric of identity and character in which this culture appears to be steeped suggests that Americans sustain a prolonged adolescent quest for selfhood and autonomy. There is much to suggest that the characterological struggle and its resultant anxiety are true of more than the adolescents and maturing adults of our culture. Theologian Robert M. Doran believes of the contemporary age that "the possibility that one may miss or lose the direction in the movement of life is disclosed as our deepest anxiety" (1990, p. 518). Confusion about whether our direction should come from the resources of tradition, from some inner path, or from acceptance and rejection by others could only exacerbate the anxiety that Doran describes as "the possibility of the loss, the futility, of our very existence" (1990, p. 518). The problem of whether shame, guilt, or anxiety should be felt toward which sources of our being could only create greater reliance upon the characterological guides our media and its rhetoric afford us.

I have tried to demonstrate only that these forms of characterological analysis are tied intimately to the rhetorical forms in which character is depicted, in which socialization occurs, and from which and toward which individual requirements for self-expression and integrity are derived. Understanding the historical relationship of rhetoric, individual psychology, and media development can enhance our understanding of the interactive dimension of social character and its functions. Such seems prerequisite to understanding the overwhelming socializing functions and effects of electronic media.

Ong's perspective suggests that this preponderance of adolescent expression is part of the displaced role of rhetoric in the noetic economy of electronic culture, whereby mass society manifests the adolescent characterological quest through the rhetoric of ego-dominance and heroic individualism. Ong holds out the possibility for transformation to higher maturity and personalism in this media ecology, although he accepts that "probably no other culture has ever had to bear the burden of so acute a self-consciousness as does the present United States" (1971, p. 327). Whether this condition leads to increased intimacy and personalism or to prolonged adolescent quest for selfhood would appear to be an ethical challenge facing the characterological resources of American society and its individuals.

The concern for and discussion of social character will doubtless continue as we observe the transformations of our culture, in its rhetoric, media, and ethical practices. Whether in the long run anxiety will mark our developing age or whether it is merely an early sign of some emergent structure remain questions. One implication of Ong's perspective is that we cannot be too quick to diagnose and judge the effects and directions of emergent media technologies. That is where many of the questions about contemporary social character linger, and where many contemporary analysts seem to have little perspective as they read the signs of character in the media they observe.

References

Only works by Walter J. Ong referred to in this volume are listed here, and reprints are not indicated. A complete annotated bibliography of Ong's published works is being prepared with his cooperation by Charles M. Kovich of Rockhurst College and James C. McDonald of the University of Southwestern Louisiana. Randolph F. Lumpp has published a chronological list of about half of Ong's published works (1987b).

Abrahamian, E. (1982). *Iran between two revolutions*. Princeton: Princeton University Press.

Abrams, M. H. (1971). *Natural supernaturalism: Tradition and revolution in romantic literature*. New York: Norton.

Abu-Lughod, L. (1989). Bedouins, cassettes, and technologies of public culture. *Middle East Report, 19*(4), 7-11.

Alberich, J. (1982). *La popularidad de Don Juan Tenorio y otros estudios de literatura Española moderna*. Barcelona: Aubí.

Alcalá Galiano, J. (1877). El poeta Grilo. *La Ilustración Española y Americana, 47*, 394-395, 398.

Alfonsus, P. (1911). *Disciplina clericalis*. A. Hilka & W. Söderhjelm (Eds.). Heidelberg: C. Winter.

Alvarado, M., Gutch, R., & Wollen, T. (1987). *Learning the media: An introduction to media teaching*. London: Macmillan.

Andreu, A. G. (1986). Diálogo de voces en *Fortunata y Jacinta*. In A. D. Kossoff, J. Amor y Vázquez, R. H. Kossoff, & G. W. Ribbans (Eds.), *Actas del VIII Congreso de la Asociación Internacional de Hispanistas* (Vol. 1, pp. 153-158). Madrid: Istmo.

Ang, I. (1985). *Watching Dallas: Soap opera and the melodramatic imagination*. London: Methuen.

Assogioli, R. (1965). *Psychosynthesis*. New York: Hobbs, Dorman.

Avotins, I. (1975). The holders of the chairs of rhetoric at Athens. *Harvard Studies in Classical Philology, 79*, 313-324.

Ayer, A. J. (1946). *Language, truth and logic* (2nd ed.). London: Gollancz.

Bacon, F. (1863). *The works of Francis Bacon* (Vols. 1-14). J. Spedding, R. Ellis, & D. Heath (Eds.). Cambridge, UK: Riverside Press.

Bally, C. (1909). *Traité de stylistique française* (Vols. 1-2). Heidelberg: C. Winter. (Reprinted. Geneva: Georg, 1963)

Barilli, R. (1989). *Rhetoric*. (G. Menozzi, Trans.). Minneapolis: University of Minnesota Press. (Original work published 1983)

Barros, J. de. (1983). *Rópica pnefma* (Vols. 1-2). I. S. Révah (Ed.). Lisbon: Instituto Nacional de Investigaçao Cientifica.

Barthes, R. (1977). *Image-music-text.* (S. Heath, Ed. and Trans.). London: Fontana. (Original works published 1961-1973)

Baumeister, R. F. (1986). *Identity: Cultural change and the struggle for self.* New York: Oxford University Press.

Bazin, N. T. (1973). *Virginia Woolf and the androgynous vision.* New Brunswick, NJ: Rutgers University Press.

Beeman, W. O. (1982). *Culture, performance and communication in Iran.* Tokyo: Institute for the Study of Languages and Cultures of Asia and Africa.

Belenky, M. F., Clinchy, B. M., Goldberger, N. R., & Tarule, J. M. (1986). *Women's ways of knowing.* New York: Basic Books.

Bellah, R. M., Madsen, R., Sullivan, W. M., Swidler, A., & Tipton, S. M. (1985). *Habits of the heart: Individualism and commitment in American life.* Berkeley: University of California Press.

Benjamin, J. (1988). *The bonds of love: Psychoanalysis, feminism, and the problem of domination.* New York: Pantheon.

Benoit, R. (1973). *Single nature's double name: The collectedness of the conflicting in British and American romanticism.* The Hague: Mouton.

Berger, P. L., & Luckmann, T. (1966). *The social construction of reality: A treatise in the sociology of knowledge.* Garden City, NY: Doubleday.

Berne, E. (1964). *Games people play: The psychology of human relationships.* New York: Grove.

Bernheimer, C. (1985). Introduction: Part one. In C. Bernheimer & C. Kahane (Eds.), *In Dora's case* (pp. 1-18). New York: Columbia University Press.

Berquist, G. F., Golden, J. L., & Coleman, W. E. (1978). *The rhetoric of Western thought* (2nd ed.). Dubuque, IA: Kendall-Hunt.

Bettelheim, B. (1977). *The uses of enchantment: The meaning and importance of fairy tales.* New York: Random House.

Biesele, M., & Tyler, S. A. (Eds.). (1986). The dialectic of oral and literary hermeneutics. *Cultural Anthropology, 1,* 131-256.

Bitzer, L. F. (1981). Political rhetoric. In D. D. Nimmo & K. R. Sanders (Eds.), *Handbook of political communication* (pp. 225-248). Beverly Hills, CA: Sage.

Bizzell, P., & Herzberg, B. (1990). *The rhetorical tradition: Readings from classical times to the present.* Boston: Bedford Books of St. Martin's Press.

Bly, R. (1990). *Iron John: A book about men.* Reading, MA: Addison-Wesley.

Bohm, D. (1980). *Wholeness and the implicate order.* London: Routledge & Kegan Paul.

Botrel, J-F. (1987). L'aptitude à communiquer: Alphabétisation et scolarisation en Espagne de 1860 à 1920. In J-F. Botrel et al. (Eds.), *De l'alphabétisation aux circuits du livre en Espagne XVIe - XIXe siècles* (pp. 105-140). Paris: Editions CNRS.

Broe, M. L. (1980). Recovering the complex: Sylvia Plath's beeline. *The Centennial Review, 24,* 1-24.

Bruffee, K. A. (1986). Social construction, language, and the authority of knowledge: A bibliographical essay. *College English, 48,* 773-790.

Burke, K. (1950). *A rhetoric of motives.* New York: Prentice-Hall.

Buxton, J. (1987). *Sir Philip Sidney and the English renaissance* (3rd ed.). London: Macmillan.

Capra, F. (1983). *The turning point: Science, society and the rise of culture.* New York: Bantam.

Carey, J. W. (1989). *Communication as culture: Essays on media and society.* Boston: Unwin Hyman.

Cervantes, M. de. (1911-1913). *El ingenioso hidalgo don Quijote de la Mancha* (Vols. 1-8). F. Rodriguez Marin (Ed.). Madrid: Ediciones de "La Lectura."

Cervantes, M. de. (1914-1917). *Novelas ejemplares: El coloquio de los perros* (Vols. 1-2). F. Rodriguez Marin (Ed.). Madrid: Ediciones de "La Lectura." (Original work published 1613)

Chesebro, J. W. (1986, December). *Media transformations: Revolutionary challenges to the world's cultures, part II*. Paper presented at the Speech Communication Association of Puerto Rico, San Juan.

Chomsky, N. (1965). *Aspects of the theory of syntax*. Cambridge: MIT Press.

Ciplijauskaité, B. (1988). El romanticismo como hipotexto en el realismo. In Y. Lissorgues (Ed.), *Realismo y naturalismo en España en la segunda mitad del siglo XIX* (pp. 90-97). Barcelona: Anthropos.

Cixous, H. (1981). Castration or decapitation (A. Kahn, Trans.). *Signs, 7,* 44-59. (Original work published 1976)

Cohen, R. (Ed.). (1984-1985). Oral and written traditions in the Middle Ages. *New Literary History, 16,* 1-206.

Coleridge, S. T. (1835). *Specimens of the table talk of the late Samuel Taylor Coleridge* (Vol. 2). New York: Harper and Brothers.

Collins, J., Green, J. R., Lydon, M., Sachner, M., & Skoller, E. H. (1985). Questioning the unconscious: The Dora archive. In C. Bernheimer & C. Kahane (Eds.), *In Dora's case* (pp. 243-253). New York: Columbia University Press.

Cottam, R. W. (1964). *Nationalism in Iran*. Pittsburgh: University of Pittsburgh Press.

Couliano, I. P. (1987). *Eros and magic in the Renaissance* (M. Cook, Trans.). Chicago: University of Chicago Press.

Davis, P. J., & Hersh, R. (1986). *Descartes' dream: The world according to mathematics*. San Diego: Harcourt Brace Jovanovich.

de Man, P. (1979). *Allegories of reading*. New Haven: Yale University Press.

de Man, P. (1981). Phenomenality and materiality in Kant. In G. Shapiro & A. Sica (Eds.), *Hermeneutics* (pp. 121-144). Amherst: University of Massachusetts Press.

de Man, P. (1985). Lyrical voice in contemporary theory: Riffaterre and Jauss. In P. Parker & C. Hosek (Eds.), *Lyric poetry* (pp. 55-72). Ithaca, NY: Cornell University Press.

Debus, A. G. (1978). *Man and nature in the Renaissance*. New York: Cambridge University Press.

Derrida, J. (1981). *Positions* (A. Bass, Trans.). Chicago: University of Chicago Press. (Original work published 1972)

Derrida, J. (1987). *The truth in painting* (G. Bennington & I. McLeod, Trans.). Chicago: University of Chicago Press. (Original work published 1978)

Doran, R. M. (1990). *Theology and the dialectics of history*. Toronto: University of Toronto Press.

Douglas, A. (1977). *The feminization of American culture*. New York: Knopf.

Dowling, J. (1989). José Zorrilla y la retórica de la muerte. *Hispanic Review, 57,* 437-456.

DuBois, P. (1988). *Sowing the body: Psychoanalysis and ancient representations of women*. Chicago: University of Chicago Press.

Duncan, H. D. (1968). *Symbols in society*. New York: Oxford University Press.

Easlea, B. (1980). *Witch hunting, magic and the new philosophy*. Brighton: Harvester Press.

Edelman, M. (1964). *The symbolic uses of politics*. Urbana: University of Illinois Press.

Ehninger, D., & Hauser, G. A. (1984). Communication and values. In C. C. Arnold & J. W. Bowers (Eds.), *Handbook of rhetorical and communication theory* (pp. 720-748). Boston: Allyn & Bacon.

El Saffar, R. (1984). *Beyond fiction: The recovery of the feminine in the novels of Cervantes.* Berkeley: University of California Press.

El Saffar, R. (1989). Anxiety of identity: Gutierre's case in El medico de su honra. In D. Fox, H. Sieber, & R. ter Horst (Eds.), *Studies in honor of Bruce W. Wardropper* (pp. 105-124). Newark, DE: Juan de la Cuesta.

El Saffar, R. (1990). Way stations in the errancy of the word: A study of Calderon's La vida es sueño. In M. B. Rose (Ed.), *Renaissance drama as cultural history* (pp. 109-126). Evanston, IL: Northwestern University Press.

Ellis, J. (1982). *Visible fictions.* London: Routledge & Kegan Paul.

Ellman, R. (1982). *James Joyce.* New York: Oxford University Press.

Ellul, J. (1964). *The technological society* (J. Wilkinson, Trans.). New York: Knopf. (Original work published 1954)

Elshtain, J. B. (1981). *Public man, private woman: Women in social and political thought.* Princeton: Princeton University Press.

Elshtain, J. B. (1986). The new feminist scholarship. *Salmagundi, 70-71,* 3-26.

Ennals, R. (1985). *Artificial intelligence: Applications to logical reasoning and historical research.* Chichester, UK: Ellis Horwood.

Enos, R. L. (1974). The persuasive and social force of logography in ancient Greece. *Central States Speech Journal, 25*(1), 4-10.

Enos, R. L. (1976). Rhetorical intent in ancient historiography: Herodotus and the battle of Marathon. *Communication Quarterly, 24*(1), 24-31.

Enos, R. L. (1977). The effects of imperial patronage on the rhetorical tradition of the Athenian second sophistic. *Communication Quarterly, 25*(2), 3-10.

Enos, R. L. (1978). The Hellenic rhapsode. *Western Journal of Speech Communication, 42*(2), 134-143.

Enos, R. L. (1986). The art of rhetoric at the Amphiareion of Oropos: A study of epigraphical evidence as written communication. *Written Communication, 3*(1), 3-14.

Enos, R. L. (1987). Aristotle, Empedocles and the notion of rhetoric. In R. J. Jensen & J. C. Hammerback (Eds.), *In search of justice: The Indiana tradition in speech communication* (pp. 5-21). Amsterdam: Rodopi.

Enos, R. L. (1988). *The literate mode of Cicero's legal rhetoric.* Carbondale: Southern Illinois University Press.

Enos, R. L. (Ed.). (1990). *Oral and written communication: Historical approaches.* Newbury Park, CA: Sage.

Enos, R. L., & Ackerman, J. (1987). *Letteraturizzazione* and Hellenic rhetoric: An analysis for research with extensions. In C. W. Kneupper (Ed.), *Visions of order: History, theory and criticism* (pp. 11-21). Arlington TX: Rhetoric Society of America.

Enos, R. L., & Odoroff, E. (1985, Spring/Summer). The orality of the "paragraph" in Greek rhetoric. *Pre/Text, 6,* 51-65.

Epstein, C. F. (1988). *Deceptive distinctions: Sex, gender, and the social order.* New Haven: Yale University Press.

Erikson, E. H. (1963). *Childhood and society* (2nd ed). New York: Norton.

Farrell, T. J. (1978-1979). The female and male modes of rhetoric. *College English, 40,* 909-921.

Farrell, T. J. (1983). IQ and standard English. *College Composition and Communication, 34,* 470-484.

Fiske, J. (1987). *Television culture*. New York: Methuen.

Flaubert, G. (1965). *Madame Bovary*. (P. de Man, Ed. and Trans.). New York: Norton. (Original work published 1857)

Fleck, L. (1979). *Genesis and development of a scientific fact* (F. Bradley & T. J. Trenn, Trans.; T. J. Trenn & R. K. Merton, Eds.). Chicago: University of Chicago Press.

Foley, J. M. (Ed.). (1981). *Oral traditional literature: A festschrift for Albert Bates Lord*. Columbus, OH: Slavica.

Foley, J. M. (1985). *Oral-formulaic theory and research: An introduction and annotated bibliography*. New York: Garland.

Foley, J. M. (Ed.). (1986). *Oral tradition in literature: Interpretation in context*. Columbia: University of Missouri Press.

Foley, J. M. (Ed.). (1987a). *Comparative research on oral traditions: A memorial for Milman Parry*. Columbus, OH: Slavica.

Foley, J. M. (Ed.). (1987b). A festschrift for Walter J. Ong. *Oral Tradition, 2,* 7-382.

Foley, J. M. (1988). *The theory of oral composition: Theory and methodology*. Bloomington: Indiana University Press.

Forrest, K. K. (1976). Speech and power: A Renaissance theme in *King Lear*. (Doctoral dissertation, Saint Louis University, 1976). *Dissertation Abstracts International, 37* (University Microfilms No. 76-22, 535).

Fox, E. I. (1986). Apuntes para una teoría de la moderna imaginación literaria española. *Homenaje a José Antonio Maravall* (pp. 341-350). Madrid: Centro de Investigaciones Sociológicas.

Fraunce, A. (1969). *The lawyer's logicke* (facsimile reprint). London: Scholar Press. (Original work published 1588)

Freire, P. (1974). *Education for critical consciousness*. New York: Seabury.

Freud, S. (1953). *Three essays on the theory of sexuality*. In J. Strachey (Ed. and Trans.), *Standard edition of the complete psychological works of Sigmund Freud* (Vol. 7, pp. 135-243). London: Hogarth Press. (Original work published 1905)

Freud, S. (1961). *Civilization and its discontents*. In J. Strachey (Ed. and Trans.), *Standard edition of the complete psychological works of Sigmund Freud* (Vol. 21, pp. 64-145). London: Hogarth Press. (Original work published 1930)

Freud, S. (1964a). Femininity. In J. Strachey (Ed. and Trans.), *Standard edition of the complete psychological works of Sigmund Freud* (Vol. 22, pp. 112-135). London: Hogarth Press. (Original work published 1933)

Freud, S. (1964b). *New introductory lectures on psychoanalysis*. In J. Strachey (Ed. and Trans.), *Standard edition of the complete psychological works of Sigmund Freud* (Vol. 22, pp. 5-182). London: Hogarth Press. (Original work published 1932)

Freud, S. (1966a). *Extracts from the Fliess papers*. In J. Strachey (Ed. and Trans.), *Standard edition of the complete psychological works of Sigmund Freud* (Vol. 1, pp. 177-293). London: Hogarth Press. (Original work published 1892-1899)

Freud, S. (1966b). *Project for a scientific psychology*. In J. Strachey (Ed. and Trans.), *Standard edition of the complete psychological works of Sigmund Freud* (Vol. 1, pp. 295-397). London: Hogarth Press. (Original work published 1895)

Fry, P. H. (1983). *The reach of criticism*. New Haven: Yale University Press.

Frye, N. (1982). *The great code: The Bible and literature*. New York: Harcourt Brace Jovanovich.

Gallop, J. (1982). *The daughter's seduction: Feminism and psychoanalysis*. Ithaca, NY: Cornell University Press.

Gallop, J. (1985). *Reading Lacan*. Ithaca, NY: Cornell University Press.

Gee, J. P., & Ong, W. J. (1983). An exchange on American sign language and deaf culture. *Language and Sign, 16*, 231-237.

Geertz, C. (1973). Thick description: Toward an interpretive theory of culture. In *The interpretation of cultures*. New York: Basic Books.

Gelb, I. J. (1974). *A study of writing* (rev. ed.). Chicago: University of Chicago Press.

Gelb, I. J. (1975). Records, writing, and decipherment. In H. H. Paper (Ed.), *Language & texts: The nature of linguistic evidence* (pp. 61-86). Ann Arbor: Center for the Coordination of Ancient and Modern Studies, University of Michigan.

Gellrich, J. M. (1985). *The idea of the book in the Middle Ages: Language theory, mythology, and fiction*. Ithaca, NY: Cornell University Press.

Gentili, B. (1988). *Poetry and its public in ancient Greece: From Homer to the fifth century* (A. T. Cole, Trans.). Baltimore: Johns Hopkins University Press. (Original work published 1985)

George, D. H. (1979). The Miltonic ideal: A paradigm for the structure of relations between men and women in academia. *College English, 40*, 864-871.

Giddens, A. (1984). *The constitution of society*. Cambridge: Polity Press.

Gilbert, N. W. (1960). *Renaissance concepts of method*. New York: Columbia University Press.

Gilbert, S. M., & Gubar, S. (1987). *No man's land*. New Haven: Yale University Press.

Gilligan, C. (1982). *In a different voice: Psychological theory and women's development*. Cambridge, MA: Harvard University Press.

Gilman, S. (1981). *Galdós and the art of the European novel, 1867-1887*. Princeton: Princeton University Press.

Gimbutas, M. (1982). *The goddesses and gods of old Europe, 6500-3500 BC: Myths and cult images*. Berkeley: University of California Press.

Golding, P., & Elliott, P. (1979). *Making the news*. London: Longman.

Goody, J. (1986). *The logic of writing and the organization of society*. Cambridge, UK: Cambridge University Press.

Goody, J. (1987). *The interface between the written and the oral*. Cambridge, UK: Cambridge University Press.

Goody, J., & Watt, I. (1968). The consequences of literacy. In *Literacy in traditional societies* (pp. 27-68). Cambridge, UK: Cambridge University Press.

Gouldner, A. W. (1976). *The dialectic of ideology and technology*. New York: Seabury.

Gronbeck, B. E. (1981). McLuhan as rhetorical theorist. *Journal of Communication, 31*, 117-128.

Gronbeck, B. E. (1990). Communication technology, consciousness, and culture: Supplementing FM-2030's view of transhumanity. In M. J. Medhurst, A. Gonzales, & T. R. Peterson (Eds.). *Communication and the culture of technology* (pp. 3-18). Pullman: Washington State University Press.

Gusdorf, G. (1965). *Speaking (La parole)* (P. T. Brockelman, Trans.). Evanston, IL: Northwestern University Press. (Original work published 1953)

Guzmán Reina, A. (1955). Valoración del analfabetismo en España. Estudio sobre sus causas y remedios. In A. Guzmán Reina et al. (Eds.), *Causas y remedios del analfabetismo en España* (pp. 11-77). Madrid: Ministerio de Educación Nacional.

Habermas, J. (1974). The public sphere. *New German Critique, 1*(3), 49-55.

Habermas, J. (1979). *Communication and the evolution of society* (T. McCarthy, Trans.). Boston: Beacon. (Original work published 1976)

Hall, E. T. (1959). *The silent language*. Garden City, NY: Doubleday.

Harding, S. (1986). *The science question in feminism.* Ithaca, NY: Cornell University Press.

Havelock, E. A. (1963). *Preface to Plato.* Cambridge, MA: Belknap Press of Harvard University Press.

Havelock, E. A. (1978). *The Greek concept of justice: From its shadow in Homer to its substance in Plato.* Cambridge, MA: Harvard University Press.

Havelock, E. A. (1982). *The literate revolution in Greece and its cultural consequences.* Princeton: Princeton University Press.

Havelock, E. A. (1986). *The muse learns to write.* New Haven: Yale University Press.

Heath, S. B. (1983). *Ways with words.* New York: Cambridge University Press.

Hekmatpour, S., & Ince, D. C. (1988). *Software prototyping, formal methods, and VDM.* Reading, MA: Addison-Wesley.

Heilbrun, C. (1973). *Toward a recognition of androgyny.* New York: Knopf.

Heim, M. (1987). *Electric language: A philosophical study of word processing.* New Haven: Yale University Press.

Henry, D. P. (1972). *Medieval logic and metaphysics: A modern introduction.* London: Hutchinson.

Hill, A. O. (1986). *Mother tongue, father time.* Bloomington: Indiana University Press.

Hillman, J. (1975). *Re-visioning psychology.* New York: Harper & Row.

Hillmann, M. C. (1981). Language and social distinctions in Iran. In M. Bonine & N. Keddie (Eds.), *Modern Iran: Dialectics of continuity and change.* Albany: State University of New York Press.

Hispanus, P. (1947). *Summulae logicales.* I. M. Bochenski (Ed.). Turin: Marietti.

Hoover, S. M. (1982). *The electronic giant: A critique of the telecommunications revolution from a Christian perspective.* Elgin, IL: Brethren Press.

Horkheimer, M., & Adorno, T. (1972). *Dialectic of enlightenment* (J. Cumming, Trans.). New York: Herder & Herder. (Original work published 1947)

Householder, F. W. (1971). The primacy of writing. In F. W. Householder (Ed.), *Linguistic speculations* (pp. 244-264). Cambridge, UK: Cambridge University Press.

Houston, J. (1980). *Lifeforce: The psycho-historical recovery of the self.* New York: Delacorte.

Howell, W. S. (1956). *Logic and rhetoric in England: 1500-1700.* Princeton: Princeton University Press.

Howell, W. S. (1960). Ramus and the decay of dialogue [Review of Ong's *Ramus, method and the decay of dialogue*]. *Quarterly Journal of Speech, 46,* 86-92.

Howell, W. S. (1971). *Eighteenth-century British logic and rhetoric.* Princeton: Princeton University Press.

Husserl, E. (1965). *Phenomenology and the crisis of philosophy* (Q. Lauer, Trans.). New York: Harper & Row. (Original works published 1911 and 1954)

Hyde, L. (1983). *The gift: Imagination and the erotic life of property.* New York: Vintage.

Illich, I. (1982). *Gender.* New York: Pantheon.

Illich, I., & Sanders, B. (1988). *ABC: The alphabetization of the popular mind.* San Francisco: North Point.

Innis, H. A. (1972). *Empire and communications* (M. Q. Innis, Rev.). Toronto: University of Toronto Press.

Irigaray, L. (1985a). *Speculum of the other woman* (G. C. Gill, Trans.). Ithaca, NY: Cornell University Press. (Original work published 1974)

Irigaray, L. (1985b). *This sex which is not one* (C. Porter, Trans.). Ithaca, NY: Cornell University Press. (Original work published 1977)

Isaacs, H. R. (1978). Bringing up the father question. *Daedalus, 107,* 189-203.

Jardine, L. (1974). *Francis Bacon: Discovery and the art of discourse*. Cambridge, UK: Cambridge University Press.

Jensen, J. (1990). *Redeeming modernity: Contradictions in media criticism*. Newbury Park, CA: Sage.

Johnson, R. A. (1986). *She: Understanding feminine psychology: An interpretation based on the myth of Amor and Psyche and using Jungian psychological concepts*. New York: Harper & Row Perennial Library.

José Prades, J. de. (1954). *La teoría literaria*. Madrid: Instituto de Estudios Madrileños.

Juana Ines de la Cruz, Sister. (1982). *A woman of genius: The intellectual autobiography of Sor Juana Ines de la Cruz* (M. S. Peden, Trans. and author of introduction). Salisbury, CT: Lime Rock Press. (Original work published 1929)

Jung, C. G. (1956). *Symbols of transformation* (R. F. C. Hull, Trans.). In H. Read, M. Fordham, & G. Adler (Eds.), *The collected works of C. G. Jung* (Vol. 5). Princeton: Princeton University Press. (Original work published 1912)

Kahler, E. (1973). *The inward turn of narrative*. (R. Winston & C. Winston, Trans.). Princeton: Princeton University Press.

Kant, I. (1908). *Kants Werke: Vol. 5. Kritik der Urteilskraft*. Königlich Preussischen Akademie der Wissenschaften. Berlin: Georg Reimer. (Original work published 1790)

Kant, I. (1909). *Critique of practical reason and other works on the theory of ethics* (T. K. Abbott, Trans.) (6th ed.). London: Longmans, Green & Co. (Original work publised 1785)

Kant, I. (1951). *Critique of judgment*. (J. H. Bernard, Trans.). New York: Macmillan. (Original work published 1790)

Katz, E., & Liebes, T. (1985). Mutual aid in the decoding of *Dallas*: Preliminary notes for a cross-cultural study. In P. Drummond & R. Paterson (Eds.), *Television in transition* (pp. 187-198). London: British Film Institute.

Kelber, W. H. (1983). *The oral and the written Gospel: The hermeneutics of speaking and writing in the synoptic tradition, Mark, Paul, and Q*. Philadelphia: Fortress Press.

Keller, E. F. (1985). *Reflections on gender and science*. New Haven: Yale University Press.

Kennedy, G. (1980). *Classical rhetoric and its Christian and secular tradition from ancient to modern times*. Chapel Hill: University of North Carolina Press.

Kennedy, W. J. (1978). *Rhetorical norms in Renaissance literature*. New Haven: Yale University Press.

Kennedy, W. J. (1987). "Voice" and "address" in literary theory. *Oral Tradition, 2*, 214-230.

Kerr, M., & Bowen, M. (1988). *Family evaluation: An approach based on Bowen theory*. New York: Norton.

Keuls, E. C. (1985). *The reign of the phallus: Sexual politics in ancient Athens*. New York: Harper & Row.

Kiparsky, P. (1976). Oral poetry: Some linguistic and typological considerations. In B. A. Stolz & R. C. Shannon (Eds.), *Oral literature and the formula* (pp. 73-106). Ann Arbor: Center for the Coordination of Ancient and Modern Studies, University of Michigan.

Kirk, G. S. (1976). *Homer and the oral tradition*. Cambridge, UK: Cambridge University Press.

Kittay, E. F., & Meyers, D. (Eds.). (1986). *Women and moral theory*. Totowa, NJ: Rowman.

Klein, M. (1975). *Envy and gratitude and other works: 1946-1963*. New York: Delacorte.

Kroll, B., & Vann, R. J. (1981). Introduction. In B. Kroll & R. J. Vann (Eds.), *Exploring speaking-writing relationships: Connection and contrasts* (pp. vii-xi). Urbana, IL: National Council of Teachers of English.

Lakoff, R. (1975). *Language and woman's place*. New York: Harper & Row.

Laplanche, J. (1976). *Life and death in psychoanalysis* (J. Mehlman, Trans.). Baltimore: Johns Hopkins University Press. (Original work published 1970)

Laplanche, J., & Pontalis, J-B. (1973). *The language of psychoanalysis*. London: Hogarth Press.

Lasch, C. (1979). *The culture of narcissism*. New York: Norton.

Lechner, J. M. (1962). *Renaissance concepts of the commonplaces*. New York: Pageant.

Leeman, A. D. (1982). The variety of classical rhetoric. In B. Vickers (Ed.), *Rhetoric revalued* (pp. 41-46). Binghamton, NY: Center for Medieval & Early Renaissance Studies.

Leiss, W. (1972). *The domination of nature*. Boston: Beacon.

Leith, P. (1988). *The LEXICAL Manual*. Belfast: Queen's University.

Leith, P. (1990). *Formalism in AI and computer science*. Chichester, UK: Ellis Horwood.

Lerner, D. (1958). *The passing of traditional society*. New York: Free Press.

Lever, J. (1976). Sex differences in the games children play. *Social Problems, 23,* 478-487.

Lever, J. (1978). Sex differences in the complexity of children's play and games. *American Sociological Review, 43,* 471-483.

Lévi-Strauss, C. (1962). *La pensée sauvage*. Paris: Plon.

Lewis, B. (1988). *The political language of Islam*. Chicago: University of Chicago Press.

Logan, R. K. (1986). *The alphabet effect: The impact of the phonetic alphabet on the development of Western civilization*. New York: William Morrow.

Lonergan, B. (1972). *Method in theology*. New York: Herder & Herder.

Lonergan, B. (1991). *Insight: A study of human understanding*. In F. E. Crowe & R. M. Doran (Eds.), *Collected works of Bernard Lonergan* (Vol. 3). Toronto: University of Toronto Press. (Original work published 1958)

Longinus. (1927). *On the sublime* (W. H. Fyfe, Ed. and Trans.). Loeb Classical Library. London: Heinemann.

López, F. (1981). 'Lisants' et lecteurs en Espagne au XVIIIe siècle. Ebauche d'une problématique. *Livre et lecture en Espagne et en France sous l'Ancien Régime* (pp. 139-148). Colloque de la Casa de Velázquez. Paris: Editions ADPF.

López-Grigera, L. (1983). Introduction to the study of rhetoric in sixteenth-century Spain. *Dispositio: Revista hispánica de semiótica literaria, 8,* 1-18.

Lord, A. B. (1960). *The singer of tales*. Cambridge, MA: Harvard University Press.

Lumpp, R. F. (1987a). A biographical portrait of Walter Jackson Ong. *Oral Tradition, 2,* 13-18.

Lumpp, R. F. (1987b). Selected bibliography of Ong's writings. *Oral Tradition, 2,* 19-30.

Luria, A. R. (1976). *Cognitive development: Its cultural and social foundations* (M. Lopez-Morillas & L. Solotaroff, Trans.; M. Cole, Ed.). Cambridge, MA: Harvard University Press.

MacIntyre, A. (1984). *After virtue: A study in moral theory*. South Bend, IN: Notre Dame University Press.

Mahler, M. (1980). Rapprochement subphase of the separation-individuation process. In R. Lax, S. Bach, & J. A. Burland (Eds.), *Rapprochement: The critical subphase of separation and individuation* (pp. 3-19). New York: Jason Aronson.

Mahowald, M. (1986-1987). A majority perspective: Feminine and feminist elements in American philosophy. *Cross Currents, 36,* 410-417.

Malone, T. P., & Malone, P. T. (1987). *The art of intimacy*. New York: Prentice-Hall.

Manuel, J. (1982). *Libro del cauallero et del escudero*. In J. M. Blecua (Ed.), *Obras completas I* (pp. 35-116). Madrid: Gredos. (Original work published 1326)

Manuel, J. (1983). *El Conde Lucanor*. In J. M. Blecua (Ed.), *Obras completas II* (pp. 7-504). Madrid: Gredos. (Original work published 1335)

Marder, H. (1968). *Feminism and art: A study of Virginia Woolf.* Chicago: University of Chicago Press.

Marrast, R. (1974). Libro y lectura en la España del siglo XIX. Temas de investigación. *Movimiento obrero, política y literatura en la España contemporánea* (pp. 145-157). Madrid: Edicusa/Editorial Cuadernos para el Diálogo.

Martínez Cachero, J. M. (1959). Biografía del poeta Emilio Ferrari. *Archivum 9,* 95-153.

Maslow, A. (1971). *The farther reaches of human nature.* New York: Viking.

Maxwell, K. B. (1983). *Bemba myth and ritual: The impact of literacy on an oral culture.* New York: Peter Lang.

Mayr, E. (1963). *Animal species and evolution.* Cambridge, MA: Belknap Press of Harvard University Press.

McLuhan, M. (1962). *The Gutenberg galaxy: The making of typographic man.* Toronto: University of Toronto Press.

McLuhan, M., & Fiore, Q. (1968). *War and peace in the global village.* New York: Bantam.

McNamee, M. B. (1960). *Honor and the epic hero: A study of the shifting concept of magnanimity in philosophy and epic poetry.* New York: Holt, Rinehart & Winston.

Menéndez Pidal, R. (Ed.). (1900). Disputa del alma y el cuerpo. *Revista de archivos bibliotecas y museos, 4,* 449-53.

Menéndez Pidal, R. (Ed.). (1905). Siesta de abril: Razón de amor con los denuestos del agua y el vino. *Revue Hispanique, 13,* 602-18.

Menéndez Pidal, R. (Ed.). (1914). Elena y María. *Revista de filología Española, 1,* 52-96.

Mercer, C. (1986). That's entertainment: The resilience of popular forms. In T. Bennett, C. Mercer, & J. Woollacott (Eds.), *Popular culture and social relations* (pp. 177-195). Milton Keynes, UK: Open University Press.

Merchant, C. (1980). *The death of nature.* London: Wildwood House.

Meyrowitz, J. (1985). *No sense of place: The impact of electronic media on social behavior.* New York: Oxford University Press.

Miller, J. B. (1986). *Toward a new psychology of women* (rev. 2nd ed.). Boston: Beacon.

Miller, J. H. (1987). *The ethics of reading.* New York: Columbia University Press.

Miller, P. (1939). *The New England mind: The seventeenth century.* Cambridge, MA: Harvard University Press.

Miller, P. (1953). *The New England mind: From colony to province.* Cambridge, MA: Harvard University Press.

Milton, J. (1982). *A fuller course in the art of logic conformed to the method of Peter Ramus* (W. J. Ong & C. J. Ermatinger, Trans.). In M. Kelley (Ed.), *Complete prose works of John Milton* (Vol. 8, pp. 206-407). New Haven: Yale University Press. (Original work published 1672)

Mitchell, T. (1988). *Violence and piety in Spanish folklore.* Philadelphia: University of Pennsylvania Press.

Modleski, T. (1983). The rhythm of reception: Daytime television and women's work. In E. A. Kaplan (Ed.), *Regarding television* (pp. 67-75). Los Angeles: American Film Institute.

Moral, J. F. del (1943). Lecturas públicas. In N. Alonso Cortés (Ed.), J. Zorrilla, *Obras completas* (Vol. 2, pp. 7-10). Valladolid: Librería Santarén.

Muñoz y Manzano, C., Count of La Viñaza. (1893). *Biblioteca histórica de la filología castellana.* Madrid: M. Tello.

Murphy, J. J. (1981). *Renaissance rhetoric: A short title catalogue of works on rhetorical theory from the beginning of printing to A.D. 1700, with special attention to the holdings of the*

Bodleian library, Oxford [and] with a select basic bibliography of secondary works on Renaissance rhetoric. New York: Garland.

Navarra, P. de. (c. 1560). *Diálogos dela differencia del hablar al escrevir. . . .* Toulouse: Iacobo Colomerio. Exemplar of the Biblioteca de la Real Academia Española, Madrid. R-78.

Navarra, P. de. (1968). *Diálogos dela differencia del hablar al escrevir. . . .* D. O. Chambers (Ed.). (Available from D. O. Chambers)

Navarra, P. de. (1985). *Diálogos dela differencia del hablar al escrevir. . . .* P. M. Cátedra (Ed.). Bellaterra [Barcelona]: Stelle dell'Orsa.

Neumann, E. (1954). *The origins and history of consciousness* (R. F. C. Hull, Trans.). New York: Pantheon. (Original work published 1949)

Neumann, E. (1966). Narcissism, normal self-formation and the primary relation to the mother. *Spring*, 81-106.

Olson, D. R. (1986). Interpreting texts and interpreting nature: The effects of literacy on hermeneutics and epistemology. *Visible Language, 20,* 302-317.

Olson, D. R. (Ed.). (1987). Special issue: Understanding literacy. *Interchange, 18*(1/2), 1-173.

Olson, D. R., & de Kerckove, D. (Eds.). (1986). Special issue: The origins and functions of literacy. *Visible Language, 20,* 248-361.

Olson, D. R., Torrance, N., & Hildyard, A. (1985). *Literacy, language, and learning: The nature and consequences of reading and writing*. Cambridge, UK: Cambridge University Press.

Ong, W. J. (1949). Hopkins' sprung rhythm and the life of English poetry. In N. Weyand, SJ (Ed.), *Immortal diamond: Studies in Gerard Manley Hopkins* (pp. 173-182). New York: Sheed and Ward.

Ong, W. J. (1951). Hobbes and Talon's Ramist rhetoric in English. *Transactions of the Cambridge [England] Bibliographical Society, 1*(Pt. 3), 260-269.

Ong, W. J. (1953). Peter Ramus and the naming of Methodism: Medieval science through Ramist homiletic. *Journal of the History of Ideas, 14,* 235-248.

Ong, W. J. (1954a). Ramus: Rhetoric and the pre-Newtonian mind. In A. S. Downer (Ed.), *English institute essays 1952* (pp. 138-170). New York: Columbia University Press.

Ong, W. J. (1954b). Fouquelin's French rhetoric and the Ramist vernacular tradition. *Studies in Philology, 51,* 127-142.

Ong, W. J. (1954c). Johannes Piscator: One man or a Ramist dichotomy? *Harvard Library Bulletin, 8,* 151-162.

Ong, W. J. (1955a). Ramus and the transit to the modern mind. *Modern Schoolman, 32,* 301-311.

Ong, W. J. (1955b). Père Cossart, Du Monstier, and Ramus' Protestantism in the light of a new manuscript. *Archivum historicum Societatis Iesu* (Rome), *24*(fasc. 47), 140-164.

Ong, W. J. (1957). *Frontiers in American Catholicism: Essays on ideology and culture*. New York: Macmillan.

Ong, W. J. (1958a). *Ramus, method, and the decay of dialogue: From the art of discourse to the art of reason*. Cambridge, MA: Harvard University Press. Preface to the paperback edition, 1983, pp. vii-viii.

Ong, W. J. (1958b). *Ramus and Talon inventory: A short-title inventory of the published works of Peter Ramus (1515-72) and of Omer Talon (ca. 1510-62) in their original and in their variously altered forms, with related material*. Cambridge, MA: Harvard University Press.

Ong, W. J. (1959). *American Catholic crossroads: Religious-secular encounters in the modern world*. New York: Macmillan.

Ong, W. J. (Ed. and co-author). (1960a). *Darwin's vision and Christian perspectives*. New York: Macmillan.

Ong, W. J. (1960b). Ramist classroom procedure and the nature of reality. *Studies in English Literature, 1*, 31-47.

Ong, W. J. (1961). Ramist method and the commercial mind. *Studies in the Renaissance, 8*, 155-172.

Ong, W. J. (1962a). *The barbarian within: And other fugitive essays and studies.* New York: Macmillan.

Ong, W. J. (1962b). Foreword. In L. J. Haigerty (Comp.), *Pius XII and technology* (pp. vii-x). Milwaukee: Bruce.

Ong, W. J. (1964). A Ramist translation of Euripides. *Manuscripta, 8*, 18-28.

Ong, W. J. (1965). [Review of P. Ramus, *Dialecticae Institutiones; Aristotelicae Animadversiones.*] *Renaissance News, 18*, 31-33.

Ong, W. J. (1966). [Review of P. de la Ramée, *Dialectique.*] *Renaissance News, 19*, 142-144.

Ong, W. J. (1967a). *In the human grain: Further explorations of contemporary culture.* New York: Macmillan.

Ong, W. J. (1967b). *The presence of the word: Some prolegomena for cultural and religious history.* New Haven: Yale University Press.

Ong, W. J. (1967c). Ramus, Peter. In P. Edwards (Ed.), *The encyclopedia of philosophy* (Vol. 7, pp. 66-68). New York: Macmillan and Free Press of Glencoe.

Ong, W. J. (1967d). Ramus, Peter. In W. J. McDonald et al. (Eds.), *The new Catholic encyclopedia* (Vol. 12, pp. 77-78). New York: McGraw-Hill.

Ong, W. J. (Ed. and co-author). (1968). *Knowledge and the future of man: An international symposium.* New York: Holt, Rinehart & Winston. Ong now likes to note that, had that volume appeared later, instead of more than two decades ago in 1968—to commemorate the 150th anniversary of the founding of Saint Louis University—he would certainly have opted for the title *Knowledge and the Future of the Human Race.*

Ong, W. J. (Ed. facsimile reproduction and author of introduction). (1969). P. Ramus & A. Talaeus, *Collectaneae praefationes, epistolae, orationes.* Hildesheim, Germany: Georg Olms Verlagsbuchhandlung.

Ong, W. J. (Ed. facsimile reproduction and author of introduction). (1970). P. Ramus, *Scholae in liberales artes.* Hildesheim, Germany: Georg Olms Verlagsbuchhandlung.

Ong, W. J. (1971). *Rhetoric, romance, and technology: Studies in the interaction of expression and culture.* Ithaca, NY: Cornell University Press.

Ong, W. J. (1972). [Review of *Eighteenth century British logic and rhetoric*]. *William and Mary Quarterly, 29*, 637-643.

Ong, W. J. (1974a). Agonistic structures in academia: Past to present. *Interchange: A Journal of Education, 5*(4), 1-12.

Ong, W. J. (1974b). Christianus Urstitius and Ramus' new mathematics. *Bibliotheque d'Humanisme et Renaissance, 36*, 603-610.

Ong, W. J. (1977a). *Interfaces of the word: Studies in the evolution of consciousness and culture.* Ithaca, NY: Cornell University Press.

Ong, W. J. (1977b). Truth in Conrad's darkness. *Mosaic: A Journal for the Comparative Study of Literature and Ideas, 11*, 151-163.

Ong, W. J. (1978a). Technology outside us and inside us. *Communio, 5*, 100-121.

Ong, W. J. (1978b). Literacy and orality in our times. *ADE Bulletin,* (Serial No. 58), 1-7. [ADE = Association of Departments of English, part of the Modern Language Association of America.]

Ong, W. J. (1979a). Comment. *College English, 40*, 871-873.

Ong, W. J. (1979b). Presidential address 1978: The human nature of professionalism. *PMLA: Publications of the Modern Language Association of America, 94,* 385-394.

Ong, W. J. (1981a). *Fighting for life: Contest, sexuality, and consciousness.* Ithaca, NY: Cornell University Press.

Ong, W. J. (1981b). McLuhan as teacher: The future is a thing of the past. *Journal of Communication, 31,* 129-135.

Ong, W. J. (1982a). Introduction [of J. Milton, *A fuller course in the art of logic*]. In M. Kelley (Ed.), *Complete prose works of Milton* (Vol. 8, pp. 139-205). New Haven: Yale University Press.

Ong, W. J. (1982b). *Orality and literacy: The technologizing of the word.* London: Methuen.

Ong, W. J. (1986a). *Hopkins, the self, and God.* Toronto: Toronto University Press.

Ong, W. J. (1986b). Writing is a technology that restructures thought. In G. Baumann (Ed.), *The written word: Literacy in transition* (pp. 23-50). [Wolfson College Lectures 1985.] Oxford: Clarendon Press of Oxford University Press.

Ong, W. J. (1987). Text as interpretation: Mark and after. *Semeia,* (Serial No. 39), 7-26.

Ong, W. J. (1988). Before textuality: Orality and interpretation. *Oral Tradition, 3,* 259-269.

Ong, W. J. (1990). Technological developments and writer-subject-reader immediacies. In R. L. Enos (Ed.), *Oral and written communication: Historical perspectives* (pp. 206-215). Newbury Park, CA: Sage.

Opland, J. (1983). *Xhosa oral poetry: Aspects of a black South African tradition.* Cambridge, UK: Cambridge University Press.

Ortega y Gasset, J. (1958). La estrangulación de 'Don Juan.' *Obras completas* (4th ed.) (Vol. 5, pp. 242-250). Madrid: Revista de Occidente.

Ortner, S. B. (1974). Is female to male as nature is to culture? In M. Z. Rosaldo and L. Lamphere (Eds.), *Women, culture, and society* (pp. 67-87). Palo Alto: Stanford University Press.

Parks, W. (1990). *Verbal dueling in heroic narrative: The Homeric and Old English traditions.* Princeton: Princeton University Press.

Parry, A. (Ed.). (1971). *The making of Homeric verse: The collected papers of Milman Parry.* Oxford: Clarendon Press of Oxford University Press.

Pastor Díaz, N. (1943). Prologue. In N. Alonso Cortés (Ed.), J. Zorrilla, *Obras completas* (Vol. 1, pp. 13-24). Valladolid: Librería Santarén.

Payne, D. (1983). Francis Bacon and the commonplaces. *Central States Speech Journal, 34,* 247-254.

Payne, D. (1989). *Coping with failure: The therapeutic uses of rhetoric.* Columbia: University of South Carolina Press.

Peat, F. D. (1987). *Synchronicity: The bridge between matter and mind.* New York: Bantam.

Perelman, C., & Olbrechts-Tyteca, L. (1969). *The new rhetoric: A treatise on argumentation* (J. Wilkinson & P. Weaver, Trans.). South Bend, IN: Notre Dame University Press. (Original work published 1958)

Pérez Galdós, B. (1986). *Fortunata and Jacinta* (A. M. Gullón, Trans.). Athens: University of Georgia Press. (Original work published 1887)

Perkins, P. (1980). *The Gnostic dialogue: The early church and the crisis of Gnosticism.* New York: Paulist Press.

Postman, N. (1985). *Amusing ourselves to death: Public discourse in the age of show business.* New York: Elisabeth Sifton Books/Viking.

Poulakos, J. (1983, Autumn). Gorgias' Encomium to Helen and the defense of rhetoric. *Rhetorica, 1,* 1-16.

Poulakos, J. (1984). Rhetoric, the sophists, and the possible. *Communication Monographs, 51,* 215-226.

Poulakos, T. (1989). The historical intervention of Gorgias' *Epitaphios*: The genre of funeral oration and the Athenian institution of public burials. *Pre/Text 10* (1-2), 90-99.

Poynton, C. (1989). *Language and gender: Making the difference.* New York: Oxford University Press.

Prigogine, I., & Stengers, I. (1984). *Order out of chaos: Man's new dialogue with nature.* New York: Bantam.

Puttenham, G. (1936). *The arte of English poesie.* G. D. Willcock & A. Walker (Eds.). London: Cambridge University Press.

Quintilian. (1920-1922). *Institutio oratoria* (Vols. 1-4). (H.E. Butler, Ed. and Trans.). Loeb Classical Library. London: Heinemann.

Rakow, L. F. (1988). Gendered technology, gendered practice. *Critical Studies in Mass Communication, 5*(1), 57-70.

Ramírez Angel, E. (1915 [?]). *José Zorrilla. Biografía anecdótica.* Madrid: Ed. Mundo Latino.

Rattansi, P. M. (1963). Paracelsus and the Puritan revolution. *Ambix, 2,* 24-32.

Rhetorical Seminar of the University of Michigan. (1983). Data format-bibliography [of Hispanic Rhetorical Treatises]. *Dispositio: Revista hispánica de semiótica literaria, 8,* 19-64.

Richards, I. A. (1936). *The philosophy of rhetoric.* New York: Oxford University Press.

Ricoeur, P. (1977). *The rule of metaphor: Multi-disciplinary studies of the creation of meaning in language* (R. Czerny, K. McLaughlin, & J. Costello, Trans.). Toronto: University of Toronto Press. (Original work published 1975)

Riemer, G. (1971). *The new Jesuits.* Boston: Little, Brown.

Riesman, D., Denny, R., & Glazer, N. (1950). *The lonely crowd: A study of the changing American character.* New Haven: Yale University Press.

Rivers, E. L. (1984). Lo escrito y lo oral: Don Pedro de Navarra. In L. Schwartz Lerner & I. Lerner (Eds.). *Homenaje a Ana María Barrenechea* (pp. 307-311). Madrid: Castalia.

Rivers, E. L. (1987). Two functions of social discourse: From Lope de Vega to Miguel de Cervantes. *Oral Tradition, 2,* 249-259.

Rojas, F. de. (1982). *La Celestina* (9th ed.). D. S. Severin (Ed.). Madrid: Alianza.

Rosenthal, A. (1983). Feminism without contradictions. *The Monist, 51,* 28-42.

Rossi, P. (1968). *Francis Bacon: From magic to science* (S. Rabinovitch, Trans). Chicago: University of Chicago Press. (Original work published 1957)

Saenger, P. (1982). Silent reading: Its impact on late medieval script and society. *Viator: Medieval and Renaissance Studies, 13,* 367-414.

Salvá y Mallen, P. (1872). *Catálogo de la biblioteca de Salvá* (Vols. 1-2). Valencia: Ferrer de Orga.

[Sancho IV]. (1968). *Los "lucidarios" españoles.* R. P. Kinkade (Ed.). Madrid: Gredos.

Santiago y Palomares, F. J. de. (1786). *El maestro de leer: Conversaciones ortológicas* (Vols. 1-2). Madrid: Sancha.

Sayers, D. L. (1949). Introduction. In D. L. Sayers (Trans.), *The comedy of Dante Alighieri, the Florentine: Cantica I, hell* (9-66). New York: Penguin.

Schaeffer, J. D. (1990). *Sensus communis: Vico, rhetoric, and the limits of relativism.* Durham, NC: Duke University Press.

Scholes, R., & Kellogg, R. (1966). *The nature of narrative.* London: Oxford University Press.

Schramm, W. (1964). *Mass media and national development.* Palo Alto: Stanford University Press.

Schwartz, K. (1988). Sound in the early poetry of Zorrilla. *Revista de Estudios Hispánicos, 22,* 31-49.

Scribner, S., & Cole, M. (1981). *The psychology of literacy.* Cambridge, MA: Harvard University Press.

Sebold, R. P. (1983). *Trayectoria del romanticismo Español.* Barcelona: Ed. Crítica.

Sennett, R. (1979). *The fall of public man.* New York: Random House.

Sharratt, P. (1987). Recent works on Peter Ramus (1970-1986). *Rhetorica: A Journal of the History of Rhetoric, 5,* 7-58.

Silberman, L. H. (Ed.). (1987). Orality, aurality, and biblical narrative. *Semeia,* (Series No. 39), 1-145.

Silverstone, R. (1985). *Framing science: The making of a BBC documentary.* London: British Film Institute.

Silverstone, R. (1990). Television and everyday life: Towards an anthropology of the television audience. In M. Ferguson (Ed.), *Public communication: The new imperatives* (pp. 173-189). Newbury Park, CA: Sage.

Singer, J. (1976). *Androgyny.* Garden City, NY: Anchor Press/Doubleday.

Solà-Solé, J. M. (Ed.). (1981). *Dança general de la muerte.* Barcelona: Puvill.

Spretnak, C. (1978). *Lost goddesses of early Greece: A collection of pre-Hellenic myths.* Boston: Beacon.

Sreberny-Mohammadi, A. (1985). The power of tradition: Communication and the Iranian revolution. (Doctoral dissertation, Columbia University, 1985). *Dissertation Abstracts International, 47,* 11a. (University Microfilms No. 86-04, 680)

Sreberny-Mohammadi, A. (1990). Small media for a big revolution: Iran. *International Journal of Politics, Culture and Society, 3,* 341-371.

St. Clair, R. N., & Giles, H. (Eds.). (1980). *The social and psychological contexts of language.* Hillsdale, NJ: Lawrence Erlbaum Associates.

Stanford, W. B. (1967). *The sound of Greek: Studies in the Greek theory and practice of euphony.* Berkeley: University of California Press.

Stephens, J. (1975a). *Francis Bacon and the style of science.* Chicago: University of Chicago Press.

Stephens, J. (1975b). Rhetorical problems in Renaissance science. *Philosophy and Rhetoric, 8,* 213-229.

Stock, B. (1983). *The implications of literacy: Written language and models of interpretation in the eleventh and twelfth centuries.* Princeton: Princeton University Press.

Sussman, H. (1989). *High resolution, critical theory and the problem of literacy.* New York: Oxford University Press.

Swearingen, C. J. (Ed.). (1986). The literacy/orality wars. *Pre/Text, 7,* 117-208.

Toolan, D. (1987). *Facing west from California's shore: A Jesuit's journey to new age consciousness.* New York: Crossroad.

Toulmin, S. (1958). *The uses of argument.* Cambridge, UK: Cambridge University Press.

Tuman, M. C. (1987) *A preface to literacy: An inquiry into pedagogy, practice, and progress.* Tuscaloosa: University of Alabama Press.

Turkle, S. (1984). *The second self: Computers and the human spirit.* New York: Simon & Schuster.

Tyler, S. A. (1987). *The unspeakable: Discourse, dialogue, and rhetoric in the postmodern world.* Madison: University of Wisconsin Press.

Unamuno, M. de (1950). El zorrillismo estético. In M. García Blanco (Ed.), *De esto y de aquello, 1* (pp. 78-85). Buenos Aires: Edit. Sudamericana.

Unamuno, M. de. (1954a). La personalidad de la voz. In M. García Blanco (Ed.), *De esto y de aquello, 4* (pp. 592-594). Buenos Aires: Edit. Sudamericana.

Unamuno, M. de (1954b). Unos versos de Zorrilla. *De esto y de aquello, 4* (pp. 575-577). Buenos Aires: Edit. Sudamericana.

Valdés, A. de. (1928). *Diálogo de las cosas ocurridas en Roma*. J. F. Montesinos (Ed.). Madrid: Ediciones de "La Lectura." (Original work published 1529)

Valdés, J. de. (1928). *Diálogo de la lengua*. J. F. Montesinos (Ed.). Madrid: Ediciones de "La Lectura." (Original work published 1736)

Valis, N. M. (1986). Pardo Bazán's *El Cisne de Vilamorta* and the romantic reader. *MLN: Modern Language Notes, 101,* 298-324.

van Beeck, F. J. (1979). *Christ proclaimed: Christology as rhetoric*. New York: Paulist Press.

van Beeck, F. J. (1989). *God encountered: A contemporary Catholic systematic theology: Vol. 1: Understanding the Christian faith*. San Francisco: Harper & Row.

Wadlington, W. (1987). *Reading Faulknerian tragedy*. Ithaca, NY: Cornell University Press.

Wallace, W. A. (1988). Thomas Aquinas on dialectics and rhetoric. In R. Link-Salinger (Ed.), *A straight path: Studies in medieval philosophy and culture* (pp. 244-254). Washington, DC: Catholic University Press.

Weaver, R. L. (1953). *The ethics of rhetoric*. South Bend, IN: Regnery/Gateway.

Weber, A. (1990). *Teresa of Avila and the rhetoric of femininity*. Princeton: Princeton University Press.

Wellek, R. (1955-1986). *A history of modern criticism* (Vols. 1-6). New Haven: Yale University Press.

Whitney, C. (1986). *Francis Bacon and modernity*. New Haven: Yale University Press.

Wimsatt, W. K., Jr., & Brooks, C. (1957). *Literary criticism: A short history*. New York: Knopf.

Winnicott, D. W. (1974). *Playing and reality*. Harmondsworth, UK: Penguin.

Winnicott, D. W. (1975). Transitional objects and transitional phenomena. In D. W. Winnicott (Ed.), *Through pediatrics to psychoanalysis* (pp. 229-242). London: Hogarth Press.

Wolf, C. (1984). *Cassandra* (J. Van Heurck, Trans.). New York: Farrar, Strauss, Giroux. (Original work published 1983)

Woolf, V. (1929). *A room of one's own*. New York: Harcourt.

Yates, F. (1964). *Giordano Bruno and the hermetic tradition*. Chicago: University of Chicago Press.

Yates, F. (1979). *The occult philosophy in the Elizabethan age*. London: Routledge & Kegan Paul.

Yates, F. A. (1966). *The art of memory*. Chicago: University of Chicago Press.

Zorrilla, J. (1925). La ignorancia. In N. Alonso Cortés (Ed.), *Poesías*. Madrid: Edición "La Lectura," Clásicos Castellanos.

Zorrilla, J. (1943). Recuerdo del tiempo viejo. In N. Alonso Cortés (Ed.), *Obras completas* (Vol. 2, pp. 654-657). Valladolid: Librería Santarén.

Zorrilla, J. (1961). *Recuerdos del tiempo viejo* (Vol. 1). Madrid: Publicaciones Españolas.

Zumthor, P. (1984). The text and the voice. *New Literary History, 16,* 67-92.

Zumthor, P. (1990). *Oral poetry: An introduction* (K. Murphy-Judy, Trans.). Minneapolis: University of Minnesota Press.

Index

About the Authors

John M. Ackerman is an Assistant Professor in the University of Utah Writing Program and Educational Studies, where he teaches courses about literacy and educational practice and business and professional writing. A recent winner of the NCTE Promising Researcher Award, his research interests include the role of prior knowledge in reading and writing, and the sociology of publishing in discourse communities.

James W. Carey is the Dean of the College of Communications, University of Illinois at Urbana-Champaign. He held the George H. Gallup Chair at the University of Iowa from 1976 to 1979. A former fellow of the National Endowment for the Humanities and the Gannett Center for Media Studies at Columbia University, Professor Carey is currently editor of the journal *Communication.* He recently edited *Media, Myths, and Narratives* (Sage, 1988) and authored *Communication as Culture* (Unwin Hyman, 1989); he has also published more than 75 essays and reviews. He has been a visiting professor at Pennsylvania State University and the University of Georgia.

Ruth El Saffar is University Research Professor at the University of Illinois at Chicago, where she teaches in the Department of Spanish and Italian. She holds doctorates in psychology and Romance languages. Her special field of research is the early modern period in Spain, with emphasis on cultural transformation and its effect on the psyche. The most recent of her four books on Cervantes is *Beyond Fiction: The Recovery of the Feminine in the Novels of Cervantes.* Editor of one collection of studies about Cervantes and of another about Spanish literature of the Golden Age, she is presently preparing a collection on Cervantes and psychoanalysis.

Richard Leo Enos is a Professor of Rhetoric in the Department of English at Carnegie Mellon University. Author of *The Literate Mode of Cicero's Legal Rhetoric* and editor and co-author of *Oral and Written Communication:*

Historical Approaches, he is the current president of the Rhetoric Society of America. His research interests include the history of rhetoric and rhetorical theory, with a specialization in classical rhetoric.

Thomas J. Farrell is an Associate Professor in the Department of Composition and in the Institute for Interdisciplinary Studies, the University of Minnesota, Duluth. His articles about orality-literacy theory have appeared in *Oral Tradition, Semeia, Pre/Text, College Composition and Communication,* the *Journal of Basic Writing, College English,* and elsewhere. His other research interests include the history and theory of rhetoric, Jungian psychology, Lonergan, Faulkner, and the Bible as literature.

Bruce E. Gronbeck is Professor and Chair of Communication Studies, The University of Iowa, Iowa City. He works in rhetorical studies, with special interests in media, politics, and cultural studies. He has authored three textbooks, two dozen book chapters, three dozen monographs and articles, convention papers, and radio commentaries on contemporary culture.

David Heckel is Raymond Allen Jones Associate Professor of English and Head of the Department of Language and Literature, Pfeiffer College, Misenheimer, North Carolina. His doctoral dissertation at Saint Louis University, which Walter Ong directed, was a study of the impact of literacy on consciousness and the transformation of the epic from the seventeenth to the twentieth century. His research interests include rhetorical and literary theory and orality-literacy studies. He is currently working on a study of the relation- ship between orality-literacy studies and poststructural literary theory.

William J. Kennedy is Professor of Comparative Literature at Cornell University. His books include *Rhetorical Norms in Renaissance Literature, Jacopo Sannazaro and the Uses of the Pastoral, Writing in the Disciplines* (as co-editor), and a forthcoming study of interpretive commentaries in early printed editions of Petrarch's sonnets.

Philip Leith is lecturer in Advanced Information Technology and Law in the School of Law at Queen's University, Belfast, Northern Ireland. He holds a Ph.D. in computer science and lectured in computer science before moving to Queen's to concentrate upon research. His current interests are the philosophy of computer science, jurisprudence, the sociology of knowledge, applications of computing in law, and the design of computer assisted legal instruction systems. Publications include *The Jurisprudence of Orthodoxy, Formalism in AI and Computer Science, The Computerised Lawyer,* and *The Barrister's World.*

Anthony J. Palmeri is an Assistant Professor in the Department of Communication, University of Wisconsin, Oshkosh. His doctoral dissertation at Wayne State University was a study of Walter Ong's work. He teaches courses in rhetorical theory and criticism, and American public address. He is currently working on a book on the rhetoric of Malcolm X.

David Payne is an Associate Professor of Communication at the University of South Florida, Tampa. Author of *Coping with Failure: The Therapeutic Uses of Rhetoric,* he conducts research in the areas of rhetoric, media studies, and the psychology of communication.

Dennis P. Seniff was Professor of Spanish in the Department of Romance and Classical Languages, Michigan State University, East Lansing. He edited several medieval texts, co-edited a bibliography on literature and law in the Middle Ages, authored a score of articles, and read numerous papers at conferences. Up to the time of his death in November 1990, he was exploring issues of orality and writing in medieval and Renaissance Hispanic literature.

Roger Silverstone is Director of the Center for Research into Innovation, Culture, and Technology and Reader in Sociology in the Department of Human Services, Brunel University, Uxbridge. He has written widely on television, technology, and contemporary culture. His current research centers on studies of the household and families' use of information and communication technologies and of the representation of science in the museum.

Paul A. Soukup, SJ, an Assistant Professor in the Communication Department of Santa Clara University, teaches courses in communication theory and communication and culture. In addition, he has explored ways of integrating theology and communication study since 1982. He is the author of *Theology and Communication: An Introduction and Review of the Literature* and *Christian Communication: A Bibliographical Survey.* His current research focuses on theological and philosophical concerns in communication theory.

Annabelle Sreberny-Mohammadi is Associate Professor and Coordinator of the Graduate Program in Media Studies, Queens College, City University of New York. Co-editor (with John Downing and Ali Mohammadi) of *Questioning the Media* (1990), she co-edited *Foreign News in the Media: International Reporting in 29 Countries* for UNESCO, which analyzed international news flow. She taught and researched in Iran from 1976 to 1980. She has published articles about communications and culture in Iran in the *International Journal of Politics, Culture, and Society,* the *Quarterly Review of Film and Video,* and the *Encyclopedia Iranica* and is currently completing a book on the subject.

C. Jan Swearingen, Associate Professor of English and Graduate Adviser at The University of Texas at Arlington, is the author of *Rhetoric and Irony, Western Literacy and Western Lies*. She works in the history and theory of rhetoric, hermeneutics, narrative studies, literary theory and criticism, and feminist approaches to gender and language. She is the editor and co-author of a collection of studies of religious doctrines of language. She has authored articles, chapters, and conference papers on narrative theory, dialogics, feminist approaches to rhetoric, and studies of gender and language in classical antiquity.

Noël Valis, a Professor of Spanish at the University of Michigan, Ann Arbor, is the author of *The Decadent Vision in Leopoldo Alas, The Novels of J. O. Picón, Leopoldo Alas (Clarín): An Annotated Bibliography,* and annotated editions of three nineteenth-century Spanish texts; co-editor (with Carol Maier) of *In the Feminine Mode;* and translator of Pedro Salinas's *Víspera del gozo* (Prelude to Pleasure, in press). She is working on a cultural history of nineteenth-century Spanish literature and society.